I SHALL LIVE

*Surviving the Holocaust
Against All Odds*

HENRY ORENSTEIN

*Foreword by
Claude Lanzmann, creator of* Shoah

BEAUFORT
BOOKS

Library of Congress Cataloging-in-Publication Data
Orenstein, Henry, 1923-
 I shall live : surviving the Holocaust against all odds / Henry Orenstein.
  p. cm.
 "revised and updated edition".
 ISBN 978-0-8253-0597-9 (alk. paper)
  1. Orenstein, Henry, 1923- 2. Jews—Poland—Hrubieszów—Biography.
3. Holocaust, Jewish (1939-1945)—Poland—Hrubieszów--Personal narratives.
4. Hrubieszów (Poland)—Biography. I. Title.
 DS134.72.O74A3 2010
 940.53'18092--dc22
 [B]
                              2009046948

For Inquiries about volume orders, please contact:
 Beaufort Books
 27 West 20th Street, Suite 1102
 New York, NY 10011
 sales@beaufortbooks.com

Published in the United States by Beaufort Books
www.beaufortbooks.com

Distributed by Midpoint Trade Books
www.midpointtrade.com

Designer: Elyse Strongin, Neuwirth & Associates, Inc.

Printed in the U.S.A.

10 9 8 7 6 5 4 3 2 1

To the members of my family
murdered by the Nazis
and
to my beloved wife, Susie,
without whose urging and inspiration
this book would not have been written

Special thanks to Dr. Lucjan Dobroszycki,
Professor of History at YIVO and Yeshiva University,
and editor of The Chronicle of the Lodz Ghetto,
for his invaluable help in the search
for documents and verification

CONTENTS

FOREWORD

T hroughout the years I spent in the preparation and making of *Shoah*, one question emerged as central for me, a question that neither the many firsthand accounts and scholarly works I read nor the testimony from survivors ever really and completely answered: How did the Jews of the villages and small ghetto towns of Eastern Europe (Poland, the Baltic countries, Byelorussia, the Ukraine) live from one day to the next during the periods of remission that followed the liquidations—or "actions," as the Nazis labeled them—in which their families and friends were brutally slaughtered on the spot by specialized teams of killers or sent off to the gas chambers of the death camps? Although the frequency and pace of extermination varied considerably according to the time and place, one general principle nevertheless prevailed: In order to deceive and lull the victims, and also because Jewish manpower was needed, the SS never "cleaned up" a ghetto in one fell swoop. Between one "action" and the next, life went on for those initially spared, days filled with anguish and terror, dominated by the anticipation and certainty of an inescapable end, yet permeated with dreams and hopes more tenacious than death, and without which their doomed existence would have been impossible.

Henry Orenstein is the extraordinary painter of this anguish, conveying a picture whose truth and sensitivity are to my mind exemplary. He makes us experience—and this is what is most profoundly unique in his story—the *passage of time,* the passing of days, weeks, and months, the deceptive calm before and after the savagery of the "actions" and executions. Quite simply, he recreates for us the *sense of duration* in the extermination of the Jews. He does so with perfect economy of means, in a spare style, without overstatement. His intellectual rigor and honesty, his accurate memory, and his keen skill for description enable us to relive each moment of this relentless martyrdom as if we ourselves belonged to the Orenstein family.

This book is above all the saga of a wonderfully united and closely knit family in which each member is prepared to give his life to save the others. Lejb, the father, Golda, the mother, the four sons—Fred, Sam, Felek, and Henry—and lastly, Hanka, the little sister, all obey the same law of love—paternal, maternal, filial, and sibling love—which bids them always to risk their own safety in order to keep the family together or to find each other again despite enforced separations, even at the price of the ultimate sacrifice. The most poignant episode in the book is undoubtedly the surrender to the Nazis on October 28, 1942, of the entire family, together for one last time in their home town of Hrubieszów, after having miraculously survived for three years. By the very austerity of its narration, the book here attains a tragic grandeur. We are witness to the final "action," the ultimate liquidation of the ghetto, the shipment of thousands of Hrubieszów Jews to the gas chambers of Sobibór. While the SS were outside with their dogs and with Ukrainian mercenaries, flushing out, house by house, the Jews who had failed to appear at roll call, the Orensteins remained hidden in a *skrytka*, a narrow concealed place behind a false wall. For eight days and eight nights—the duration of the "action"— they waited. Henry, the youngest son (who was nineteen years old in 1942), escaped implacable reality by devouring a Polish transla- tion of *Gone with the Wind* with its last twenty pages missing. "I shall never know the end of the story," he thinks, indicating thus his sense of impending death. Dirty, starving, with their strength and hope exhausted, the Orensteins decide to make an end of it and surren- der to the murderers. Golda and Lejb are taken to the cemetery and killed with a bullet in the neck. The mother, before being dragged away from her family, cries out to her oldest son the four piercing words which express the most absolute gift of self: "Fred, save the children!"

For the five children, the hell of the camps would now begin. Until now, we have been reading a meticulous account of a manhunt, rich with fresh insights into relations between Jews and Poles, the habitual anti-Semitism of the Polish population, but also the simple heroism of a handful of men and women who risked their lives to help the victims (Mrs. Lipińska remains unforgettable); we learn, too, about everyday life in this part of Poland, occupied by the USSR between 1939 and 1941, during which period anti-Jewish discrimination was banned, and lastly about the solitude and the unbelievable feeling of abandonment experienced by Jews desperately trying to survive in a totally hostile environment, a desert bereft of all humanity.

But then the tenor of the book suddenly alters, and in trailing the path of Henry Orenstein, we plunge into the most harrowing of adventure stories. An adventure of horror to be sure, as lived hour after hour for thirty interminable months, but at the same time, one that is almost novelesque in the extraordinary succession of mira- cles which enable the young man to remain among the living so as

to eventually tell his story forty years later, with Voltairesque ferocity and often with sheer and invigorating joy. From one ordeal
to another, outwitting death time after time, Henry Orenstein, an
intelligent, soberly pessimistic Candide, is possessed by a will to
live so prodigious that he seems able to maintain his spirit while
overcoming the most improbable odds. One of the most hazardous
of these was his enrollment in an ultra-secret *Kommando* of phony
chemists, engineers, and mathematicians, whose task was to em-
ploy Jewish intelligence for the purpose of inventing a unique gas
that would save the Third Reich from disaster by paralyzing the
engines of enemy tanks, aircraft, and all other motorized vehicles.
Readers will have to discover for themselves this truly delusionary
scheme, a sheer product of the Nazi phantasmagoria. As a member
of a *Chemiker Kommando,* our hero was sheltered to some extent in
each of the five camps to which he was deported: Budzy´n, Majdanek, and Płaszów in Poland; Ravensbrück and Sachsenhausen
in Germany. The news from the front, Hitler's defeats, the advance
of Soviet troops (he rightly considers the battle of Moscow in the
winter of 1941–1942 to be the decisive turning point of the war),
together with the Allied landings helped sustain Henry Orenstein
during his worst moments: The reader must imagine the horrible
torture in Ptaszów of being confined in the *Stehbunker* (a tiny, foul,
coffin-like cell with barely room to stand), waiting his turn to be
hanged, escaping in his imagination into the realm of military strategy, identifying with the generals of the victorious armies—Zhukov
and Eisenhower, Montgomery and Rokossovsky—correcting and
perfecting their battle plans, but also maintaining his equilibrium
when on the brink of death by visualizing Hitler's suffering on seeing his world crumble.

The end of the book is admirable. In a series of hallucinatory
scenes which would lend themselves to cinematic treatment, the

author has us relive the death march of the prisoners from Sachsen-hausen during the last days of the war. At that point, impelled by an overwhelming need to tell, Orenstein attains such perfect mastery that his work achieves the rank of literature.

CLAUDE LANZMANN

Translated from the French by Toby Talbot

INTRODUCTION

■

I am writing this introduction to add another dimension to the masterful foreword by Claude Lanzmann. This renowned artist and author has captured the special significance of this book and it cannot be improved upon.

I have been privileged to know many of the most outstanding personalities of our time, from world leaders to renowned religious figures and cultural icons. None has had a greater impact or more profound impression on my life as did Henry Orenstein. Beyond my deep affection and admiration for Henry and Susie, I have come to rely on his incisive and substantive command of world events. Henry is a keen observer, largely self-educated, with remarkable insight sharpened by his life experience. His remarkable story is movingly recounted in *I Shall Live*, but it offers only part of the full account of this unique and special man.

His resourcefulness, creativity, and intellect are evident in his ability to survive against the greatest odds. Only those who had firsthand experience with the unfathomable evil of that period can fully appreciate the miraculous nature of his survival.

I Shall Live is much more then another personal account of that terrible era. Rather, it is the inspiring story of the remarkable triumph of an individual who by virtue of extraordinary will and courage was able to overcome incredible challenges that would have doomed a lesser person. He repeatedly faced almost certain death, yet by his wit, courage, and determination he confounded the plans of his Nazi tormentors. Not given to despair or self-pity, despite his incredible experiences, which might have deterred those lacking his zeal for life, he went on to establish a family, successful businesses and engage in significant philanthropic endeavors. These qualities enabled him as well to overcome reversals of fortune, from which he emerged stronger and went on to even greater accomplishments. His creativity and imagination continue to produce new inventions and innovations up to the present time.

While *I Shall Live* is largely Henry's story, he places the events in an historical context, enhancing the reader's experience and education. The lessons of Henry's life are particularly important for the younger generations. The increased visibility and vociferousness of Holocaust deniers underscores the importance of his work. Similarly, the mood of our time makes his real-life demonstration of the indomitable spirit so vital.

The word chosen to symbolize the Holocaust was "*zachor*," remembrance. In our tradition, remembrance is also about the future, because only those who learn the lessons of the past are able to meet the challenges of the future. *I Shall Live* sounds an alarm for this generation so that the pledge of "Never again!" will be fulfilled.

I hope—I urge—that young people of every faith, ethnicity, and national origin, in and outside of the classroom, will be encouraged to read and benefit from *I Shall Live*. I have no doubt it will inspire, sensitize, and instruct them as they draw lessons for their own lives.

Henry's caring for so many individuals from every walk of life, his devotion to Israel and the Jewish people, his love for and commitment to the United States and the vitality of our society, cannot be adequately recounted in this volume. Perhaps it is best left for others to recount. Henry never sought recognition, thought it was rightly earned. In fact, he shunned the limelight, preferring to have his deeds speak for themselves.

We are indebted to Henry for sharing his life story and for enabling us to be, directly or indirectly, part of it. May he and Susie be blessed with many more years of health, happiness, and good deeds.

MALCOLM HOENLEIN
Executive Vice Chairman,
Conference of Presidents of
Major American Jewish Organizations
April 2009

PUBLISHER'S NOTE

∎

I Shall Live was originally published in 1987 to great critical acclaim. Henry Orenstein's extraordinary account of the way he and his family struggled to survive the atrocities perpetrated on European Jews by the Nazis has resonated with readers ever since. The narrative opens on Henry's domestic life with his family in Poland prior to its invasion by the Germans and the Russians in 1939. His words portray in brutal detail the nightmare that descended upon Poland and the rest of Europe.

Throughout his book he sets his personal struggle against the larger backdrop of war-torn Europe, giving readers a better perspective on the war as he and his siblings are moved from one concentration camp to another.

Since the original publication of *I Shall Live*, more information has come to light about a specific aspect of his story. When the Nazis ordered all scientists to sign up for a special assignment, Henry, his brothers, as well as a number of other Jewish prisoners who were not scientists, signed up anyway. They gambled their lives hoping that the war would end before the SS found out that they were not who they claimed to be.

The idea of creating the scientists "Kommando" was originated by a number of German professors who worried that they would be drafted into the German Army and sent to the Russian front. After the professors interviewed the Jewish prisoners who enlisted in the "Kommando," they realized that these were not real scientists. They were so anxious to avoid fighting the Russians that they decided to gamble themselves and give the prisoners make believe "scientific" work.

After the war Henry Orenstein engaged two German historians, Dr.Gotz and Dr. Strebel, to conduct a search in the German archives to try to find documents relating to the phony "Kommando." The enclosed letters show how far-reaching the deception was. In one of them, the head of SS in Poland, Wilhelm Koppe, writes to Heinrich Himmler, the head of the SS, asking him for permission to move the "Kommando" to Germany, and telling him how important its work is to the German war effort. In another, Himmler, apparently very impressed, writes to Pohl, a key SS leader in Berlin, and asking him to set up an advisory committee to supervise the "Kommando."

I Shall Live puts a very human face on those who survived the camps and those who were not fortunate enough to make it. At its root, it is a story of a bright young man who grows into adulthood in the most unimaginable circumstances, but somehow becomes a good and decent man who puts the love of his family above all else.

Beaufort believes it is important to keep alive this unique story of strength and survival. For this new edition we have kept the original introduction by Claude Lanzmann, creator of "Shoah," and included a brand new introduction by Malcolm Hoenlein.

ERIC KAMPMANN
President, Beaufort Books

PREFACE

■

I wrote this book primarily from my own experiences, which for the most part are etched in my memory with unusual clarity. Some of the people and events from more than forty years ago are more vivid to me today than are those of only yesterday.

At times I was aware, while they were happening, that I was a witness to extraordinary events, and I tried to remember them as fully and as accurately as possible, with the conscious intent of recording them, should I be fortunate enough to survive the war. Such an event, for example, was Dr. Blanke's "selection" in Płaszów.

A few events were so terrible and were buried so deep in my memory that only when someone who had shared the experience reminded me of them would the whole scene suddenly flash before me, intact in every detail and as fresh as though it were happening at that moment.

In many cases I verified my recollection by conversation with other survivors who had been with me during the extermination actions and in the concentration camps. These included Adam Folman and Clara Herman, now living in Israel, both members of the *Chemiker Kommando*.

I describe my personal experiences against the background of events on the fighting fronts during various stages of the war, because of their crucial importance to our chances for survival and because the gigantic struggle between Hitler and the coalition of western countries and Soviet Russia became almost an obsession with me.

The following pronunciation guide will help English-speaking readers to pronounce the names of Polish locales that figure prominently in the story:

Bełzec	Bel´ zhets
Hrubieszów	Hr$\overline{oo}$ bye´ shoov
Kraśnik	Krash´ nēk
Łęczna	Len´ chna
Lublin	L$\overline{oo}$´ bleen
Łuck	L$\overline{oo}$tsk
Majdanek	Mīda´ nek
Ołyka	O ly ka
Sobibór	Sōbē´ bo˘or
Treblinka	Trĕblĭn´ ka
Uściług	$\overline{Oo}$st see´ loog
Włodzimierz	Vlōdzee´ miezh

I shall not die

I shall live

I shall tell the story . . .

Hrubieszów:
Before World War II

∎

When they met for the first time, my father, Lejb, took one look at my mother, Golda, and promptly fell in love. And no wonder: Golda was a beautiful young girl with a sweet face, perfect features, big brown eyes, brown hair, and a peach-like complexion.

Lejb was an aggressive, impatient young man who didn't believe in the customary matchmaking; he decided on the spot that Golda was the girl he would marry. Since he was on a business trip from Łęczna, where he lived, to Hrubieszów, where Golda lived, he couldn't stay long that first time, but as soon as he returned home he began writing her love letters every day. Unfortunately he could write only in Yiddish, and not very well at that. His youngest brother, Moshe, remembered Lejb sitting for hours writing letter after letter, tearing each one up and starting again. Moshe, a mischievous and inquisitive boy of six, would later collect the torn bits, and with the help of his older brother,

Hejnach, try to decipher the language of their brother's ardor, but they never succeeded.

It took a couple of years, but at last Golda succumbed to Lejb's persistent courtship. They were married in 1908, when both were twenty-six. Golda's one condition was that they make their home in Hrubieszów, to which Lejb agreed.

Lejb's father, Jankel, and his mother, Sarah (Surcia), were money lenders and dealers in grain; they also held an exclusive license from the Russian government to sell salt in Łęczna. Jankel and Sarah were unhappy with Lejb's decision to move to Hrubieszów, which was fifty miles away, but they knew that once he had made up his mind, no amount of persuasion would change it. Of their seven children—Usher, the eldest, Lejb's younger brothers, Bucio, Hejnach, and Moshe, and the younger sisters, Golda and Ryfka—it was Lejb who showed the greatest promise as a businessman.

The Strum family had been in Hrubieszów for many generations; Golda, her parents, Mordche Hersh and Sarah, and her brother Abraham (Abuś) were all born in Hrubieszów, and the family had lived there from as far back as anyone could remember.

At the turn of the century Hrubieszów was a sleepy town, built around a central square where the important stores and the best apartments were located. The rest of the town, consisting mostly of small one- and two-story houses and shops, fanned out from the square. Only a few streets were paved, and most of those were of cobblestone, over which horse-drawn carriages clippity-clopped. On rainy days in the spring and fall the mud in the unpaved streets was so deep that wagons often got stuck and had to be pulled out.

Jews had been living in Hrubieszów since the Middle Ages, the first Jews having arrived there not long after the village was granted the status of a town by the king of Poland in 1400. The first historical reference to a Jewish settlement in Hrubieszów dates back to the year 1444. Mention is made of a Hrubieszów Jew, Eliaser (Elias) who in 1445 made a trip to Kiev to obtain merchandise from the East. He and the other Jews in Poland were part of a Jewish migration from Western Europe to the East which began in the eleventh century and continued for hundreds of years, under the pressure of massacres by the Crusaders and of many other religious persecutions.

Polish Jews and Gentiles alike suffered the depredations of successive waves of invaders—Tartars, Cossacks, Turks. But the Jews had always lived almost totally separated from the Gentile population, as was the case in most of the towns and villages of Poland and Russia. Many Jews did not speak Polish at all, or at best only broken Polish. At home they spoke Yiddish, and their customs and culture were different, too, as was their appearance: most of them wore beards and long earlocks, yarmulkes on their heads, and black caftans.

Their religion was the key to their existence, and precluded any assimilation; life on earth was secondary in importance to the one hereafter. Because they had caused them so much misery, Christianity and Christians were viewed with deep suspicion. Although Jews had lived in Poland for centuries, it was still to them a foreign land. Many civil rights, privileges, and sources of income were denied them; to earn a living they had to depend on crafts and trade. They were the tailors, the shoemakers, the candlemakers, the money lenders, the tradesmen, and the storekeepers. By 1897, Jews constituted about half the population of Hrubieszów, more than 5,000 out of 10,500.

Life was hard in Hrubieszów, as there was virtually no industry. The Polish peasants were poor, and opportunities for Jews were limited. There were a few well-to-do families, but most lived in poverty. The daily diet consisted of bread, potatoes, herring, and soup; the more fortunate families had chicken and fish on Saturdays, but for hundreds there wasn't even enough bread, and many Jewish children were undernourished, pale and hollow-cheeked.

These conditions and many restrictions caused a few of the Jews to resort to questionable business practices. This gave the anti-Semitic Poles a reason to brand all Jews as dishonest. Most Poles viewed the Jews with suspicion; to them they were a strange people, a foreign body thrust into the midst of Polish society. They couldn't understand why Jews held to their traditions and religious beliefs with such fanatic dedication, and they resented them for it. Danger was everywhere: Polish hooligans threatened pogroms and Catholic priests spread anti-Jewish propaganda, poisonous lies, even telling their congregations that Jews killed Polish children and used the blood to make matzohs for Passover.

But later, when some Jews tried to become assimilated into Polish society, the Poles resented that too. Jews were thus faced with a dilemma: If they kept to their traditional language and culture, they were hated and mocked for being different; when they tried to behave like Poles, they were laughed at and rejected.

The relationship between Jews and Poles had become a vicious cycle. Each had good reason to mistrust the other, but it was the Jews who bore the brunt of the abuse because they were the minority. And the centuries of invasions, destruction, and mass killings in this part of Europe had hardened the local population to bloodshed, which was an all-too-common sight. It didn't take much to start a fresh outbreak of violence against the Jews.

This, then, was the town Lejb came to settle in. Golda's family was poor and could do little to help the young couple. Her mother, Sarah, had borne sixteen children, but in such primitive conditions that only Golda and Abuś had survived, the others having died either at birth or as infants. Golda's father, Mordche Hersh Strum, was a likable and respected man, but he never made much money; he dealt in grain, occasionally selling it to the army, but that wasn't enough business to support a family. He was also an *eytse geber* (adviser) to people with problems, and although he didn't charge for his services, neither did he protest when a client discreetly left some eggs, a chicken, or a loaf of bread with Sarah; after all, a man had to feed his family. And he was a specialist in repairing hernias, at which the townspeople believed him to be more expert than any doctor.

The first few years were hard for Lejb and Golda. They lived in a small cottage on the outskirts of town, and there were many days when they had no other food than milk from their cow. But gradually, with Lejb's industry and intelligence, their situation improved.

At first the Jews in Hrubieszów were suspicious of Lejb, but he was smart and energetic, and soon people began to take notice of the hard-driving young newcomer who often beat his competitors to the punch. It was not long before he won their respect and even admiration, which was not unmixed with envy. Here was a young man without connections who was making more money than most of the established businessmen.

With the outbreak of World War I, Lejb, Golda, and their three small children—Fred (Niuniek), born in 1909, Felix (Felek) (1910), and Sam (Shlojme) (1911)—faced many dangers. The opposing armies—first the Germans and the Russians, later the Poles and the Russians—were often fighting in and around Hrubieszów, and whenever the Cossacks were in the neighborhood they ran amok, looting and burning houses. My parents liked to tell of an incident that occurred during one of the Cossack raids. A huge Cossack armed with a rifle came into their house, put some of the family's valuables into a sack he was carrying, and was about to take the only loaf of bread they had. Food was scarce during the war and the children started to cry, so Lejb with great courage pleaded with the Cossack to take pity on them and leave the bread, as he had nothing else to feed his children. At that the Cossack pulled out a large knife. The children started screaming, but the Cossack smiled and cut the loaf in two, saying, "I'm a fair man—half for me, half for you."

It was at about that time that Abuś, Golda's younger brother, whom she loved very much, was arrested by the authorities on suspicion of being a Leftist and jailed in Lublin, the largest city in the region. Ignoring the dangers of an area that was infested with bands of army deserters and bandits, Golda left the three small children with Lejb and went to Lublin on foot, hitching a ride by horse and wagon whenever she could. In Lublin she went directly to the chief of the Russian police and made an eloquent plea on behalf of her brother. Impressed by her courage, the chief promised he would release Abuś soon, and indeed did so.

On her way back home Golda heard rumors that there was a food shortage in Hrubieszów, so she bought as much food, mostly bread and potatoes, as she could carry. With twenty or thirty miles to go, she couldn't get transportation and had to walk, carrying about forty pounds on her back. When she finally arrived back in town, she learned that there had been no food shortage after all, and her Herculean effort had been unnecessary. She did, however, win the admiration of many for her courage and tenacity.

The war brought not only danger but opportunities as well. In the winter of 1918, all supply routes to and from Hrubieszów were cut off, causing a severe shortage of coal and wood. Houses went unheated in bitter cold weather. A neighbor happened to mention to Lejb that he had heard of an area not far from town where the soil was especially rich in peat; supposedly the local farmers were burning it in their stoves to heat their houses. Lejb immediately went to see for himself, discovered that the story was true, and set about hiring farmers to dig the peat. He organized a caravan of thirty wagons to carry it back to Hrubieszów, riding at its head. At first the townspeople were skeptical, but Lejb showed them that it worked, and they gladly bought the peat from him for fuel.

Lejb repeated this operation several times, making a good profit on the venture. By the end of the war he was prosperous enough to buy the largest building in Hrubieszów. Real estate prices were then very low, and he knew a bargain when he saw it; he bought the only three-story building in town and moved his family into the second-floor apartment, which consisted of six large rooms and a maid's quarters. This was by far the most luxurious apartment in town, since most of Hrubieszów's houses amounted to little more than one-room shacks. Soon after that, Lejb took on a partner, Moshe Lichtenstein, a dealer in fabrics, and in one of the shops on the first floor of Lejb's building they opened the largest fabric store in town.

After the war ended Lejb continued to prosper; he was quick and decisive, and not afraid to gamble when the odds were in his favor. He began buying great quantities of corn, wheat, and other grain from the local Polish gentry, who owned most of the land. Most of the grain he sold for export, but he also opened his own granary and bought a half interest in a local flour mill.

Lejb and Golda had wanted a little girl, so they may have been disappointed at the first sight of me, on October 13, 1923. By then Lejb had become the wealthiest man in Hrubieszów. My first memories are of being catered to by servants and being made much of by my parents and three brothers, who were twelve to fifteen years older than I. My parents still wanted a girl, however, and at last their wish was granted in February 1926, when my sister, Hanka, was born. My mother was forty-three.

Hanka was a beautiful little girl, fair-skinned, with large, shining brown eyes and straight brown hair. She was adorable, and everyone wanted to play with her. As the only girl in the family, for a while at least she became the center of attention, but my parents evidently made sure I was getting plenty of love too, because I seldom remember being jealous of my sister.

Fred was a tall, very handsome young man with wavy dark hair and brown eyes. Felek was of medium height, nice-looking, with expressive brown eyes, brown hair, and smooth skin. Sam, the youngest of the three, was about Felek's height, with grayish-brown eyes and wavy blond hair, which became darker as the years went by.

I was a shy little boy, always absorbed in my own thoughts. One of my earliest memories is of a resort where my mother and we five children stayed one summer for two or three months. I was not quite four, and remember vividly the thousands of flowers surrounding the small villa we had rented. Father used to come for weekends, and once he brought his sister Ryfka (Regina) with him. There weren't enough beds, so Regina slept in my bed. Already I was conscious of the difference in our sexes, and can still remember how embarrassed I was, sleeping in the same bed with a woman. At home I still slept from time to time with my parents in their big bed, but of course that was different—Golda was my mama.

Regina was then in her early twenties, a pretty, full-bodied girl. When we were in bed she tried to hug and kiss me, but I turned my back to her and pressed myself against the wall as hard as I could. I refused to face her. The whole episode upset me very much. It upset my aunt too; she couldn't understand my behavior. She stayed with us for about a week, and throughout that time I avoided looking her in the eyes.

Another early memory was of a Christmas tree. At that time the tenants on the third floor were a Polish teacher and his wife, who had a little boy about my age named Jasiek. At Christmastime they would invite me upstairs to see their Christmas tree and play with Jasiek. I remember being overwhelmed by the beauty, warmth, and glitter of the tree; an aura of charm and mystery surrounded it, and Jasiek and I spent hours playing around it. I thought of the tree often during the following months, and couldn't wait for the next Christmas to arrive.

Although I loved all my brothers very much, my memories from that time of Fred, the eldest, are rather hazy because he went to study medicine in France when I was only four or five. He had been at the head of his class in the Hrubieszów *gimnazjum* (gymnasium, or high school), but by then the Polish universities were admitting very few Jewish students, and practically the only way Polish Jews could get into medicine was by going abroad.

It was at about that time that I had my first experience of violence. I was five, and until then the only violence I had known was when Mother gave me a spanking. She never hit me hard, and if I cried it was mostly from injury to my pride.

But one day I was playing out in front of our shop when I noticed a commotion a few doors away, near the leather-and-shoe store. I had strict orders from Mother not to wander away from our building, but curiosity won out and I went to see what was going on. A customer was arguing with Shlojme, the owner of the store, who was a large man with a brutish face. Shlojme made leather boots from large pieces of hide, which he had hanging both inside and outside the store and from which customers could make their selections. The man was complaining about the fit of some boots Shlojme had made for him, and Shlojme refused to fix them. The argument grew louder, and I saw Shlojme raise his arm and strike the customer. Apparently he had been holding a knife in his hand—for cutting leather, probably—because suddenly the man's head and face were covered with blood, which dripped onto his shirt. A wave of nausea and terror seized me. I ran back to our shop and threw myself into Mother's arms, crying hysterically. I couldn't speak for some time afterward, and had nightmares for months. Even several years later I would wake up with the image of the man's bloody head vivid in my dreams.

I learned to read when I was four. It came to me very easily, and I don't remember anyone ever teaching me. Soon reading became an obsession. Hrubieszów had a library with several thousand books, and from the time I was six I used to visit it every day except Sunday to pick out books to take home. My first love was Westerns. I read dozens of Zane Grey's tales of the Wild West, but my favorite Western author was Karl May, a German who never visited America but could spin marvelous yarns about cowboys and Indians. I remember feeling sorry for the poor, brave Indians whose lands were gradually being taken from them, and yet at the same time admiring the dynamic, rambunctious Americans who were continually on the move, vigorously expanding across the vast continent.

When I ran out of Westerns, I turned to mystery writers like Edgar Wallace. One evening when I was about six I was sitting at my table with a thriller whose Polish title was something like *The Fraternity of the Large Frog*. It was about a murderous English secret society, and I was utterly engrossed in it when Mother came in and told me it was time to go to bed. I promised her I would in just a few minutes, when I had finished the chapter I was reading, but by then I was too caught up in the story to stop. It scared me so that I was afraid even to move, and besides, I couldn't tear myself away; it was late into the night when I finished the book. By then I was so petrified I could only stare straight ahead, not daring to look either left or right. I was even breathing shallowly, from terror that at any moment the villain would come and get me. I remained frozen in that position until around four in the morning, when Mother woke up and saw the light on in my room. I was so relieved when she came in that I fell into her arms and would not let go of her for a long time.

When I was six, it was time to start school. I was to go to the large state elementary school, the only one in town. The first day Mother helped me dress, packed me a lunch, walked me to the entrance, wished me good luck, and left. Inside the schoolyard I was overwhelmed by the sight of all the screaming kids chasing one another around and fighting while waiting for the classes to begin. Suddenly a loud bell rang. That was the last straw; I decided this wasn't for me and ran back home.

My parents were very surprised, and tried to explain that attending school was compulsory, but I was adamant and refused to go. Reasoning, cajoling, pleading, all had no effect. Finally Father gave in and got permission for me to be tutored at home, a concession for which he had to pay off a local official.

My tutor, Samuel Hubel, was a short, likable man who came to our house three days a week for a few hours and taught me a variety of subjects. He gave me quite a bit of homework to do, and I actually learned more from him than I would have had I gone to school with the other children.

But as far as my religious education was concerned, I was not doing so well. My parents didn't observe religious holidays or attend the synagogue with the dedication of the majority of Jews in Hrubieszów, but they still felt I should learn some Hebrew as well as the fundamentals of the Jewish religion. At the time, however, I was more interested in secular subjects, and learned very little from the private tutors in religion my parents hired for me.

I remember in particular one embarrassing moment with the last religion teacher I was to have, a little man with a bright red beard and black yarmulke. I had felt so bored and frustrated with his predecessors, I told him that unless he played ping-pong with me I'd refuse to have any lessons. The poor man needed the money badly, so we started playing ping-pong. He was a fast learner, and after a week or so he liked the game so well that we abandoned the lessons altogether and only played ping-pong. Soon he became a terrific slammer; he even beat me, because I was still too short to play the game really well. My mother was usually in the shop during the middle of the day, when I was supposedly having my Hebrew lessons. One day she happened to go upstairs during lesson time and surprised us in the middle of a hot match. That was the end of my "Hebrew lessons."

Religious tradition was still very strong in our town, and during the major holidays nearly all Jews were at prayer in the synagogues, especially during Yom Kippur, when practically everyone fasted. No more than perhaps fifty or so nonbelievers in the whole town, almost all of them young, committed the ultimate sin of breaking the fast during Yom Kippur. But even they would never dare eat at home; on this, the holiest day of the year, most of them bought ham sandwiches from a Polish butcher, Krasnopolski, who sold cold cuts down the block from us. Krasnopolski, who was not the brightest man in the world, used to get a little mixed up. For weeks before Yom Kippur he would anxiously ask me, "Tell me, Mr. Heniek—when is it, this day of the year when Jews are allowed to eat ham?"

I especially loved to read history and geography, and soon became stuffed with facts and figures. When Sam and Felek were preparing for their final gymnasium exams, a few of their friends would come to our house to study with them. Soon they discovered that I knew the dates of virtually all the major battles in history, the names of generals, of famous travelers, the populations of cities. They got a kick out of this boy, not yet seven, who could give them all the answers.

Mother was very proud of her precocious child, and one day she overheard these eighteen-year-olds quizzing me. I loved to show off, and was snapping out one answer after another. After a while she summoned Felek and said, "Felek, isn't he a real genius?" Totally preoccupied with his forthcoming exams, Felek replied impatiently, "Mama, I don't have time to discuss this now. Yes, he is a very smart boy." But that wasn't enough for her. "Well," she said, "I think he is at least *half* a genius."

My first personal experience of death occurred when I was seven. My maternal grandmother, Sarah, died. Once a week Hanka and I had visited her in her tiny cottage across the bridge, and although she was very poor she always had a piece of candy or a little gift for us. She was a shriveled-up little woman who had lost her husband, Mordche Hersh—after whom I had been named, although I was called Heniek—years before I was born, and who was now supported by my mother. I remember well how bare and poor Grandma's house looked, and how meticulously clean it always was.

After she died, the only remaining member of Mother's family to whom she was close was her younger brother, Abuś. He was ill with heart trouble and in failing health generally, and Mother worried about him. He was a very intelligent man who had educated himself, and we all loved him. He had a beautiful voice and was the leading singer in the town's small amateur theatrical group. Abuś was a dental technician, and his wife, Lisa, a beautiful girl from Warsaw, was a dentist. Their combined incomes were not enough to make ends meet, and Mother would often help them out with gifts of money. They had only one child, a boy, Józiek (Joseph), who was not quite a year older than I, a very good-looking and lively child, much spoiled by his parents. When I was small, Joe was my frequent companion. He loved to jump up and down; he would jump on sofas, chairs, tables, floors—wherever he got a chance. One day when he grew tired of doing it alone, he asked me to join him. I replied, "Józiek, you jump, and Sianiu [as I pronounced Heniek] will watch you." My brothers overheard this exchange and teased me about it for a long time afterward.

Abuś and Lisa finally decided that they were never going to make a go of it in Hrubieszów and moved to Warsaw, hoping for better luck there. Their departure, which took place when I was only seven, made me very sad and left an emptiness in my life.

Father was an unusually courageous man. Our cook told me the following story: One day he and a group of other Jews were talking together in the town square. A Polish policeman, who was known to be anti-Semitic, came over and pushed one of them down and contemptuously called him *"parszywy żyd"* (rotten Jew). Father happened to be standing nearby, and without hesitation he hit the policeman in the face, calling him *"Polska świnia"* (Polish swine). Such an act was comparable to a Black punching out a small-town Mississippi sheriff and calling him "Whitey pig." This episode cost Father a lot of money, and at that he was lucky the authorities did not put him in jail. But the whole town was proud of him.

I was six or seven when I had the opportunity to see for myself how fearlessly Father would stand up to anyone who challenged him. He had made a deal with a Polish nobleman, a Count Chrzanowski, the scion of one of the oldest families in Poland, who owned many villages not far from Hrubieszów. He was very rich but always short of cash, because every winter he would travel to the French Riviera, where he lost heavily at the casinos. Father had already made enough money to buy the whole crop of certain commodities from Chrzanowski and other Polish landowners. He would pay cash for them during the preceding winter, and receive the shipments after the harvest. That year he bought Chrzanowski's entire crop of poppy seed. It so happened that after he had paid Chrzanowski for it, bad weather destroyed virtually all of Poland's poppy seed crop, except in the Hrubieszów region. The price of poppy seed rocketed to four or five times its normal price.

Harvest was over, and still there was no word from Chrzanowski. A great deal of money was at stake, and with the passing of each day my parents became more anxious. It was a sensitive situation; demanding one's rights from a Polish aristocrat was no light matter. At last Father decided to go to see the count in person. He hired a *droshka* (a horse-drawn carriage) for the trip, and at the last minute decided to take me along. After several hours' drive along country roads, we arrived at the count's mansion, where we were told to wait in the anteroom. In a few minutes Father was summoned to the main reception room, while I waited apprehensively. At first I could hear nothing through the closed doors, but soon voices were raised. Suddenly I heard a loud bang, and Chrzanowski shouted, "Remember to whom you are speaking! My name is Chrzanowski!" Immediately came another bang, and Father shouted, "And my name is Orenstein!" I was frightened for his safety, but soon he reappeared in the doorway, put his arm on my shoulder, and said, "Let's go." We got back into the droshka and started home.

No one could guess what the outcome would be, and the intervening time was tense. But a few days later, with no advance notice, a caravan of wagons appeared outside Father's warehouse. He had won the battle of wills in a confrontation with a Polish aristocrat—a victory to be treasured always by our family.

Father was a highly unusual man. He had an open mind, never accepted anything at face value, and refused to trust anyone's opinion on any matter until he himself had examined the facts. Once when Mother developed an internal infection of some kind, the local doctor insisted that she had to have an operation, but Father was opposed to it; probably he didn't trust the doctor. He wanted to take Mother to Warsaw, but the doctor maintained that if the operation was not performed within a few hours, Mother would die. At that point Father was called away for a short time, and the doctor took advantage of his absence to persuade our relatives and friends to get Mother to agree. She was ill and confused, and the doctor assumed he had her permission to go ahead. He was going to perform the operation in our house, and he told the women to get buckets of boiling water ready. He had his instruments spread out on a bed sheet and was all set to start operating when Father returned. He took in the situation at a glance, seized the bed sheet, threw the instruments on the floor, and chased the doctor out of the house. Later, when Fred was told what had happened, he said it was almost certain that Mother would have died from hemorrhage had she been operated on then.

Mother and Father were true partners. Although he trusted his own judgment, he consulted her on every important matter in his life. She in turn looked after Father's interest in the shop, took care of the house, did the marketing, and cared for the children. She could also bake the most delicious cakes and cookies, and these were the first things my brothers would ask for when they came home on vacation.

Mother could be both very gentle and very determined. When I was about eight she discovered that Fred had become seriously involved with a French girl while studying medicine in Montpellier, France. The question was: Should Fred marry a *shiksa* (Gentile girl)?

One subject of many discussions between my parents was: If he did, would their children be brought up as Jews or as Catholics? Finally Mother decided to take matters into her own hands. She set off on a three-day journey across Europe, arriving in Montpellier without knowing a word of French. When she left, she took a surprised Fred back home with her for a cooling-off period.

This, however, was not the end of the story. The girl, who apparently was very much in love with Fred, decided to follow him, and soon she too arrived in Hrubieszów. She, naturally, spoke not a word of Polish, and the poor thing must have had a terrible time of it making her way to our little town. Somehow my parents got word of her imminent arrival and sent Fred away to visit a relative. I well remember the girl's brief visit. I was told to stay in my room out of her way, but I managed to catch a glimpse of the pretty young thing as she walked by. She couldn't communicate with anyone, and it must have been heartbreaking for her to have made such a long, difficult journey without even seeing Fred. My heart went out to her, and I was angry with my parents for breaking up the romance and with Fred for not standing up to them.

Another troublesome romance involved my brother Sam, who fell in love with Bluma Brandt, a pretty girl who was from a well-known but poor family. Mother didn't want him to marry her, and claimed that Bluma was too frail and sickly. Later I learned there were other objections as well. Not only was there no money in the family; Bluma's older sister, Syma, was known to go out with the officers of the local Polish army regiment. But Sam persisted; he continued to see Bluma. He didn't, however, go so far as to insist on marrying her.

After Felek graduated from the gymnasium, he, like Fred, went to Montpellier to study medicine. But Sam, who had studied particularly hard, was able to get into the Warsaw Law University. Fred and Felek returned home on vacation from France only once a year, but Sam would come home often from Warsaw, and I used to love the long talks we had on the sofa in Father's study. We always had so much to talk about.

By now I was reading more serious authors. I read every book in the library by Gogol, Chekhov, Dostoyevski, Tolstoy, Thomas Mann, Feuchtwanger, Wassermann, and Balzac. Philosophers like Spinoza were more difficult, but I persisted, even though reading them sometimes gave me a headache.

My favorite writer was the Polish author Henryk Sienkiewicz, who had written a famous historical trilogy. The first part, *Ogniem i Mieczem (By Fire and Sword)* covered the 1648 Chmielnicki rebellion; the second, *Potop (The Deluge)*, the Swedish occupation of Poland in 1656, and *Pan Wołodyjowski* (Mr. Wołodyjowski), a number of subsequent wars. I read and reread those three volumes until I could recite whole pages from memory. So anxious was I to discover the world through books that I would start reading a new one the minute I left the library with it, and continued reading all the way home. Mother, fearful that I would be run over by a horse and wagon, made me promise at least to be careful crossing the streets.

When I was eleven I at last agreed to go to school. I attended the junior class of the grade school, and soon discovered that thanks to the private tutoring and so much reading, I was easily at the head of my class. I was the best reader aloud, and our Polish-language teacher usually chose me to read to the rest of the class. This gave me some prestige, but it wasn't enough to protect me from anti-Semitic abuse; the Polish boys pushed me around just as they did the other Jewish kids. They used to chant, "Jews, go to Palestine," and write anti-Semitic slogans on the blackboard. I dreaded the morning roll call. Every time my official name, Mordche Hersh Orenstein, was called, there were nasty chuckles and snickering. Morning prayer was another source of embarrassment; the Polish kids would pray aloud, repeating the teacher's words, while we Jews stood in silence. Before I started school I had been aware of anti-Semitism, but for the most part only to the extent of having overheard conversations about it. Now it was hitting home. Occasionally a Jewish boy would resist and put up a fight, but whenever that happened a whole gang of Polish kids would set upon him and really beat him up. There was no one to complain to, because most of the teachers, the police, and the town officials were leading the way in teaching anti-Semitism to the young.

This was very depressing to me. Suddenly I realized that the future was clouded. The fascinating world I had discovered in books, and the sense of that world opening up to me, somehow no longer seemed so exciting.

Nevertheless, there were moments of triumph too. The following year I had to take the crucial entrance exams for admission to the Hrubieszów State Gymnasium. In my brothers' time it had been a little easier for Jewish boys to be accepted, but now, with anti-Semitism increasing everywhere in Poland, the school administration was restricting the admission of Jews to only one or two a year, out of a class of about thirty—in a town in which fully half the population was Jewish. There were no other high schools within fifteen miles. There were no automobiles either, and few Jewish parents who could afford the high tuition fees were sending their children to Jewish high schools in other towns. But a diploma from one of those schools counted for little in the Polish universities; the tiny number of Jewish students admitted by the universities came almost exclusively from the Polish state gymnasiums.

About five hundred kids applied for the thirty or so places in the freshman class of the gymnasium. There were two written examinations, in Polish language and in mathematics. I was well prepared and breezed through the math exam—I was the first to turn in my paper. The Polish-language exam took longer. The subject was "My First Adventure in a Forest." I wrote a story that started on a beautiful sunny morning and ended with an evening storm full of thunder and lightning. In between, I described baking potatoes, searching for hidden treasure, and generally experiencing the beauty of nature.

About a week later the applicants and their parents assembled in the auditorium to learn the results. It was packed, with standing room only. The director of the school read the results, calling out the students' names in alphabetical order. The marks ranged from "very good" to "failing," and were mostly very low. One student, Bienkiewicz, the son of a Polish landowner, got "very good minus" in Polish language and "average" in math. When my turn came, the director read "Orenstein: Math—very good. Polish language—very good minus," and a murmur went through the crowd. The director stopped and looked around, but he didn't know who I was and I was too shy to raise my hand. He then read through the rest of the students' marks. There wasn't another "very good" among them.

I was embarrassed to see people staring at me and bowed my head, but in my heart there was great joy. I fought my way through the crowd to my parents, who hugged and kissed me without saying a word. We walked home together, with Father on one side and Mother on the other, each holding one of my hands.

Two weeks later a list was posted of the thirty students who had been accepted in the freshman class of the gymnasium. Chaim Ajzen and I were the only two Jews admitted, although there were many other Jews who had gotten better marks than the Polish students who were accepted.

As time passed, I became increasingly disturbed at the upsurge of anti-Semitism in Poland. Marshal Piłsudski died in 1935, and the new government under Rydz-Śmigły wasn't strong enough to withstand pressure from such anti-Jewish groups as the Endeks, a nationalistic Polish party. Such minimal protection as was offered to Jews by the police and other government agencies was weakening. Diverse groups found it in their interest to arouse urban mobs and ignorant Polish peasants to violence. One such group was the rising Polish merchant class, who were finding it difficult to compete with Jewish shop owners, with all their centuries of experience in trade. Another was the professional class, who were anxious to see Jews excluded from the practice of law and medicine. Propaganda from Germany expounding Hitler's "master race" theories further incited Polish anti-Semites. Newspapers and radio broadcasts were full of reports of actual pogroms. These usually occurred during fairs in small towns and in a few cities, when large crowds would descend upon a village or town, and the local authorities found themselves completely inadequate to cope with the situation. In addition to the farm products they were selling, peasants would arrive at these fairs with empty sacks and boxes, hoping for an outbreak of violence or perhaps even a full-fledged pogrom that would permit them to plunder Jewish houses and shops.

I spent many sleepless nights fearful of the approaching 1936 summer fair in Hrubieszów. Visions of rampaging mobs armed with clubs and knives breaking down our doors and physically attacking us haunted my dreams.

Father reinforced all our doors with heavy metal bars, but we knew this wouldn't be enough to save us in the event of a full-fledged pogrom. Sam, who at that time had already graduated from law school, went with Father to the police and the mayor's office to ask them for protection during the fair, but all they got was a shrug and the excuse that what few policemen there were would be unable to cope with a large mob.

The day of the fair came at last, and although there were a number of broken windows and some minor attacks on Jews, there was nothing like a pogrom or even the serious threat of one. We all sighed with relief, and life returned to normal—for the time being.

Since starting school, I was spending more time with a few of my friends. Among them were Józiek Peretz, my second cousin on Mother's side of the family, and Chaim Ajzen. Józiek had a beautiful voice, and as we strolled the quiet streets of Hrubieszów after supper he would lead us in the latest hits, like "Bolero" and "Caravan."

There were other pleasant memories as well from that apprehensive time. Our tenant on the third floor was a Mr. Zelpowicz, who used four or five of his small rooms as a hotel. Every few months touring performers stopped off in Hrubieszów for a one-night stand and would stay overnight at his place. Our apartment had an elegantly furnished salon, with a large chandelier and a grand piano, and Mother often invited the performers to come there after the show for drinks and a buffet supper. There wasn't much to do in Hrubieszów, and most of them were happy to accept Mother's invitation, so we got to meet some of the best-known dancers, actors, singers, and comedians of the day. I remember in particular Dzigan and Shumacher, the most famous Jewish comedy team in Poland. I laughed so hard I needed a handkerchief to wipe away the tears.

When Josephine Baker, the American entertainer, came to town she almost caused a riot. She was the first black person ever to visit Hrubieszów, and crowds of children, including a number of adults, followed her through the streets, many trying to touch her to see for themselves that the black of her skin wouldn't rub off. She spent an hour or so in our salon, but unfortunately none of us spoke English. When she switched to French, I managed to exchange a few pleasantries with her.

Another sensation was the first automobile in town, bought by our mayor. At first kids would run after it, but eventually the novelty wore off. And after that, the streets never seemed safe again.

Naturally we went to see every movie that came to Hrubieszów. Westerns were my favorites, but I was also secretly in love with Deanna Durbin. I saw *A Hundred Men and a Girl,* starring Deanna, the conductor Leopold Stokowski, and Adolph Menjou, three times, and that must have been the Hrubieszów record. I had erotic dreams about Deanna, and whenever I heard her beautiful voice my heart would melt. Shirley Temple was adorable too, and everyone was crazy about her. Movies were a great pleasure, except that whenever the newsreels preceding the feature film included items about Jews, they were inevitably accompanied by derisive catcalls and laughter. Our lives were not immediately affected by such things—we had grown used to them by then—but deep down there was an inescapable awareness that our situation was getting worse. It was with great foreboding that we looked toward the future.

Only the better-educated or well-to-do Jews, however, were preoccupied with these matters; poor Jews were so caught up in the daily struggle for survival that the dangers of anti-Semitism and the deteriorating situation for Polish Jewry generally were to them of only remote interest. But young Jews were becoming more politically active and were more acutely conscious of what was happening. They organized for political action. The most popular groups were the Betar, on the right, under the leadership of Żabotynski, and the labor-oriented Hapoel, on the left. Each had a small headquarters, where its members gathered occasionally to discuss the events of the day and to play ping-pong.

The goal of both groups was the establishment of a Jewish state in Palestine, but although each year one or two young people managed to emigrate to Palestine to join the *kibbutzim*, for the great majority it was only a dream. As far as the older generation was concerned, the traditional greeting "Next year in Jerusalem" was just a greeting and not even a dream. Their roots were in Poland and they knew that, for better or worse, their remaining years were going to be spent there. A few families with relatives in America had emigrated before World War I, when it was relatively easy, but by the 1930s the immigration quotas had been drastically cut, the cost of travel in any case was beyond the reach of most, and for all practical purposes America was no longer a real alternative.

At the time I didn't get involved in any of this, and only went to the Hapoel or Betar to play ping-pong.

September came, and I began my freshman year at the gymnasium. I was very excited about putting on my new blue uniform with gold buttons and matching hat, and I marched off to my first class. Most of the kids knew that I had received the highest score in the entrance exams, and the prestige that went with that helped to compensate for the indignities I had to suffer as a Jew. My lessons with Mr. Hubel had proved useful, and except for physical education I got straight A's in every subject. I especially loved Latin, and soon was able to read and even converse in Latin with my teacher. That first year I studied hard and continued to read a great deal.

A few months after the term started, Bienkiewicz, the Polish landowner's son, began making trouble. Since I was not as strong and athletic as the average boy my age, Bienkiewicz used to pick on me to bully. During recess he would push me into a corner and press me against the wall with his back, hit my ribs with his elbows, and make fun of me. He was taller than I, so I was afraid to fight him, especially since I suspected the other Polish kids would gang up on me if I did. I was too embarrassed to tell the teachers or my parents about it, and so I suffered in silence. Since I offered no resistance, Bienkiewicz was soon bullying me as a matter of routine, and scarcely gave me a moment's peace. It got so bad I dreaded going to school in the morning. Mother sensed that something was wrong, but I was ashamed to tell her about it.

This went on for some weeks, and I grew desperate. Chaim Ajzen urged me to fight Bienkiewicz even if it meant getting beaten up. I was afraid of that, but I was still more fearful of being expelled from the gymnasium. No matter what happened, the authorities would never blame Bienkiewicz because of his father's position, and they might well be just as happy to have an excuse for getting rid of a Jew. However, Bienkiewicz's tormenting got worse and worse, until at last one day when he cornered me yet again and wouldn't let me go, I shouted, "Enough! I challenge you to a fight."

All the kids around us immediately picked it up and started chanting, "Fight! Fight! Fight!" Such issues were usually settled after gym class in the game room, and we all crowded in there. My coach was Chaim Ajzen. He explained to me that Bienkiewicz was actually very clumsy, and that I should have no problem with him: "Just feint with your left and punch his face with your right." I was scared before the fight, but once the kids had surrounded us and begun urging us on, I calmed down. I was determined now to pay Bienkiewicz back for all I'd suffered from him.

I quickly discovered that Chaim was right: Bienkiewicz was ludicrously clumsy. Every time I feinted with my left he covered with both hands, and I punched him from the right at will. For the first few minutes all the Polish kids were on his side, egging him on with cries of "Hit the Jew in the gut," "Punch him all the way to Jerusalem," but Bienkiewicz was such a poor fighter that no amount of encouragement could help him. He could do nothing but cover himself, while I must have hit him forty or fifty times, receiving back from him just a few glancing blows.

I was exhilarated. I punched him so many times my knuckles were hurting; I showed him no mercy. At last I was having my moment of revenge for all the weeks of humiliation, and it was sweet. Even the Polish kids were beginning to enjoy the show, which had become almost comical. When Bienkiewicz's nose started to bleed badly, I decided he'd had enough. Chaim shook my hand, and even a few of the Poles came over and congratulated me. I was so happy I didn't even notice when our gym teacher came in. The crowd immediately dispersed, and to his credit, Bienkiewicz, when the teacher asked about his bloody nose, made some excuse and didn't complain about me. But he never spoke to me or even looked me in the eyes again during the remaining two and a half years we spent together in the same class.

One day while I was standing outside our shop with a couple of my friends, a droshka drove up and stopped in front of it. A man in his early forties wearing a striped suit and shiny leather shoes stepped down and paid the driver. He was clearly a stranger in town, and asked me in broken Polish, "Is this the Orenstein building?" I told him it was, and he asked, "Is Mr. Orenstein here?" By chance Father was in the shop, and I told the man to wait and I would get him. When Father came out, he took one look at the man and shouted, "Moshe!"

It was indeed my uncle Morris from America. He and Father had not seen each other for twenty-four years. In 1912 Morris, then sixteen, had committed an unpardonable sin. He was observed by several Jews holding hands with a *shiksa* in a little park behind the church in Łęczna, where his family lived. On Saturday the rabbi reported the shameful event to his congregation, and Jankel, Morris's father, was so humiliated that he slapped the youthful offender in front of everyone.

That night Morris took whatever money he could find in the

house and ran away from home. He arrived in Hrubieszów and told my parents he wanted to go to America. Father hesitated to help him for fear of antagonizing Jankel, but Mother was on Morris's side. To Morris this was a momentous event in his life, and when he was a very old man the details were still as vivid as ever: "Your mother, Golda, was so beautiful. She had the face of an angel. She told me, 'Moshe, this country is not for you; you belong in America. Don't be afraid. You have your two hands to work with; you won't get lost in America.'" Mother helped him get the papers he needed to emigrate, and Morris was on his way to start a new life in the New World.

He never saw his father again; Jankel died a few years after World War I. Morris wrote letters home for a couple of years, but after the outbreak of the war the family heard no more from him until his return in 1936. He had married Minnie, a girl from Poland whom he met in New York, and had two sons, Seymour and Danny, and a daughter, Annette. When he arrived back in Poland he first went to visit his mother and the rest of his family in Lublin, where they had moved after Jankel's death. Always a practical joker, Morris put on a pair of sunglasses and pretended to be "Morris's friend" from America. No one recognized him until he told them who he was; Father was the only one Morris couldn't fool. His visit caused great excitement among us. I remember sitting on his lap and asking him all sorts of questions about America. He was surprised at how much I already knew about it from the books I had read, and he gave me his Waterman fountain pen as a reward.

Soon after Morris left, Felek came back from France. Studying wasn't as easy for him as it had been for Fred, so it was decided that he would help run the shop, learn the business, and eventually start one himself. At first Felek was unhappy working for Father, and I felt sorry for him. But after a while he fell in love with a girl from Galicia. There was talk of marriage, and Felek would go to visit her and her family. This brightened his mood considerably, and we were all happy for him.

In the spring of 1937 my first year of gymnasium was drawing to a close. I continued to be the only straight-A student in my class. At the end of the school year a prize-giving ceremony was held, which was attended by all the students and their parents, with the director of the school awarding a prize (usually an inscribed book) to the best student in each class. When our turn came, to everyone's surprise the director announced that the award committee had decided that no one in the freshman class had reached the required level of excellence, and that therefore no prize would be awarded.

I sat in a state of shock, realizing that this was their way of preventing a Jew from getting the prize. To give it to another student would have been impossible, a travesty of justice; therefore, ours was the only class without a prize. My parents were saddened, but not surprised. Father said to me, "This is our fate, and we must deal with it as best we can."

This incident had a profound effect on me. It made me very bitter, and when the sophomore year began in the fall, I had lost all interest in my studies and didn't bother to do any homework. This caused no difficulty at first, because by this time the teachers assumed that I knew all the answers and seldom checked up on me. I actually was ahead of the others anyway, so I could afford to coast for a while. I even stopped reading books, and instead played a lot of ping-pong, read the newspapers, and listened to the radio with great interest.

Hitler was now the undisputed dictator of Germany. Many, if not most, Jews had begun to realize that this former "painter," the butt of many jokes and initially not taken seriously by most Germans and other Europeans, was now becoming a serious threat to our very existence. Polish anti-Semites were encouraged more and more by the example of their powerful neighbor to the west, and talked openly of the necessity of finding a "solution" to the Jewish "problem," which meant nothing less than finding a way to get rid of the Jews altogether. Signs reading "Jews to Palestine," even "Jews to Madagascar," appeared everywhere. Palestine was not a realistic possibility, because the British had no intention of letting any substantial number of Jews into their protectorate, but the Madagascar option was widely discussed. This former French island colony is located east of Africa, not far from the equator, and consists mostly of tropical jungle—a highly unsuitable spot for mass immigration from Europe. It was symptomatic of how desperate the situation in Poland was becoming for Jews that some of them considered the "Madagascar option" as a feasible possibility.

In 1938 Uncle Morris came to visit us again. This time we were expecting him, and after he spent a few days with us, Father took him for a week's vacation to a spa. This was shortly after Chamberlain's visit to Hitler in Munich, from which he had returned to England waving a piece of paper signed by the Führer and proclaiming that he had achieved "peace in our time." Chamberlain then stood by and watched helplessly as the German soldiers trampled brutally over what was left of Czechoslovakia.

The morning after Morris left, I spoke with Father about Hitler and the threat he represented to our future. I was eloquent, talking about Hitler's concentration camps. I said I was convinced that the invasion of Poland was inevitable and imminent, and that I thought we should all go to America.

Father agreed with me about the approaching danger, but felt that it would be very difficult for him to begin a new life elsewhere. All his roots, his business, his friends, and most of the family were in Poland. "How can I now, at the age of fifty-six, start from scratch in a foreign land, without understanding a word of English?"

I sensed that I was making no headway, and in desperation I did something I had never done before: I threw myself on the bed and started crying almost hysterically, repeating over and over, "But you don't understand. He will kill us all. He will kill us all."

Surprised at the intensity of my feeling, my parents looked at each other, not sure how to handle the situation. Finally Father sat down on the edge of the bed, put his arms around me, and said, "I cannot go, but if you feel so strongly about it, I will send you to America to study after you graduate from the gymnasium." I realized then that it was useless to try to change Father's mind, and I never brought up the subject again.

In fact, although a few families in Hrubieszów had relatives abroad and the financial means to emigrate, only one family actually did so. Dr. Grynspan had a very successful medical practice and his family had lived in Hrubieszów for generations, but one day he and his wife and children said farewell to their relatives and friends and left for Argentina. This event was much discussed by the Jews of Hrubieszów. Some felt that the doctor might well prove to have been the smart one in the end, but no one else followed his example. I admired his courage and wisdom, and wished that my family would follow the Grynszpans' example.

By now I was well into my junior year of gymnasium, and still riding on my reputation as a good student. Then one day, when our history teacher asked me to lead a discussion on a subject we had been studying for weeks, he discovered that I was totally unfamiliar with it. He was shocked and angry that he had let me get by with bluffing for so long, and threatened to fail me. He notified other teachers of his discovery as well, and suddenly I was in trouble.

I began studying day and night, frantically trying to regain the ground I had lost. My parents were surprised and troubled to learn of my drastically lower marks. In the end I managed to get promoted to the senior year, but for a while it was touch and go.

Our last summer before the war we spent in Domaczów, a resort deep in the woods about a hundred miles north of Hrubieszów. There was some talk of an impending German attack, but most people dismissed it from their minds. Our villa was surrounded by trees and I enjoyed myself lying in the hammock, reading, swimming, and playing poker with the other kids. We returned home in the middle of August. The radio and newspapers were full of rumors of concentrations of German troops on the Polish border. Hitler was rattling his saber and demanding Danzig and the "corridor."

On August 23 Germany and Russia stunned the world with the announcement of their "nonaggression pact." We couldn't believe it. Polish Communists who had been rotting in Polish jails for years and had been taught by their leaders that Hitler and fascism were the devil incarnate were bewildered by the sudden flip-flop. White was black now, and black was white. Colonel Józef Beck, the Polish foreign minister, was seeking a peaceful solution, but the country was in a hopeless position. England and France, unwilling to subject their people to mass destruction in a war that promised to be even more savage than World War I, were searching desperately for an honorable way out, all the while knowing deep in their hearts that there was no way to deal with Hitler except by going to war.

On August 28 German troops moved toward the Polish-Slovakian border, effectively surrounding Poland on three sides. On August 30 the German foreign minister Joachim von Ribbentrop presented Nevile Henderson, Britain's foreign minister, with a sixteen-point memorandum that amounted to an ultimatum demanding Poland's capitulation to all Hitler's demands. That same day Poland ordered the mobilization of the Polish army. On August 31, on direct orders from Hitler, the Germans staged a phony "Polish attack" on the Gleiwitz radio station in Upper Silesia. The attack was carried out by German soldiers dressed in Polish army uniforms. This charade provided Hitler with the "proof" of Polish "provocations" he needed to present to his own country, and gave him an excuse for his impending invasion of Poland.

Western civilization thus saw itself slowly slipping into the abyss of the greatest catastrophe in its history, fully aware of what was happening, yet totally unable to do anything to prevent it.

World War II Begins

■

I remember the morning of September 1, 1939, very well. After days filled with tension, the German army attacked Poland. The Polish state radio announced the news with bulletins that spoke of German assault forces, led by tanks and supported by Stuka bombers, penetrating Poland's frontiers from the north, west, and south. The bulletins emphasized the brave resistance of the Polish army, and even reported a counterattack by the Polish cavalry, which supposedly had advanced into German territory, but we were skeptical about the latter.

It was a depressing morning. We all knew that we were in for very tough times, but it was Mother especially who, perhaps thanks to her feminine intuition, sensed the enormity of the impending disaster. The minute we heard the news she began weeping and sobbing, which was very uncharacteristic of her. "This is the end," she kept repeating. "This is the end of everything." But she soon stopped crying and became our positive, energetic Golda once again. From her experience in World War I she knew that food and fuel would soon become scarce, and she set about at once to lay in supplies of these and other necessities.

The German radio was boasting of deep penetrations by German armor, but most people dismissed this as propaganda. The hope we clung to was that the Polish army, which, although inferior to the Germans, was famous for its patriotic bravery, would be able to hold off the Germans long enough to give the Western powers time to mobilize, come to the rescue, and crush their common enemy.

We assumed that Hitler, who had begun building up his military machine only in the last few years, would be no match for the combined Western forces; we believed that Churchill's repeated warnings of the huge increases in German armed strength were exaggerated. England and France we thought of as lazy giants, who at the moment were pacifying Hitler in order to prevent bloodshed, but whose powerful armies, once unleashed, would dispatch the Germans with one swift mortal blow. We were hoping that after the fiasco of Munich and all Hitler's broken promises, the Allies, faced now with the invasion of Poland, would see at last that the only way to deal with him was through force of arms, and would immediately declare war on Germany.

But September 1 and then 2 passed, with no declaration of war from either France or England. We were shocked and frightened, unaware of the frantic efforts on the part of both countries during those two days to persuade Hitler to halt his advance into Poland— efforts that were unavailing. Hitler, exhilarated at the success of his Blitzkrieg, would not be denied his victory. Finally, on the afternoon of September 3, England, convinced that she had exhausted all possibilities for a peaceful settlement, declared war on Germany, and a few hours later France followed suit.

A tremendous wave of relief and joy surged through Poland.

Now the great armies of the West would teach Hitler a lesson. Most people believed that Western arms superiority was so overwhelming that for all practical purposes the contest would be over before it had properly got started. Hitler had bluffed and lost. We expected to see him on his knees any day now, suing for peace.

But amidst our rejoicing, news from the front continued to be ominous. Polish communiqués were vague and confusing, but it was clear that the Germans were advancing rapidly, and shortwave radio from the West seemed to confirm German claims of victory. We began hearing horror stories of German Stukas attacking peaceful towns and strafing civilians, singling out the columns of refugees that were beginning to jam the roads. Our euphoria over the entry of the Western powers into the war soon gave way to the immediate problem of what to do in the face of the approaching Germans.

German planes began to appear in the skies over Hrubieszów, often flying so low that we could see the black crosses on their wings. For several days that was all they did; at first we ran for cover, but after a few overflights without incident, we assumed that we were safe, especially since there was neither industry nor Polish army units, at that time, in Hrubieszów.

On September 7 or 8 I was walking through a field about half a mile from home when I noticed a single plane flying toward me. I assumed it was German because by then the Polish air force had virtually ceased to exist, but I didn't run for cover because there was only one other person anywhere in sight, and surely the two of us didn't present enough of a target for the pilot to bother with. Suddenly I saw the Stuka go into a dive, with a horrifying, ear-splitting shriek. I threw myself on the ground as the *rat-tat-tat* of bullets tore through the air. My heart was pounding wildly. As the sound of the plane faded in the distance, I stayed frozen on the ground for several minutes, afraid it might return. On reaching home, I learned

that the same plane had made several other strafing runs over Hrubieszów. Fortunately, only a few people had sustained any injuries,
and all of them were slight.

Refugees fleeing the oncoming Germans began to appear on the
roads leading south and east through Hrubieszów. A few drove
cars, some had horse-drawn wagons, others walked. The wagons
had obviously been loaded in a hurry; piles of mattresses, trunks,
loose clothing, boxes, umbrellas, even pieces of furniture were all
heaped on every which way. The wagons were so overloaded that
there was no room for anyone to ride on them; even the driver
walked alongside, holding the reins. Only small children occasionally sat on top of the piles of family belongings. Those who had
no transportation either for themselves or their possessions walked,
carrying large packs on their backs. From time to time we saw Polish soldiers, some in groups, others singly, many without weapons,
walking dejectedly along with the civilian refugees. Once or twice
high-ranking officers drove by, but even they had lost all their usual
dash and bravura.

On September 10, 11, and 12 the stream of refugees rose steadily,
the most-traveled roads becoming flooding rivers of humanity. People pushed and shoved, cursing the owners of wagons that had got
stuck in the mud and were blocking the road. Children were crying,
and often people knocked on our door asking for food.

What were we to do? All of us were at home, except for Fred, who
was in Warsaw. We had to decide whether we should join the masses
fleeing the Germans or stay where we were. There were arguments
for either alternative, and we spent many frantic hours weighing
the pros and cons. On the one hand, we all knew that as Jews we
were in great danger. We had the example of Hitler's treatment of the
German Jews to warn us of what we could expect: "Crystal Night,"
when Jewish shops had been smashed, the concentration camps, all

had been well publicized. At the very least, all Jews would suffer great hardships, with beatings, confiscation of property, even atrocities, and some would certainly be sent to concentration camps.

A minority, of whom I was one, had a sense of much more serious danger: perhaps great numbers of Jews would actually be killed. But these forebodings were not clearly defined, and no one certainly, seriously considered the possibility of mass killings that would include old people, women, and children. Most of us believed too that, however harsh, the occupation would be brief; perhaps a few weeks would be enough for the Allies decisively to defeat Hitler.

But attempting to escape presented many problems as well. In the first place, transportation was virtually unobtainable. The Polish army had requisitioned all the horses. In defiance of the orders the peasants had kept some, but they were unwilling to sell any because the future of the Polish złoty was so uncertain. To the owners of the few horses still remaining in the area, a horse was worth more than almost any amount of paper money. Besides, we could see that even those few fortunate refugees who had horses had the greatest difficulty keeping them moving in the mud. Many animals were collapsing on the roads, weakened from lack of fodder and from being forced to pull enormous loads day after day.

Nor was there any clear escape route to follow. The Germans were approaching from three directions, leaving open only the east, toward the Russian border, and the southeast, toward Rumania. The Russians were very unpredictable, and there was no telling whether they would open their borders to refugees. Certainly we couldn't count on any compassion from Stalin—we knew all too well how many millions of innocent people had been deported to Siberia, and how cold-bloodedly he had murdered most of his closest associates. Rumania was more likely to open its borders, but it was much farther away. The speed of the German advance and the slow pace of movement through muddy roads with horse and wagon meant that our chance of reaching the border before the Germans overtook us was almost nonexistent.

Both options were risky, but time was running out and we had to make up our minds. In the end we decided to join the tens of thousands of refugees. Father went all over Hrubieszów looking for a horse to buy, but found that even his Polish so-called friends who still had several horses were unwilling to sell him one. Eventually he managed to buy a horse from a peasant whom he had helped many times before the war, but not before the man demanded and received in gold coins much more than the horse was worth. We decided to head east, toward Russia. The Soviet border was nearer, and time was running out.

On the morning of September 15 we loaded the wagon with a few belongings, mainly food and clothing. Having seen so many refugees get stuck in the mud from overloading their wagons, we were careful not to take too much. Mother supervised the packing to make sure we didn't leave behind anything essential, such as Father's asthma medicine.

We took the road to Włodzimierz, but it soon became obvious that we were going to have trouble with our horse. We already knew that he was underfed; now we discovered that he lacked spirit as well. We walked alongside the wagon, from time to time climbing on to ride for a while. The roads were full of refugees. Fortunately it wasn't raining. Even so, the ground was muddy, but most of the traffic was moving, more or less. Our horse was capricious; from time to time he would stop without warning and look defiantly back at Father, who was holding the reins. I hated to see him whipped, but it was the only way we could get him going again.

By midday we had crossed the river Bug and stopped to eat. With all her other preoccupations, Mother had thought to prepare and bring with her many of our favorite dishes. We couldn't stop for long, though, and before dark Father found a Ukrainian peasant who was willing to let us sleep in his barn. As we lay down exhausted in the hay, it smelled good. Despite all our worries, our flight, I thought, at least had an element of adventure.

It rained that night, and when we started out early in the morning, we found the road very muddy. We kept getting stuck, and it took all our combined efforts to get the wagon moving again. The horse was not cooperating; now even whipping him didn't help.

At last we reached Włodzimierz, a town of about twenty-five thousand inhabitants, and passed through it without much trouble, since most of its roads were paved. But after we left the town it started to rain again, and the going became even rougher. The horse grew weaker, and we had to push the wagon to help him. Late in the afternoon the wagon got stuck so deep in the mud that we couldn't get it out by ourselves. Father went searching and found a peasant who brought another horse with him to help pull us out. After we got going again traffic was lighter because of the rain, but our horse was too tired to make much progress.

We decided that we had traveled enough for one day. Luckily we found a *karczma* (inn) with a room available. They even served us a hot meal, which was a comfort after all the hours on the road. We slept fully dressed. In our room there were two beds, which made it very uncomfortable for the six of us, and the next morning we were all tired. It had begun raining again, and soon after we got started we realized that we were fighting a losing battle—our progress was too slow. A couple of times the horse actually fell down, and it was harder each time to get him up again. At last it stopped raining, but we were moving at a snail's pace.

Father, who normally dealt very energetically and capably with any problem, found himself helpless. We were dirty and exhausted, and we still had covered no more than a quarter of the distance to the Russian border. In a small town twenty miles or so east of Włodzimierz we found a Jewish family who were willing to take us in for the night. We were gratefully resting and drinking tea when a neighbor came in and said, "Did you hear the news? The Russians are coming."

We were stunned, but the man assured us that it was true. The Soviet government had announced on the radio that because of the "unstable situation" in Poland they felt compelled to enter eastern Poland in order to protect the Ukrainians and White Russians who constituted the majority of the population.

This changed everything as far as we were concerned. Obviously, it made no sense to proceed toward the Russians when they were coming toward us. We knew of course that the Russians hadn't made a major move of this kind without the prior knowledge and probably the cooperation of the Germans. The critical question for us was: What would happen to Hrubieszów? Would it be occupied by the Russians or by the Germans? It seemed clear that the Russians would occupy the entire territory east of the river Bug. Hrubieszów was on the other side of the Bug, but there were many Ukrainians in the area, and it could therefore be considered part of the Ukraine.

We discussed these new developments late into the night. For the time being, at least, we didn't have to face the onrushing German army. As far as our hosts were concerned, of course, the war was over. The nightmare of German occupation no longer threatened them. Our own situation, though, was different. We were glad of the respite, however temporary, but now we were faced with a new set of difficult decisions. Should we go back to Hrubieszów, perhaps now occupied by the Germans, or should we stay where we were, with only a few of our belongings?

We decided that in the morning we would head back west and

see what developed as we approached Hrubieszów. Early the next morning we were on our way home. The skies had cleared, and we found the going a little easier, although the roads were still very muddy and we all had to help push the wagon. But we felt much better. At least we knew where we were going.

Soon we were back in Włodzimierz, where we learned that the Russian army was not far away. We stayed overnight there, and the following morning the Russian soldiers entered the town. They were friendly; clearly they were under strict orders to behave like liberators, not conquerors, which was a pleasant surprise. The local people didn't know what to expect, but soon they felt at ease and even began telling Russian stories and jokes.

It was obvious from the soldiers' behavior that the newly "liberated" territories were far more prosperous, with a much higher standard of living, than they were used to in Soviet Russia. Butter and meat were a tremendous luxury to them, and they were avidly buying things like fabrics and watches, which apparently were scarce in Russia. The soldiers were too proud to admit to any shortages of consumer goods in the Soviet Union and always asserted that everything was abundant in the Socialist paradise. The local Jews soon made a joke of it, and would ask the soldiers, "Say, soldier—you got plenty of *tsures* [troubles, in Yiddish] in Russia?" The soldiers standard reply was, as always, *"Dovolno"* (plenty).

The day after the Russians arrived in Włodzimierz, we learned that the Soviet army was also in Hrubieszów. Immediately we set out for home, arriving there in the evening. The horse collapsed just before we reached the house, and the last couple of blocks we had to push the wagon ourselves. But here everyone knew us and helped us. It was a relief, too, to find the house undisturbed and everything in order.

We unpacked, bathed, and rested. Mother was just as tired as everyone else, but she immediately started cooking dinner, and soon we were all sitting around our dining room table enjoying one of her delicious meals.

For the next few days the town buzzed with conflicting rumors. The Russians were in Hrubieszów, but the Germans were not far away. No one could predict what would happen.

To our surprise and disappointment, the Western front was strangely silent. Our hopes and expectations of a quick Allied victory had proven groundless. The "phony war" was on between the Allies and the Germans, and Poland was once again occupied by both Germans and Russians, just as it had been for more than a hundred twenty years before World War I.

Near the end of September, a new set of rumors swept through Hrubieszów: The Russians would be withdrawing behind the Bug River after all, and Hrubieszów would soon be taken over by the Germans. This unhappy news was soon confirmed by the Russian troops in Hrubieszów as they began preparing to depart.

Once more we were faced with hard choices and the tortuous process of analyzing the pros and cons. Should we leave our home again and start a new life in a Communist country? We knew it would be very risky to stay in Hrubieszów and face the dangers of Nazi occupation, but the other choice was scarcely preferable. Father was known to be a rich man, and sooner or later would be singled out by the Soviets as a capitalist enemy. He and perhaps his family too might well be deported to the Siberian labor camps. The prospect of undertaking to make a new life for ourselves under the oppressive Soviet regime was almost as difficult to face as was the grim possibility of life under the Germans.

Should the Allies finally launch their long-awaited offensive and defeat the Germans, then Poland, and Hrubieszów, would be liberated from them—but what would happen in that event to eastern

Poland, recently occupied by the Russians? Would the Allies be in a position to force them to give it back?

At last, after prolonged and agonizing discussions, we arrived at a decision. The men in the family—Father, Sam, Felek, and I (Fred was still in Warsaw, and we had had no contact with him)—would go to the Russian side. Mother and Hanka would stay home. Men, we thought, would be in much greater danger from the Nazis than women, who might be subjected to fines and indignities but whose lives wouldn't be at risk. Mother and Hanka would be more comfortable at home, where they could look after our property, perhaps even get some income from the shop. As refugees under the Soviets we knew it wouldn't be easy to make ends meet, and we hoped Mother would be able to send us some money. We believed too that, especially in the beginning, it would be possible to cross the border between German- and Soviet-occupied territory. Perhaps we could return home before long, and be with Mother and Hanka again.

With heavy hearts we packed some of our clothing, hugged and kissed Mother and Hanka, got into a waiting horse-drawn wagon we had hired, and waved good-bye as we left on our second journey to Włodzimierz.

Under the Soviets

■

We arrived in Włodzimierz that afternoon and spent the rest of the day looking for a place to stay. We found a small house in which an elderly Jewish couple lived and arranged for room and board with them. We had with us a substantial amount of cash in złotys, which were still in circulation along with the new Soviet rubles, and Father had also brought along a few of the gold coins that he had prudently saved for such an emergency. There was only one room with two beds for the four of us, but it was the best we could do for the time being. We unpacked, and soon our landlady called us for dinner.

She was not a very good cook, and I had been spoiled by Mother. I could hardly eat a bite. Not wanting to hurt our hostess's feelings, I told her that I was too tired to eat. After dinner, Father took me aside and explained that I could not expect to find the comforts of home in our new situation. "You're going to have to learn to adjust to a new set of realities," he told me.

During the next few days we walked around town getting acquainted with Włbdzimierz. It was a livelier and more civilized place than Hrubieszów, with a large Jewish population of about twelve or thirteen thousand. I was very curious to learn about life in Soviet Russia, and engaged in conversations with Russian soldiers who could speak a little Polish. They were very friendly, but wary of talking about life in the Soviet Union. They gave only the typical, stereotyped answers, and it was obvious that they were afraid to speak openly with a stranger.

Finally I came across a Jewish soldier from Leningrad who at first was unwilling to talk, but after a while he sensed that I could be trusted and he loosened up. He told me that for the time being, Stalin was friendly to the Jews, so things were not too bad. But he warned that Stalin was unpredictable, and there was no telling when his mood would change. He told me how the people in the Soviet Union were scared of the NKVD (now the KGB), and how one had to be constantly on guard. He warned me to be careful whom I spoke to, because one could never tell who might turn out to be an NKVD agent.

Life grew more normal, but there were significant changes. All businesses and farms, except for very small ones, were being nationalized. The NKVD left most people alone as long as they behaved "correctly" (a favorite word of the authorities), but people learned to be cautious when discussing anything of a remotely political nature. Former officials of the Polish government and people who were considered wealthy were apprehensive about their future in a Socialist-Communist state, but for the time being they were left alone.

The big question in our minds concerned Soviet policy with regard to the hundreds of thousands of refugees from Poland, mostly Jews, who were arriving here to escape Hitler. Some were Polish

Communists. In prewar Poland the Communist party had been out-
lawed, and its members who were arrested by the Polish police rotted
in jail for years. Many were idealists who were prepared to give their
lives to the cause of social justice. They had been stunned to learn in
September of the flip-flop in the Party line on Nazi Germany, and arrived in the newly acquired Soviet territories breathing fire and eager
to assume their well-deserved place of honor in the new Socialist society. They then received a second shock, from which most of them
never recovered: The Soviet leadership decided that there was a danger some of them were spies, saboteurs, or "plants" sent in by the
"reactionary West to do their usual dirty work against the forces of
Communism and Socialism." Since it was impossible to prove that
one was *not* a spy, the NKVD came up with a simple solution: Most of
these people, who had spent their lives fighting for Socialist ideals,
were dispatched to Siberian labor camps. Many of them did not survive the hardships of the camps, and those who did either became
the bitterest and most dedicated enemies of the Soviet regime, or
turned into cynical apparatchiks—the ones who made things work—
cold-bloodedly playing the game according to Soviet rules.

At that time the Soviet government did not discriminate against
Jews, which made things much easier for us. The schools were re-
opening, and I enrolled in the Włodzimierz high school (a *desatiletka*,
a ten-year school; the term *gymnasium* was no longer used, as having a decadent, capitalist ring). In education and in the professions,
such as medicine and engineering, Jews were treated well. There
were a few exceptions, where local anti-Semites were in power, but
they had to be careful. Using abusive language, such as calling a
Jew *"parszywy Żyd"* (rotten Jew), was illegal and punishable by a
prison sentence. This of course was balm for my nerves, still frayed
from the insults and name-calling and all the other injustices Poles
habitually inflicted on their Jewish countrymen.

Attending high school was compulsory in the Soviet Union, and the attitude of the teachers toward the students was in general much friendlier than that in the Polish gymnasiums. The official language was Ukrainian, and classes were taught in that language. Fortunately, Ukrainian is very similar to Polish, and I had occasionally heard it spoken in Hrubieszów, so I had no difficulty with it. Writing presented more of a problem because Ukrainian uses the Russian alphabet, but I learned that too within a few weeks.

Russian language was a compulsory subject, and I well remember my first class. Many of the local students knew a little Russian, and some spoke it fluently. Before the war I had never heard anyone speak it. The Russian and Polish languages both have a Slavic base, but even words that look similar are often pronounced very differently. (It's like French and Italian, which are both Romance languages, but the French and Italians are nevertheless unable to understand one another unless they learn the other language.) So when our new Russian-language teacher, a big man from Smolensk, came in and introduced himself to the students in Russian, I had no idea what he was saying. At the end of the class he called on a few of us to translate Polish and Ukrainian words into Russian. When he asked me to repeat a Russian word, I put the accent on the next-to-last syllable, as it is in almost all Polish words. It must have sounded funny, because the whole class burst into laughter. I promised myself right then and there to learn to speak Russian better than they.

To learn the language quickly, I decided to read aloud and listen to the Russian radio. Every evening I listed to the Moscow radio for several hours, and within a few weeks I had the feel of the accent and was beginning to master the language. The rest of my free time I spent reading Russian novels aloud. I had difficulty at first and had to consult my dictionary frequently for both meaning and pronunciation, but soon it began to jell, and before the end of the year I was speaking fluent Russian.

After a few weeks we moved to another house in Włodzimierz, in which we were able to rent two rooms. Father and I occupied one, Felek and Sam the other. Mrs. Burstyn, our landlady, was a good cook and anxious to please. The Burstyns had a son in his late twenties who was very bright and a terrific chess player. I had considered myself pretty good, but Burstyn soon showed me how wrong I was. Even spotting me a rook, he won almost every time.

The border between German- and Soviet-occupied Poland was not yet closely guarded, and we were in frequent communication with Mother and Hanka. They were still living in our house, but the shop as well as all of Father's other businesses had been confiscated by the Germans. Mother had managed to hide many of the fine wool fabrics, and she and Hanka were living on the proceeds from selling them off little by little.

The Gestapo was ordering the *Judenrat* (Jewish Council) to pay them large sums of money, which they called "contributions." Mother was asked to make substantial cash contributions. She explained to the leaders of the Judenrat that Father's net worth had been in real estate and other businesses that we had lost, but to no avail. The Judenrat continued to put great pressure on her, and she was forced to hand over most of her dwindling reserves of cash.

She had managed to stay in touch with Fred, who still had his office in Warsaw. We missed them all very much, but there was still no military action in the West, and our early hopes for a reunion faded, for the time being.

In December we received news of the Hrubieszów "march." Without warning, SS *Einsatzkommandos* (special units) had arrived in town. They went from house to house searching for men, and soon they had gathered together a group of seven hundred Jews, whom they marched at a brisk pace to Sokal, a town farther south, giving them no chance to rest. Those who couldn't keep up with the rest were shot on the spot. Only two hundred of the men survived. Similar Einsatzkommando *Aktionen* (actions) took place in a number of other Polish cities and towns.

It was clear that Hitler had escalated his anti-Jewish policy to a new level of ferocity, an ominous development that supported the pessimists' view that he was prepared to carry out the threats against the Jews he had expressed in *Mein Kampf.* Many people we knew had been killed in the march. We were deeply troubled, and it was becoming clear that our decision to leave Hrubieszów had been a wise one.

The Soviets now announced that all inhabitants of the western Ukraine, including the refugees from Poland, would be given Soviet citizenship. The local inhabitants had little choice; their town was now part of the Soviet Ukraine, and they intended to remain there, for better or worse. With us, it was a different story. We were refugees, and hoped to return home as soon as the war was over; we didn't want to live under the Soviets, who denied their citizens what was to us the most important thing in life: liberty. We were worried that accepting Soviet citizenship might jeopardize our freedom to eventually leave Soviet Russia. We knew that not following orders to apply for citizenship was taking a great risk, but we decided it was better to take the risk than lose the chance to leave, whenever that became possible.

The deadline set by the government for signing up came and went, and we, together with most of the other refugees, did not comply. I felt very uneasy, fearing the Soviets would consider our refusal an act of defiance and ingratitude, and that the NKVD would now consider us "unreliable" and perhaps deport us to Siberia. However, several weeks passed and no action was taken against us, to our intense relief. We couldn't vote in the forthcoming "elections," but that was a small price to pay.

Meanwhile, I was doing very well in school. Once again I was getting all A's, and soon was at the head of my class in most subjects. Father was very proud of me. He had very little to occupy him, and I suggested that he try reading, which he had never had time for at home. I got him some interesting Polish books, and at first it was hard for him because he had never learned to read Polish well, but he was a quick learner, and in no time he was reading easily. Totally devoted to business before the war, he now became engrossed in books, in which he discovered a whole new world.

Winter came, and we learned of the Soviet attack on Finland. At first it seemed impossible that this tiny country, with a population of only a couple of million, would dare to challenge the Soviet colossus, but it did. It seemed certain that the Russians would defeat the little Finnish army in a matter of days. But days became weeks, the fighting continued heavy, and the Red Army was making no progress. The whole world watched in amazement as the brave Finns resisted all Russian attempts to gain ground. On the BBC and other Western radio stations we heard marvelous stories of Finnish fighters on skis suddenly appearing behind the Russian lines, wreaking havoc, and then as suddenly disappearing in the dark of night. My friends and I rooted enthusiastically for the Finns, waited impatiently for the war communiqués, hoped fervently that they could continue their miraculous stand. But the embarrassed Soviet High Command threw many fresh new divisions and thousands of additional tanks and planes into the battle, and with this overwhelming advantage in men and matériel they slowly gained ground. The Finns were finally forced to accept Soviet terms and cede part of Karelia.

They had lost the war but won the admiration of millions of people all over the world, and the Soviets had lost a great deal of prestige, revealing themselves to be inept in planning and strategy, and questionable in the quality of their equipment and the fighting ability of their soldiers.

This evidence of Soviet weakness might, we thought, encourage Hitler to strike at Russia, a possibility we viewed with mixed emotions. Fighting on two fronts might prove as disastrous for Germany as it had in World War I; on the other hand, we were only fifteen miles from Hitler's army and didn't relish the thought of falling into his hands.

About this time I became friendly with a girl in our class, Itka Kaufman, a blue-eyed blonde with lovely skin—and, unfortunately, a somewhat prominent nose. Itka was the first real girlfriend I had ever had, and it was very exciting. In Hrubieszów I had been shy with girls, and except for a quick kiss stolen here and there, I had never been at all close to a girl. For three years I was in love with a Polish girl in my class in the gymnasium and often had erotic dreams about her, but I doubt that she ever knew of my feelings; I was so afraid of rejection that I never allowed them to show.

The furthest I dared to go with Itka was prolonged kissing, after which I would open her blouse and feel her breasts. I occasionally played chess with Itka's father and got to know him rather well. I felt it would be highly improper to "take advantage" of his daughter.

But apparently Itka didn't agree. One evening after we started kissing, we leaned over on the sofa and I wound up on top of her. We were both fully dressed—I even had my jacket on—but we started moving our bodies in rhythm, until Itka asked, "What if I have a baby?" I thought she was joking, and laughed. Only later, back in my room, did it occur to me that Itka had seemed some-how disappointed, and the thought suddenly struck me: Might she have been willing to go all the way? I never found out, be-cause whenever I was alone with Itka after that, the very thought of betraying Mr. Kaufman's trust made me avoid any horizontal positions.

The winter of 1939–1940 was exceptionally severe. On many days the temperature reached –30°C (–22°F). This didn't bother me. All in all, this was not an unhappy time. I was young, I had a girl-friend, I enjoyed studying and playing chess, and, most important, as a Jew, I had a feeling of equality with the Gentiles. Stalin, known for his ups and downs with regard to Jews, was, at that time, strict-ly enforcing Soviet laws protecting all nationalities from slander. I could see many of the inefficiencies and the brutality of the Soviet system in other areas, but for the time being, at least, those did not affect us personally.

The precariousness of our situation, however, was soon force-fully brought home to us. One night we were sleeping in our beds when we heard heavy knocking at the front door. Mrs. Burstyn got up to see who was there. A loud voice said, "Police. Open up." Suspecting that this might have something to do with us, and showing great presence of mind, she whispered to her hus-band to go and tell us to hurry and hide in the attic, while she held the police off for a couple of minutes, long enough for us to straighten our beds and climb the ladder to the attic. An NKVD officer came in with two local policemen asking whether there were any refugees from Poland in the house. Mrs. Burstyn as-sured him that there were none. She must have sounded very con-vincing, because they promptly left the house and drove away in their truck.

The next morning we learned that the night visit had been part of an NKVD citywide sweep arresting refugees who hadn't applied for Soviet citizenship. Those they picked up were given ten minutes to pack their belongings, then were loaded onto waiting trucks and taken to the Włodzimierz railroad station, where they were put on a train that departed the following morning, heading east. Over a thousand people were in this transport—men, women, and some children. The same thing took place all over Western Ukraine and Byelorussia; more than a hundred thousand Polish refugees who had failed to register—mostly Jews—were shipped to Siberian camps. In addition, many local people who were suspected of disloyalty to the regime were arrested and shipped east as well.

A couple of months later the first letters from the deportees began to arrive from several Siberian labor camps. Between the lines they told of the cruel cold and hunger. Fortunately, the NKVD permitted them to receive food and clothing packages. We had known all along that by not taking out Soviet citizenship papers we were risking reprisals; nevertheless, we were shocked and unnerved.

For the next few nights we slept fully dressed, ready to run and hide in the attic at the sound of a knock on the door. Our presence was now "illegal," and I stopped going to school. We had no idea how to cope with this situation, but the Soviets, with a wonderful lack of logic, solved the problem for us. They announced that if those refugees who had escaped the roundup would register immediately, they would receive Soviet citizenship papers or temporary residence permits. So those who had not hidden from the NKVD had been sent to Siberia, while those of us who had disobeyed were now safe from persecution, at least for the time being.

When spring came, letters from home were less frequent. It was now much more difficult to cross the border, and there was no regular mail service. We did hear, at least, that Mother, Hanka, and Fred were all in good health, and that, since the initial wave of shootings in December, mass killing of Jews had stopped.

In April we learned of the German invasion of Denmark and Norway. Hitler's audacity surprised us. We had thought that England's mastery of the seas would surely prevent the Germans from crossing the Kattegat and Skagerrak straits in the North Sea. But with the help of paratroops, they succeeded in occupying every major Norwegian city. Only in the north did the British finally manage to land, at Narvik and a few other points, but even there they were unable to hold out for long, and eventually were forced to evacuate their troops.

This was gloomy news, but we were still hoping that the "phony" winter war in the West would soon come to an end and the Western armies would launch their long-awaited offensive—although we were no longer quite so confident as we had been. After Hitler's successful occupation of Denmark, and especially of Norway, the British no longer seemed so invincible. We tried to rationalize their defeat by telling ourselves that Norway, after all, was of only peripheral importance, and that the Allies must have decided to concentrate all their efforts on a massive attack on Germany itself later on.

The Danish people and their king now provided a shining example of courage and character to the whole world. Immediately upon occupying the country, the Nazis exacted heavy "contributions" from Danish Jews, and in general made their lives as miserable as possible. The Danes, led by their king, went to great lengths to demonstrate wholehearted support for their Jews and, at a considerable risk to themselves, resisted the German orders in every way they could. Such behavior was in striking contrast to that of many other occupied countries, and stands out as one of the proudest chapters in human history.

That spring Felek and Sam were able to get jobs in Uściług. Felek became a teacher, and Sam started off on the Uściług schoolboard and eventually became the head of it. He became friendly with Mojsejenko, who was the Secretary of the local Communist Party. Because of his friendship with Mojsejenko, he was able to help a number of people who were considered "unreliable" by the Russian secret police and had problems with them.

All our hopes came crashing down during the next few weeks. On May 10 the German army struck on the western front. Against all our expectations, it was they and not the Allies who opened a major offensive in the west. In a lightning attack they surged across the Belgian frontier, following the strategy of the Schlieffen Plan and, supported by mobile tank formations and diving Stuka fighter-bombers, quickly scored their first successes. The French and British sent forces into Belgium as well, but they had no chance against the efficiency of the German war machine. Belgium soon capitulated and the German flood poured through the gap, sweeping across into France, sending the British and French forces into disorderly retreat. The celebrated Maginot line, boasted of for so long as impregnable, was attacked from both sides—a contingency not anticipated in its planning—collapsed with little resistance, and fell to the Germans.

Farther north, the rapidly advancing German mobile attack forces drove deep into France, taking hundreds of thousands of prisoners. The roads were jammed with refugees fleeing the onrushing Germans. It was a catastrophic rout. The victorious invaders drove a deep wedge between the French and the British. In a swift enveloping movement they swept around the British Expeditionary Force, now retreating toward the sea, and reached the English Channel west of Dunkirk. The British were now cut off from the main French forces and surrounded, with their backs to the sea, while the French army was escaping south, completely demoralized.*

The French, who were now isolated, made a halfhearted stand on the river Somme, but the Wehrmacht broke through in a matter of days and the French resistance collapsed. Paris was occupied on June 14, and the French wept in the streets as they watched the hated Boche marching in triumph down the Champs-Elysées.

On June 22 Hitler went to Compiègne to receive personally the surrender of the French army. The ceremony took place in the same

---

*The German general Heinz Guderian, who commanded the tank formations, saw an opportunity to wipe out the entire BEF of several hundred thousand men, which would deal the British a crippling, perhaps a knockout, blow. Knowing they had not had time to organize the evacuation of their troops, he wanted to strike the final blow before they got a chance to do that. To his astonishment, Hitler ordered him to hold off. Again and again Guderian, knowing that this unique chance to wipe out the British army en masse was slipping away with every passing hour, pleaded with his Führer for permission to press the attack and drive the British into the Channel. And again and again Hitler denied permission, until it was too late. An improvised armada of ships of every size and description was forming in England's ports, and would soon come to the rescue of their countrymen. Under intense and continuous bombardment by Goering's air force, the British navy, and civilians as well, plying steadily back and forth across the waters of the Channel, managed to evacuate over three hundred thousand British soldiers and thousands of French in the space of a few days. All their equipment was lost, but they lived to fight again.

Military historians are still debating the reasons for Hitler's fatal hesitation. The prevailing view is that he was so surprised by the lack of resistance to Guderian's attack that he began to suspect some sort of trap for his overextended forces. Whatever the reason, Hitler's failure to act had a far-reaching effect on the course of the war. Without those hundreds of thousands of their best-trained officers and men, the English would have found it much more difficult, if not impossible, to fight the victorious Germans alone, for more than a year.

railway car in which the victorious Allies had received the German surrender on November 8, 1918. In a single stroke Hitler had accomplished what the Kaiser had never, in four bloody years, been able to do. The incredulous world watched with astonishment as this barbaric madman became master of the European continent. Nightmare had become reality. It was clearly of no use resorting to logic or common sense to predict what would happen next. Churchill vowed that England would continue to fight on alone, but her armed forces were still pitifully weak and only the English Channel stood between the Nazi border and their homeland. America was not yet anywhere near to entering the war. Even Mussolini, who had stalled until the last minute, fearful of repeating the mistake Italy had made in World War I in coming in on the losing side, now jumped into the fray and stabbed France in the back after she had already been defeated.

These events were a terrible blow to us. Our hopes for a quick end to the war evaporated. The outlook for our future was bleak. We were refugees in the Soviet Union, with no home or reliable source of income; Mother, Hanka, and Fred were in Hitler's clutches. Our chances of being united again in the foreseeable future were slim. Our hearts were heavy with apprehension; only a miracle could help us now.

The school year came to an end, and as the best student in my class I was awarded a prize: a book, which Father proudly showed off to the neighbors. I became a chess fanatic, spending almost every day of my summer vacation playing chess from morning till night. The trouble was that young Burstyn was getting bored because he was so much better than I. I had to beg him to continue playing with me, with Mrs. Burstyn interceding on my behalf as well. Although we played an average of eight to ten hours a day, I don't think I ever won a game from him. I actually improved tremendously, but he had a psychological edge: I saw danger in his every move. I did much better against all the other players, and placed third in our school tournament.

Toward the end of August many of the refugees, including Father and me, were ordered by the authorities to move east to a distance of at least a hundred kilometers from the border. Evidently they didn't trust us.

The nearest town beyond the hundred-kilometer limit was Ołyka, so we said good-bye to the Burstyns and our other friends in Włodzimierz and set out by train for Ołyka. Soon after arriving we arranged for room and board with an elderly lady who owned a small house in the center of town. Ołyka had a population of nine thousand, of which three or four thousand were Jews. It was a pretty town, with small houses and many gardens with fruit trees. In it were a high school, a library, and a Russian military base. The people were friendly and easygoing. I started attending the Ołyka high school, and Father joined the library. We frequently heard from Sam and Felek, but very rarely from Mother and Hanka.

The war news was not encouraging. Hitler's expected invasion of England did not take place; instead, there were furious air battles over the Channel between English and German fighter planes, the "Battle of Britain," as it later was called. None of it had much effect on our situation. Our one hope now was that America would soon decide to enter the war and with her enormous production capacity bring about the rapid defeat of Hitler.

Ołyka high school was much easier and less competitive than the one in Włodzimierz. I was far more advanced in my studies than the local students, and my reputation as a top student spread rapidly. Before long the principal was referring to me in meetings as "the best student in our school."

The Soviets placed heavy emphasis on scholastic achievement. Sports such as soccer, volleyball, and basketball were encouraged,

but the emphasis was on academic excellence. Teachers were greatly respected, and promising students received frequent praise and
pampering. The principal and the senior teachers met often with
the students to stress the importance of studying and good grades,
which would lead to a high position in Soviet society. There was a
great deal of rhetoric about youth and its vital role in the Socialist
and eventually Communist world of the future.

A classmate of mine was called Yuri. He had been born in Moscow, and his father was an officer in the local unit of the Red Army.
Yuri was tall and blond, with blue eyes and a very engaging smile.
We became friends and spent a lot of time together, playing chess
and volleyball and discussing all kinds of things. He was bright, but
completely unaware of what the world was like outside the Soviet
Union. He really believed all the propaganda about the decadent
West; he thought the majority of the American people were starving
on the streets. Father warned me to be very careful when I talked
to him, and never to be critical of the regime; his father was a Party
member. So I avoided all conversation that might lead to a discussion of life in capitalist societies. We spoke about books, but this was
dangerous too because so many of my favorite writers were taboo
in Soviet Russia. Talking to Yuri helped me to become very fluent
in Russian, which I soon spoke without any Polish inflection. Sometimes when I met a Russian I would pretend to be from Russia too,
and was never challenged. I quit doing that when Father pointed
out that this too was a dangerous game that might cost us our freedom. What if I should happen to run into an NKVD agent?

However, to be known as "the best student in the entire school"
in such an atmosphere made me a prominent figure. At almost every school meeting, the principal singled me out as an example for
the other students to follow, which was embarrassing but pleasant
nonetheless. This together with relief at not being threatened as

a Jew compensated to some extent for being a refugee, separated from the family.

But I greatly disliked the "political meetings." All too often, all the students, teachers, senior members of the local Communist party, town officials, and representatives of the local Red Army unit and the various trades would gather in the school auditorium. Seated on the stage, in a single row of chairs, was the "meeting committee." Because of my scholastic standing I was on that committee representing the students. Seated next to me were the representatives of the teachers, the Red Army, the workers, and so on. The meeting was always chaired by the Party secretary, a man in his late fifties. He came from somewhere in Russia; apparently the Party would not entrust this important position to a local man so soon after the takeover of the Western Ukraine.

There were several speakers, each more boring than the last. They seldom spoke critically of anything or anyone, and most of the speeches were leaden exhortations to ever-increasing effort in building the great Soviet society of the future. The Party secretary always spoke last and longest, and invariably finished by reciting the names of the nine members of the ruling Politburo, large posters of whom hung in the background, praising them for their efforts on behalf of humanity. He began by calling out the name of the least important of the nine, listing his achievements in the service of the Soviet nation, and then worked his way up the hierarchy in reverse order of importance (following of course the line laid down by the radio and newspapers). Thunderous applause followed each encomium.

After he had finished with that, it was Stalin's turn to be praised. I never ceased to be amazed at the range and variety of glowing superlatives the Party secretary came up with to describe this despot, who had sent so many millions of his innocent countrymen to their deaths. Stalin was "the brilliant leader, the wise teacher, the pacesetter for new ideas, the master theoretician, the prudent guide of the nation's destiny, the visionary architect of the new society, the far-seeing builder of new cities, the heroic defender of our country, the fearless leader of the Red Army, the Sun that shines upon us all and to whom we are so grateful," and on and on. A thunderous standing ovation would follow, which seemed to go on forever. Everyone knew that NKVD agents were scattered throughout the crowd, observing the people's reactions, and no one would risk being the first to stop clapping or sit down before the Party secretary. During this period Stalin's deification was at its height, and to me the whole spectacle was both sad and comical. I suspected that the Party secretary enjoyed playing this game of cat and mouse, and at times I found it difficult to keep a straight face.

Unexpectedly, we received a letter from my cousin Józiek, who had been seized by the NKVD during the wave of refugee arrests in December. He was now in a Siberian labor camp not far from the North Pole, had managed somehow to get in touch with Fred, and had learned from him where we were. We gathered that there was hunger in the camp, and we mailed a food parcel to him. From a local farmer we bought over ten pounds of fatback, which was high in calories and would stand up well in the long transit to Siberia. We also sent him some biscuits, sugar, and fruit preserves. After a month or so he wrote to tell us that he had received the food, and how much it had helped. Over the next several months we were able to send him a few more parcels.

To a great extent I was now the center of Father's life. Before the war he had always been too busy, and I too young, for us ever to have had much in the way of conversation. Now we talked about many things. He was very proud of my scholastic achievements, and whenever there was a school meeting with the parents he would attend, to hear praise and compliments from my teachers. It made me happy to give him such pleasure, and for the first time we became very close.

Thanks to my academic record, the head of the local Komsomol approached me about joining the Communist youth organization. One could not advance far in the Soviet hierarchy without joining the Communist party, and the Komsomol was a preliminary step to becoming a Party member. He told me that even though I was a refugee, it was important that the best student set an example politically as well as academically. I was unprepared for this and became somewhat flustered. To gain time, I told him how grateful I was, but that I wanted to think over such an important decision, and would let him know.

It was a real dilemma. On the one hand, it would be helpful if we were forced to stay for any length of time in the Soviet Union, and in any case refusing might mark Father and me as "enemies of the people," which could result in a long trip to Siberia. On the other hand, it might present a problem in the more distant future; assuming Hitler's eventual defeat, it could jeopardize our chances of returning home. And more immediately distasteful was the prospect of having to attend still more of those boring, phony political meetings. In the end, we decided that I should say nothing, and wait to see whether the Komsomol leader would pursue the matter. He never did, but I suspected that I had made an enemy and felt uneasy about it.

May 1 was Labor Day, and one of the two most important Soviet holidays. (The other was November 7, the anniversary of the Communist Revolution.) The Party scheduled a big parade, in which all strata of society were to be represented. Students were to march first, followed by members of the various trade organizations, farm co-ops, municipal employees, members of the local Communist

Party, and so forth. As always, the units of the Red Army, featuring a tank brigade, came last.

May Day 1941 was a beautiful day. We were all gathered in the schoolyard, where the teachers were trying to organize us, when the principal rushed in breathlessly and informed me that I had been chosen to lead the parade. I was given an enormous red flag to carry; luckily it wasn't windy, or I might have been swept away.

So here I was, marching all alone at the head of the parade, the great red flag rippling and swirling around me. As I entered the town square, I saw that it was jammed with thousands of spectators. Trying to keep a straight face at the thought of Father's astonishment when he saw me leading the procession, I marched past the stands filled with local dignitaries, looking for him in the crowd. Unfortunately I couldn't spot him, but this story became one of our favorites.

On the war front, nothing much was happening. England seemed safe now from invasion; Hitler had missed his chance, if ever there had been any. Still, Hitler's domination of Europe was complete for the time being, and we knew we were in for a long wait. Our only hope for the future was still America. We heard rumors that the Germans were concentrating their forces on the Russian border, which was alarming; the Russian-Finnish war had lowered our estimate of the Red Army's strength.

I became friendly with our math teacher, Mr. Urbaniak. He was a Pole who had spent most of his life in the Soviet Union, a graduate of Leningrad University who had taught high school there before being sent to Ołyka. He realized that I was capable of much more than our school curriculum required, and offered to tutor me in advanced math at his house after school. He and his wife, who was also a teacher, were near retirement age and had no children. They both took a liking to me, and I spent hours learning math from Mr. Urbaniak while Mrs. Urbaniak fed me tea and cookies. I developed a fondness for trigonometry, and spent many hours at home solving the complicated problems that Mr. Urbaniak set for me.

Graduation day came, and again I received a prize as the best student. I was even prouder of a gift from Mr. Urbaniak, an old trigonometry book that he had received as a prize when a student in Leningrad. He inscribed it, "To Henry Orenstein, the best student I ever taught." Later, when we were on the run, I carried this book with me as long as I could.

At the end of May, Sam and Felek arrived in Ołyka to spend their summer vacation with us. We were a little cramped all in one room, but very happy to be together again. The weather continued beautiful; we went swimming together and took long walks. But we hadn't heard from Mother in weeks, which worried us.

Talk of German troop concentrations on the Russian borders intensified. The BBC was predicting that an attack was imminent; one broadcast even pinpointed June 22. We weren't sure whether these reports represented anything more than wishful thinking by the English, who were naturally weary of resisting Hitler all alone. But in any event, Ołyka was more than a hundred kilometers from the border, and we didn't feel immediately threatened even if war should break out.

The Soviet radio and press gave no hint of potential trouble. Soviet freight trains loaded with grain and other supplies continued rolling to Germany. Whenever she was mentioned on the Soviet radio, it was in the usual neutralist vein. Soviet criticism was still reserved for the capitalist West. We decided that since the Russians weren't worried, why should we be, and continued to enjoy the beautiful spring and summer of 1941.

The Germans Attack the Soviet Union

■

J une 22 1941, was a beautiful sunny day. It wasn't hot yet, and a gentle breeze made it even more pleasant. I got up early that morning and went to a park where school kids played soccer and basketball. I noticed a few people in a cluster, talking excitedly. Early that morning the Germans had attacked Russia.

So this was it. All kinds of thoughts were racing in my mind: the excitement of a gigantic struggle between two large armies, fear of the Germans, hope that all this could somehow lead to the end of the war. I rushed home with the news. Sam, Felek, Father, and I spent the whole day talking, worrying, hoping. Since we were a hundred kilometers from the border, we felt that we were in no immediate danger. The Soviet army was very large and well equipped; even at worst, it would certainly not collapse as quickly as had the Polish army.

The Soviet radio made no announcement until late in the day. When it came, it was, of course, typical Soviet propaganda: "The heroic Soviet army will deal the treacherous fascist invaders a crushing blow," and so on. Even the master of treachery himself, Stalin, apparently found it difficult to believe that Hitler, his new friend and ally, would launch such a massive attack against him without the slightest provocation or warning. Even though we were caught in the middle, we felt a certain satisfaction at the ignominious end of the cynical pact between those two despots.

Once again, as in September 1939, it was likely that Sam and Felek—and this time perhaps I as well—would be mobilized. And once again, it all became academic because of the rapid advances of the German army. By the third day of the war we watched, with disbelief and broken hearts, Russian tanks and soldiers fleeing east in a disorderly retreat. Soon the BBC confirmed German claims of having dealt the Soviets a smashing defeat, and those menacing low-flying Stukas appeared in the skies without challenge from Soviet fighter planes.

Once more we discussed our options. We might flee with the Russians; the problem there was that Father was ill with asthma and had a double hernia, and it would have been very dangerous for him to embark on a long journey without knowing whether medical care would be available at any point along the way. We felt—as events were to prove, correctly—that almost certainly we would have been caught by the rapid advance of the German armies, and would have found ourselves somewhere in the Ukraine without the conveniences of our temporary home in Ołyka. The idea of escaping into the forests, as a few young people were thinking of doing, we never seriously considered, mainly because of Father's health.

Hitler had not yet begun his systematic destruction of the Jews. After the collapse of Poland there was a wave of atrocities, usually forced marches on which tens of thousands of Jews, mainly men, were killed by the Einsatzkommandos. That was followed by a period of increasingly dehumanizing policies: Jews were sealed into ghettos, were forced to surrender most of their money in the form of "contributions," and were made to suffer many indignities. But there had been no mass killings including women and children, as yet. The speeches of Hitler and his lieutenants included a great deal of rhetoric concerning their plans for rendering Europe free of Jews (*Judenrein*), "stamping out the Jewish vermin," and so forth, but only the extreme pessimists could believe that Germany, a nation of poets, philosophers, musicians, and scientists, a nation that had given the world Beethoven, Goethe, and Kant, could actually embark on a program of deliberate mass extermination of the Jewish people as a whole, including innocent children, helpless old people, and women.

So we decided to wait for the arrival of the Germans and their occupation, hoping that we would survive somehow, that the Russians, with the help of "General Winter," would eventually defeat Hitler as they had Napoleon in 1812, and that America would sooner or later enter the war and rescue Europe once again as she had in World War I.

We thought too that in the meantime we might find a chance to rejoin the rest of our family in Hrubieszów. It was now a year and nine months since we had left home, and we missed them more than ever.

Meanwhile, the Russian retreat was becoming a rout. Demoralized Soviet soldiers came through Ołyka, sometimes without their weapons. On June 27 we heard for the first time the threatening rumble of artillery in action. The Stukas were flying low over the town, attacking anything that moved. Clearly it was a matter of hours before the Germans arrived, and so we, together with many others, sought refuge in caves in the hillsides of the main road on the outskirts of Ołyka.

Never will I forget the entry of the German army into Ołyka.
First we heard the distant roar of hundreds of approaching vehicles, which became louder and louder. Then we heard commands
shouted in German, and a large column of the German army came
into sight—first motorcycles, then tanks, trucks filled with soldiers,
artillery, and hundreds of foot soldiers. The column was moving
along in a very orderly fashion; the soldiers' uniforms were clean
and fresh, as though they had never seen battle. Officers in open
command cars were barking orders and talking to each other loudly. It looked more like a parade of a victorious army than a combat
force. There was fear in our hearts; the Germans sounded harsh
and arrogant, and we were awed by the power and efficiency of the
German war machine.

Even though we had expected it, we were still surprised by the
warmth and enthusiasm with which the Ukrainian population met
the Germans. Women threw flowers at the soldiers, people ran up
to them waving greetings and offering them bread and salt as a

---

*Looking back now, from the perspective of time, I believe that Hitler's greatest
blunder in World War II was his treatment of the local populations in the territories the Germans captured from the retreating Soviets. Most of these people
hated Stalin and his regime. In the Ukraine—and, judging from the accounts
of friends and relatives who were there at the time, in Byelorussia as well—the
great majority of the inhabitants wanted to see Communism destroyed. They
had always dreamed of an independent Ukraine and Byelorussia, even though
throughout most of their history they had lived under the dominion of others.
For centuries, Russians, Poles, Swedes, Turks, and Mongolians had taken turns
occupying these areas; only sporadically, as in Chmielnicki's rebellion three
hundred years earlier, had the Ukrainians had a taste of independence.

I am convinced that had the Germans announced the immediate formation
of Ukrainian and Byelorussian governments under nationalist leaders, and had
they treated the people well, played down occasional partisan activity, and conducted themselves as liberators, they would have enjoyed considerable support
from the local population. Even in Russia itself, had they come in with such

symbolic gesture of friendship. There was no sign of any hostility. Apparently the Ukrainians were not aware of Hitler's opinion of them—indeed, of all Slavs. They didn't know that they were classed as *Untermenschen* (subhumans), and that plans were already under way to exterminate most of them to make room *(Lebensraum)* for the Germanic peoples.*

slogans as "Liberty from Communism," or "We want to give Russia back to the Russian people," Russian resistance both on the fighting fronts and in the conquered areas would have been much weaker. By behaving like brutal aggressors, treating the local population as racial inferiors, confiscating their possessions, and literally starving to death hundreds of thousands of prisoners of war, they gave the people no choice except to fight to the bitter end, even under the hated leadership of Stalin. Had Hitler turned this simmering dislike of Communism to his advantage, he probably would have succeeded in occupying Moscow and Leningrad, perhaps bringing about the collapse of the Soviet armies late in 1941. And without the enormous pressure the Soviet army exerted on the Germans later on, it would have taken the Allies many more years, perhaps decades, to win the war. It is not even inconceivable that in such circumstances the British, and perhaps the Americans as well, would have concluded that a temporary truce with Hitler, however uneasy, might be preferable to a very long, costly war—and, given the uncertainty as to which side might first develop devastating new weaponry, perhaps an unwinnable one.

Under the Germans:
Ołyka

■

T he first couple of weeks under the German occupation were not so bad for the Jews as we had feared. The German army passed quickly through the Ołyka area in pursuit of the Russians, meeting only sporadic resistance. If any Germans remained behind in Ołyka, we didn't see them. A few Ukrainians had been appointed by the Germans to take over local government, and there was no shortage of food or other basic commodities.

The rapid advance of the German army and the Red Army's inability to hold any defensive lines took everyone by surprise. Every day German newspapers and radio gave the names of the cities newly fallen to the onrushing Germans: Zhitomir, Minsk, Smolensk. The German war communiqués spoke of gigantic encirclements, with entire Soviet armies surrounded and annihilated. Five hundred thousand Russians were trapped in a huge pocket in Byelorussia, six hundred thousand in the Ukraine. Most were killed or taken prisoner. The Germans seemed unstoppable.

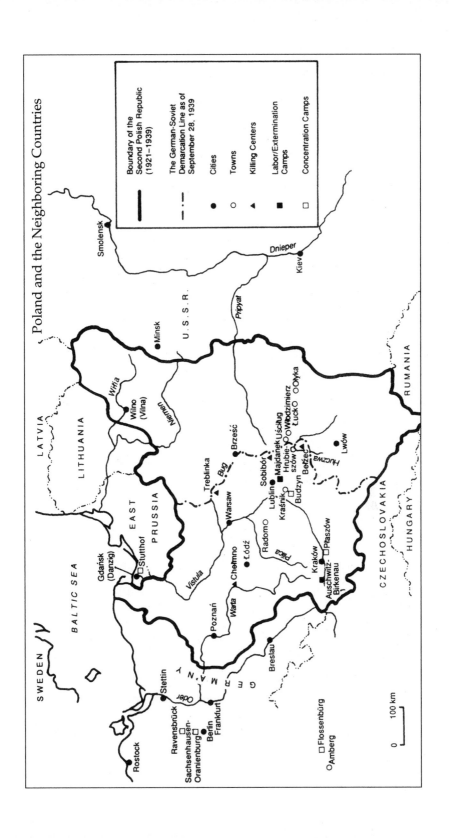

Poland and the Neighboring Countries

Boundary of the
Second Polish Republic
(1921–1939)

The German-Soviet
Demarcation Line as of
September 28, 1939

Cities

Towns

Killing Centers

Labor/Extermination
Camps

Concentration Camps

SWEDEN

BALTIC SEA

Rostock

Stettin

Oder

Ravensbrück
Sachsenhausen-
Oranienburg
Berlin
Frankfurt

G E R M A N Y

Breslau

Flossenbürg
Amberg

0   100 km

Gdańsk
(Danzig)

Stutthof

E A S T

P R U S S I A

LATVIA

LITHUANIA

Wilno
(Vilna)

Niemen

Wilia

Minsk

U. S. S. R.

Smolensk

Dnieper

Pripyat

Kiev

Poznań

Warta

Vistula

Łódź

Chełmno

Radom

Warsaw

Treblinka

Bug

Brześć

Sobibór

Lublin

Majdanek Uściług
Hrubie-   Włodzimierz
szów   Łuck
Budzyn   Bełżec
Kraśnik

Włodzimierz

Horochów

Łuck

Wołyka

Pilica

Kraków

Auschwitz
Birkenau

Płaszów

Lwów

RUMANIA

CZECHOSLOVAKIA

HUNGARY

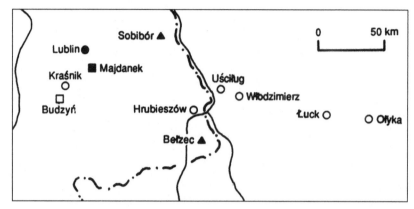

Enlargement of the area in Poland where the Orenstein family was moving from town to town during the 1939–t1943.

One day in the middle of July, Felek, Sam, Father, and I were sitting in our room, discussing the situation. Father wasn't feeling well and was lying on the sofa. Our landlady looked through the open window and told us, "The Germans are going from house to house rounding up Jews for work." We quickly decided to go upstairs to the attic. Father wouldn't join us. "I'm not going," he said. "I'm sick—they can't use sick people to work for them."

A minute later, from the little attic window, we saw an SS man and two Ukrainian policemen enter the house. First we heard the Ukrainians shout in broken German, *"Juden—Arbeit"* (Jews—work). Then we heard the German screaming, and there was a great deal of commotion. We saw them leave our house and enter the one next door, from which they soon emerged, taking our neighbor and his son with them. They continued down the street, looking for more Jews.

Our landlady came to the foot of the attic stairs and called, "They're gone. Hurry, your father needs help." We ran downstairs. Father was sitting on the sofa, the top of his head covered with blood. "Don't worry, it's not bad," he reassured us. We cleaned and bandaged the cut, which was superficial, while our landlady told us what had happened.

The SS officer had been angry at not finding any men in the house except for Father, and ordered him to get up from the sofa. "I'm sick. I can't go to work," Father replied. The German put his revolver right to Father's temple and said, *"Verfluchte Jude* [Damned Jew], you come or I'll shoot you." "Go ahead and shoot," Father answered. "I can't go. I'm sick." The German then struck Father on the head with the butt of his gun, spat, repeated "Verfluchte Jude," and walked out, followed by the two Ukrainians.

As she recounted this, the landlady shook her head. "Your father is a *meshugene* (crazy). He tells a German, 'Go ahead and shoot.' I thought he was a dead man for sure." Once again Father had demonstrated his extraordinary coolness and toughness; how many men would refuse to obey an order with a gun to their heads?—especially when at the time it seemed to be merely a matter of a day's work.

We learned within an hour or so that the Germans and their Ukrainian helpers had gone searching through the main Jewish section of Ołyka, taken all the men they could find, about four or five hundred, loaded them into trucks, and driven off. The men's families were not particularly concerned; most thought they would be back by the end of the day. By evening, when the men had not yet returned, their families were beginning to worry, but not for their lives; it was more a question of their being hungry and perhaps mistreated.

The following morning a man came back with a bone-chilling tale. A Ukrainian school friend of one of the Jewish boys who had been taken away told his parents that from a distance, just outside the town, he had seen the Germans and the Ukrainians shoot all the Jews they had taken to "work" and bury them in ditches left over from World War I.

The general reaction was of disbelief. One of the men started shouting, "He is a liar, an anti-Semite! He's trying to torture us with worry. The Germans wouldn't do that." Sam, always the pessimist, thought the boy might be telling the truth. Felek and I didn't believe it. Father didn't say much; perhaps he agreed with Sam but didn't want to worry us. So many men had been taken away that in about half of all the Jewish families in Ołyka someone was gone—a father, a son, a son-in-law, an uncle, a cousin.

They waited nervously all that day, but there was still no news from the men. By next morning the nightmare was becoming a reality. One of the Ukrainian police confided in his girlfriend that it was true, the Jews had been killed. She in turn repeated the story to a Jewish friend of hers. Even then, faced with this confirmation, many people refused to believe it. They still thought the stories were being spread by anti-Semites who wanted to scare the Jews.

But as days passed and none of the men were heard from, the terrible truth had to be accepted—especially since we were now hearing similar stories from other nearby towns. Worse yet, actual eyewitness accounts of the mass killings of thousands and thousands of Jews, including women and children, were coming from the Russian side. A wounded German officer on the way home from the Russian front told one of the men working at the Ołyka train station of an unbelievable slaughter in Kiev: a hundred thousand Jews—men, women, and children—murdered in a ravine.*

This was the first time we had heard of mass extermination, and at first I rejected the monstrous thought. Women, old people, babies, being murdered on such a scale—it was simply not conceivable. But while my mind pushed the thought away, my heart was gripped with terror. Most people refused to believe the story, unable to accept such a possibility, that not only they themselves, but

---

*It was the infamous massacre of Babi Yar.

their entire families, the whole Jewish people, might be wiped out. They seized upon any rationalization, however improbable; perhaps the Germans considered all Jews inside "Old Russia" to be Communists. We, the "Europeans," they would surely leave alone. These were frantic days and frantic discussions. It was difficult for us to absorb the thought of mass slaughter of little children and old people. How could we begin to grasp the fact that we were going to be killed just for having been born Jews—and that there was nothing on this earth we could do to prevent it?

In the meantime, the Germans continued to advance on all fronts. They surrounded Leningrad, occupied Kiev, then Kharkov, and were approaching Moscow. It seemed only a matter of days before Leningrad and Moscow would fall. How long could the Russian army continue to resist? Then I saw a bold red headline in a German army newspaper dated October 3, 1941: HITLER: THE WAR IS WON. ONLY MOPPING-UP OPERATIONS REMAIN.

I was crushed, my heart broken. This was the end of hope. I wept silently, in despair. Now that Hitler was the master of Europe, all her resources at his disposal, how long would it be before the free world could defeat Germany? Ten or twenty years—maybe never. It seemed unbelievable, illogical, insane, that this maniac, this mass murderer could control the destiny of hundreds of millions of lives, but he did. It seemed that nothing and nobody could stop him now. True, there was still America, with her fantastic productivity, but what good was she, an ocean away? And America hadn't even declared war on Germany. Only helpless little England was still free, fighting on alone, her sole defense the waters of the English Channel.

The world was dark, dark, dark! Even to an optimist like me, everything looked hopeless. For the first time ever I began questioning whether life was worth living. Hitler seemed invincible. In 1939 he had conquered Poland in days, in May and June of 1940 he had dealt a crushing blow to the combined Anglo-French armies, and now the world was witnessing the quick destruction of the Soviet army.

It never occurred to us to doubt the truth of that headline; until then all Hitler's announcements of victory had proven completely accurate. We had no way of knowing then that for the first time Hitler had announced a victory that wasn't really his. I was so depressed that for days I wouldn't look at a newspaper or listen to a radio.

In the meantime the Germans and their Ukrainian henchmen stepped up their persecutions. They formed a Judenrat, a Jewish council like the one in Hrubieszów, composed of elders whose terrible job it was to see that German orders with respect to the Jewish community were carried out. All Jews were ordered to wear the yellow star. Arbitrary and exorbitant fines were imposed, which the intimidated Jews paid, often out of the savings of a lifetime. Jews were brutally beaten and kicked while at work and in the streets. The brutalizing process was in full swing, and we felt totally helpless in this small town, where we were strangers even to the local Jews.

We still had a little money left, but it wouldn't last long. We started thinking of moving west, closer to home, hoping to get to Hrubieszów, even though we had heard that the Germans were still guarding the border. But perhaps they were treating the Jews better in Poland; after all, we told ourselves, Ołyka was part of eastern Poland, which had been "contaminated" by the Communists for two years. These were foolish rationalizations, but we grasped at any notion, however ridiculous, that offered even the feeblest ray of hope.

We met a local Ukrainian truck driver who transported oil drums for the German army, and made arrangements with him to take us as far as Włodzimierz.

It was a cold day in October. We met the truck driver after dark on a narrow street not far from where we were lodging. He told us to climb inside some empty oil drums in the back of the truck, and laid more drums over us. The road was full of potholes; crouched inside the drums, we were nearly deafened by the clanging as the truck jolted and lurched along. Approaching Łuck, a large town between Ołyka and Włodzimierz, we suddenly heard a German command: "Stop!" We could see nothing, only heard the soldiers questioning our driver, and his replies in broken German. At last we heard *"Los, los"* (Out, out). The truck started up and we breathed again as it picked up speed.

Włodzimierz

■

The trip to Włodzimierz seemed endless. My knees hurt and I developed a tremendous headache from the banging and clanging of the steel oil drums. At last we stopped. The driver came back and moved the empty drums so that we could get out. "All right, we made it," he said, "but I wouldn't take a chance like that again for any money in the world."

We got out of the drums and climbed down from the truck to find ourselves on a dark, deserted street in Włodzimierz. Our legs were so stiff from crouching for so many hours that we needed a few minutes before we could even start to walk.

We went to the Burstyns', where Father and I had roomed during the Soviet occupation. Mr. Burstyn greeted us warmly, but had no room for us in his house. The town was already overcrowded with Jews from neighboring villages who had been forced by the Germans to move there; twenty thousand Jews were now in Włodzimierz, compared to a prewar population of twelve thousand. Mr. Burstyn was very helpful, though, and in the morning found a small room for us in the same neighborhood.

Conditions in Włodzimierz were even worse than they had been in Ołyka. Everybody was terrified; the stories of mass killings on the Soviet side of the Ukraine had had a paralyzing effect on people here as well, and the brutalizing process we had seen beginning in Ołyka was far more advanced here. Beatings and killings were no longer isolated incidents, but commonplace. The Germans were tightening the screws with increasing cruelty. There were only about a dozen Gestapo in Włodzimierz, but these were sufficient to control twenty thousand Jews, for they had recruited about a hundred Ukrainian policemen, who enthusiastically did most of the Gestapo's dirty work for them. These Ukrainians had had nothing before the war; now they had plenty of food, carried weapons, which they used freely, and were encouraged to beat and torture Jews whenever they felt like it.

The Judenrat, executing the orders of the Germans, supervised the distribution of food, registered Jewish workers, and delivered them to the places to which they had been assigned. Most members of the Judenrat had no choice but to do the Germans' work for them; either they had served in the Jewish town administration before the war, or they were prominent citizens and appointed by the Germans specifically to this post. Refusing such an appointment would have meant certain death.

The Judenrat in turn set up the Jewish police, mostly a bunch of riffraff who were more than willing to enforce German regulations against their Jewish brothers in exchange for more favorable treatment for their own families. And in some cases they were beating and otherwise abusing their fellow Jews entirely on their own initiative.

To make matters worse, I now developed water in my lungs. I

was running a high fever, and the doctor couldn't get me the medicine I needed. I was growing weak, and the family was worried. I often thought while I was ill how much better it would be for me to die then and there, in bed, than to survive only to be murdered later by the Germans. I used to kid the doctor, who was a very nice man: "You know, Doctor, with you around I might get lucky and die right now." The doctor would smile ruefully, recognizing how true this was.

News of "actions" against Jews were now arriving thick and fast from neighboring towns and cities: Łuck, Równo, Pińsk. As yet there had been no total exterminations in this area, but thousands of people who had been captured by the Gestapo had been taken to the outskirts of town and killed. An "action" was clearly imminent in Włodzimierz.

This meant a new and urgent need for hiding places, which had to be very cunningly disguised. Many families were constructing these *skrytkas* (hideouts) in their houses, and people who didn't have one tried desperately to secure a hiding place elsewhere. Our landlord built a double wall with a door that perfectly matched the paneling of the wood, and in front of the door he placed a wooden cabinet. In order to get into the skrytka between the two walls, one had to open the cabinet door, swing out a shelf, crawl inside the cabinet, push through its back wall, and open the hidden door leading to the skrytka. Then you closed the cabinet door, got into the skrytka, swung the cabinet shelf back into position, and closed the door in the wall. We congratulated our landlord on his masterpiece. The Germans would never find us.

In some houses, skrytkas were built in a crawl space between the ceiling and the roof, again with a cleverly disguised entrance. The actions in the Western Ukraine during this period of the occupation were only partial. All the Jews who were captured by the Germans during these searches were killed, but those whom the killers were unable to find returned to their homes once the action was over. It was a game of hide-and-seek in which the prize was one's life, and a cleverly constructed skrytka meant the difference between life and death.

The Włodzimierz action started on a rainy morning in November. Everyone was on the alert, and the moment we saw the trucks arrive with the Germans and Ukrainians we got into our skrytka. It was about twenty feet long and two and a half feet deep, and there were sixteen or seventeen people in it: the four of us, the landlord's family, including his daughter and son-in-law, and another tenant and his family. There was barely enough room for us all to squeeze in. It was impossible to sit or crouch; even standing up, our bodies were pressed tight together. It was pitch-dark.

Soon we heard the sounds of a search party in the house. We could hear them walking about, laughing and cursing, knocking on the walls listening for secret openings, alert for the cry of a baby. They went down to the cellar, up to the attic. They were in the house for only three or four minutes, but it seemed an eternity. My heart was pounding so hard I was sure they could hear it. One sneeze from any of us, and it would all be over. Finally we heard the German in charge say, "There's nobody here. Let's not waste any more time."

As soon as they left the house the landlord's son-in-law let out a whoop of joy. He was instantly hushed. We knew that the Germans often left one of their party behind after the rest had gone, hoping to catch Jews as they came out of hiding. This son-in-law was a dangerous fellow; even before the war he had never been quite right in the head, and the anxieties of the occupation had unhinged him still further. He now started complaining that everybody was pushing him, but in fact no one was; it was just too crowded in there. He was standing near one wall, so he put his hands on it and started pushing the others back, to make more room for himself. He was strong, and the rest of us were being squeezed unmercifully. A few people started complaining and apparently he found this amusing, because he suddenly started to laugh very loudly, terrifying us all. His father-in-law kept apologizing for him and pleading with him to be quiet. The ventilation was very poor, and after two or three hours the air became so heavy that some of us were close to fainting. Finally we took a chance and opened the door a crack.

We stood in the skrytka all day, until dark. At last the landlord opened the door, stepped out, walked cautiously over to the window, and returned to tell us that the street was quiet. The action seemed to be over. We decided to go back to our rooms but remain dressed, while one of us, hidden behind the curtains, kept watch at the window. I slept for a while, then woke up and couldn't go back to sleep. When my turn came to stand guard, I peeked through the window. It looked like a ghost town outside, with no sign of life, no lights anywhere.

In the morning a Jewish policeman appeared in the street, running and shouting: "The action is over. You can come out." Immediately people appeared in doorways; some even went out into the street to see what had happened to the others. There was a great clamor of anguished cries when they discovered how many were missing.

Later in the day we learned from the Judenrat that about two thousand Jews had been seized by the Germans. They had hidden in cellars, under beds, or in attics, and many were found by the SS and taken away to their deaths.

There were now few optimists left among us. We had had too many eyewitness reports of the mass killings, both from Jews who had not been mortally wounded and had managed to escape from the execution pits after the Germans had left, and from Gentiles who had watched the killings from a distance. We all knew what had happened to the two thousand Jews from Włodzimierz.

But about that time, in November, hope started creeping back into our hearts. The German advance seemed to be slowing down. Leningrad, although surrounded, was holding out. German communiqués spoke of battles near Moscow, but their advance had slowed to a crawl. Their tanks and trucks were foundering in the deep mud. In the Kharkov and Rostov areas fighting was intense; the Soviets had even briefly recaptured Kharkov, a major city, but they had lost it again. Nevertheless, this unexpectedly strong resistance so deep into Russian territory bought time for the Russians, which was what they needed; it prolonged the war enough to bring her most powerful ally into action: "General Winter" came to the rescue of "Mother Russia."

The situation on the front now changed dramatically. German supply lines were dangerously overextended, and military vehicles found it almost impossible to move in the deep snow. The Luftwaffe was often immobilized by the bad weather. Worst of all, the soldiers were totally unaccustomed to the terrible Russian winter and could not fight. Those supposedly infallible German strategists had underestimated the length of the Russian campaign—it was supposed to have been another Blitzkrieg, with total victory before winter set in—and had failed to provide the men with warm clothing. It is hard to handle machines or guns with frozen fingers. On the other hand, the Red Army, which only weeks before had seemed on the verge of disintegration, was resisting ever more staunchly and was gaining in strength and confidence every day. The Russians, at first demoralized by the speed of their defeat, now came into their own. They could withstand the cold, and they suddenly saw their enemy turn from Übermenschen to half-frozen, frightened, hungry men, far from home, unprepared psychologically or physically to fight this kind of war. It gave a tremendous lift to the Russians' spirits, and changed the whole complexion of the war.

All this was music to our ears; at last there was hope. We began hearing stories of German soldiers literally freezing to death on the Russian front. Troop trains were returning to Germany full of soldiers who had lost arms and legs. Visions of a full-scale Napoleonic retreat danced in our heads. So Hitler could be beaten after all. The Russians had not been defeated; the miracle we had been waiting for was here. Our excitement grew daily: "Hold out—just hold out!" Then doubts flooded back. Perhaps it was only temporary, perhaps the Germans were merely resting and regrouping in order to launch a new attack. It was hard to believe in such a sudden reversal, from a total rout to a quick victory. Was it possible?

Now a new order was announced: Jews and Gentiles alike were to deliver all their furs to certain designated depots. Anyone found keeping back a fur coat would be shot. People were laughing: "Look at the son of a bitch! Now he needs Jewish furs to cover German bodies! The soldiers of the Master Race are to be warmed by furs from the Jewish vermin." What delicious irony!

Early in December German war communiqués told of German troops reaching the area of Moscow. The Russians were evacuating the capital, transferring the government to Kuybyshev. What a disappointment! Was Moscow going to fall after all? Then days went by, while German newspapers continued to carry stories of fighting in the suburbs, with photos of the Russian capital in the background of the advancing German troops. After that, for a few days, there was little or no news at all from Moscow.

Then suddenly, for the first time ever in World War II, a new word appeared in the German communiqués: "Defensive." Defensive battles were being fought. My heart leapt with joy. Then another new term: "Shortening the lines"—a euphemism for pulling back.

The English shortwave radio went crazy with the news. The Germans were in retreat! They were suffering heavy casualties. Hundreds of thousands of them were freezing to death in the snow. We heard the names of towns fifty, a hundred miles west of Moscow in the German communiqués; they were being pushed back from the Russian capital. Returning German soldiers told horror stories of the Russian front: the troops stuck in the deep snow in their light summer uniforms, unable to walk, their legs frozen—a disaster. It was sweet music to our ears.

For the first time we heard of Germans actually criticizing Hitler. Right at the start of the war there had been some skeptics who thought the victory in Poland was not indicative, since the Poles were so weak. But after the triumph in the West and the occupation of France, most of these critics were silenced. Hitler had achieved what the Kaiser could never do: He had taken Paris, and he'd had the British on the run at Dunkirk, happy to get away with their lives. Finally, at the peak of the German victories in the East, when he was on the verge of subjugating all Russia, there were virtually no critics left. Hitler was God, he could do whatever he wanted.

Now, with this unexpectedly stiff resistance from the Russians, and with the Germans in retreat, doubts reemerged. We were working at a railway depot at the time, under the supervision of German army officers, and we clearly sensed the change in the atmosphere. One officer told our foreman that he personally had never believed that the "painter" knew what he was doing. "And look at how he treated the poor Jews. The crazy bastard!"

These were exhilarating days. Even if Hitler killed us, we would die knowing he was going to hang for it. And just think of the Russians! What fantastic fighters! To us, who were helpless, the thought

Countries and territories incorporated into, occupied, or controlled by the Third Reich from March 1938 through September 1943.

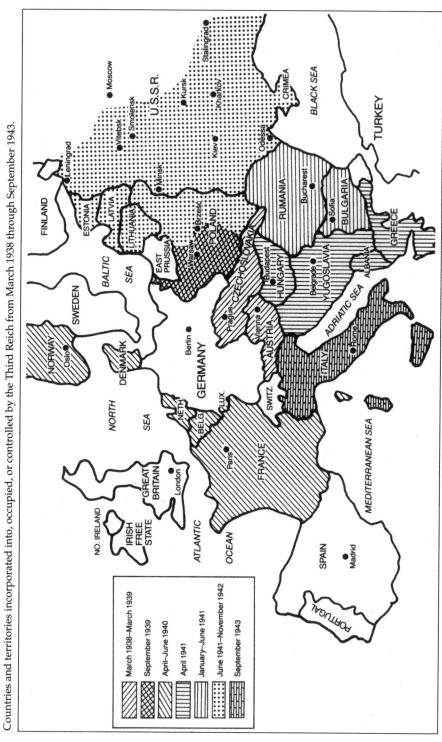

of the Russians turning on their tormentors and giving them a taste of what it was to suffer was like a breath of life, an infusion of energy and hope. Hitler's savagery toward the Russians now came back to haunt him with a vengeance. They fought back like tigers. They could resist the brutal cold, the hunger, the discomfort far better than the Germans. They were used to it, the terrible winter was their element. And they had heard about the hundreds of thousands of Russian prisoners who were being starved to death. There was a large prisoner-of-war camp not far from Włodzimierz, with close to sixty thousand Russian prisoners. For weeks the Germans had given them no food. There were horrible scenes, even cannibalism. The peasants sometimes threw loaves of bread over the barbed wire, and packs of soldiers would fall on each loaf, tearing it and themselves to pieces. After a few days, an order came: No more bread. German guards shot at anyone approaching the fence. A few courageous women tried anyway; one was shot to death. In ten weeks, sixty thousand men—virtually the entire population of the camp—starved to death.

The Russian people knew they had nothing to lose. Most of them hated Stalin—but now he was leading the fight against their tormentors. And he knew how to appeal to them. Not for the cause of Communism; no, it was to something much deeper, to their love of country. He spoke to them in the name of "Mother Russia," words long forgotten in the Communist dictionary. Women worked sixteen-hour shifts in the new factories in Siberia, going full blast even before the roofs were on. At the front, the soldiers fought like men possessed. Behind the German lines, partisans derailed German trains, exploded ammunition dumps. The Russian nation rose as one to fight the invader.

Life in Włodzimierz was becoming extremely difficult. There were shortages of food, and the Ukrainians were going wild, beating people in the streets at the slightest whim. We decided to leave Włodzimierz and move to Uściług, a small town on the Bug, eight miles west of Włodzimierz. It was right on the border, and on the road to Hrubieszów on the other side of the border. Felek and Sam had worked in Uściług during the Soviet occupation, and had friends there. Sam was able, through his connections in Uściług, to register us there with the Judenrat. We made arrangements with a Ukrainian peasant who took us to Uściług at night.

Uściług

■

As soon as we got to Uściług, we rented a room with a Jewish family. It wasn't bad; we had two wide beds, and we could sleep more comfortably than in Włodzimierz. Here life was more orderly, and the local Germans and Ukrainians seemed less vicious. Food was more readily available from local farmers, and it was cheaper too, which was important, because we didn't have much money left. We had about five thousand rubles, and we knew that would not last us long.

Money was not our main concern, however; at the moment the burning question was: What were Hitler's intentions for the Jews? Would his Gestapo continue their limited "actions," in which some Jews were killed and the rest allowed to go on living, or would they start total extermination actions in our area, like the ones they had conducted in Kiev and other cities and villages across the former Polish-Soviet border?

What kept our spirits up was the situation at the front. We were hoping that the German soldiers, shocked by the sudden turn in the fortunes of war, cold, exhausted, and stuck in the snow, would break, abandon their arms, and flee home, as Napoleon's armies had done one hundred and thirty years earlier.*

As the winter progressed, the situation at the front became stalemated. Seriously weakened by the loss of millions of soldiers in their initial defeats, the Russians could not maintain a counterattack. Most of their industrial production capacity was lost. They had succeeded in evacuating a number of large plants and equipment, but these were in the process of being set up in the Urals, and only a few were yet in operation. Men, women, and children worked night and day in the bitter Siberian cold to get these plants going. They realized now that this was no ordinary war, but a fight to the finish. Either they defeated the Germans, or they would perish. So they labored for their lives, without sleep, frostbitten, half starved. Their heroic efforts, together with the sacrifices of their fathers, brothers, and sons at the front, saved Russia, and perhaps Western civilization as well. As the grim winter of 1941–1942 wore on, both sides were close to exhaustion.

On the whole, this was good news. Although our hopes for a total German collapse and a speedy end to the war had not materialized, there was reason to take heart. Hitler's advance had been halted; he had even been pushed back a little. England was still alive, and building up her armed forces. We had something to hope for.

---

*Hitler's generals did advise retreat in order to save the army. Had Hitler taken their advice, the retreat might have turned into a rout. But he refused, and ordered anybody retreating to be shot. The generals were dismayed. They had never liked Hitler, and now they hated him. "The man is mad," they said. "He knows nothing about military strategy." But the generals were also frightened that Hitler would order the Gestapo to kill them, so they obeyed. The German soldiers followed their orders. They died by the hundreds of thousands, they froze to death, but they gave ground grudgingly.

At the same time, however, I sensed an increased danger. Hitler had to be enraged at his setbacks, and I felt sure that the Jews would bear the brunt of his fury. If there had ever been any hope for the survival of those Jews already in Hitler's clutches, our chances were surely now much diminished. It was ironic: Good news was bad news for us. But even though we lived in fear, we nevertheless felt relief. The thought of Hitler and his demented henchmen ruling the world was hard to bear.*

In the meantime, hope rose from another quarter when the Japanese attacked Pearl Harbor. America was now in the war, and the world's greatest industrial power would save Western civilization.*

---

*In his memoirs Churchill speaks of the later German defeats at Stalingrad and El Alamein, toward the end of 1942, as the turning point of the war. With all due respect to the great man, I disagree. I think the real turning point was the cruel Russian winter of 1941–1942. Until then the German soldiers, buoyed by their victories, had expected the war against the Soviets to be quick and easy. "The Russians are dumb animals," they said. "They run from us like rabbits. Their planes are being shot down by our Messerschmitts. Their tanks and artillery are pretty good, but no match for ours. The German soldier is invincible. Hitler is right; we should have won World War I. We lost only because we were betrayed."

Suddenly all this had changed. The Russians were fighting back, and fighting well. They were tougher than the Germans, and more tenacious; they could take the cold. The Germans were not such a superior race after all. This shift in the Germans soldiers' view of their Russian foe was, I believe, decisive. In the great battles that followed—Orel, Kharkov, Stalingrad, Kursk— the Germans became frightened, even demoralized. They began to realize the enormity of what they had gotten into. The huge Russian landmass confronting them looked overwhelming. They were oppressed by a sense of futility, which put them at a critically important psychological disadvantage in the battles to come.

*Churchill wrote in his memoirs that on December 7, 1941, for the first time since the beginning of the war, he had a really good night's sleep. He was certain now of victory.

We felt that way too, but for us it was less a question of ultimate victory than of immediate survival. We too believed that it was only a matter of time now, perhaps a year, two at the most. But how could we hold out that long? The Russian front was five hundred miles away, and the vast majority of the local population was hostile to Jews.

I found a job with a dentist as an assistant in his office. Our first two or three months in Uściług were relatively peaceful. We knew that our situation could only worsen, but it was a welcome relief, for the moment, after the hard times in Ołyka and Włodzimierz.

Sometime in April the Germans tightened the screws, and there were no more easy jobs. Felek and I were assigned to work in a small shop making roof tiles. We would mix clay and water, put the mixture into a form, beat it with a special tool to shape and harden it, sprinkle the newly formed tiles with a cement additive, and set them on a rack to dry. It was hard work, but no policemen supervised us, and we were happy to have the job.

I was also giving math lessons to a boy named Lipiński. The Germans had appointed his father mayor of Uściług. Occasionally Mrs. Lipińska would give me a little money or food in payment for the lessons.

Evenings we spent at home reading or discussing the latest news of the war and of Jews in other towns. We were only six or seven miles from Hrubieszów, but for some incomprehensible reason, the Germans were maintaining guards all along the old border. For the first time since the German attack on Russia, we managed to exchange a few messages with our family in Hrubieszów. Their life was much the same as ours in Uściług: living in fear of the Germans and hoping to survive. But at least they were alive and in good health.

There was little news from the Eastern front. Both armies were resting, resupplying their troops, and preparing for new battles. But we were shocked to learn of the smashing Japanese victories. How could America have let herself be caught like that, unprepared for war in the Pacific? We had always known the Japanese soldiers were fanatical fighters, but we were amazed at the apparent superiority of their planes and ships. After the disaster at Pearl Harbor, they seemed unstoppable. First the Philippines were lost, then many more key islands, one after another. Finally Singapore itself, that supposedly impregnable British fortress, fell in a matter of days. Tens of thousands of British soldiers surrendered, the worst British loss so far.

These were sad days for the once mighty British Empire, which seemed to be in retreat everywhere: first in France, then in Greece, then in the Far East. Even in Africa the British army was beaten by a relatively small Afrika Korps, led by the brilliant General Rommel.

We were naturally distressed at this news, but still confident of ultimate victory. Now America was in the war, and Germany could never stand up to that great industrial machine once it was converted to wartime production. We heard about the fantastic capacity of American factories. Could it possibly be true? Could they produce one hundred thousand planes a year? One hundred thousand tanks? We shook our heads in wonder. "Leave it to those Yanks. They are just incredible, with their mass-production assembly lines."

Of more immediate concern, however, was the Russian front. Would the Germans, now that the winter was over, be able to march again? Had the Russians learned from their past mistakes, and would they be able to hold the Germans off, or at least continue fighting until the following winter? Or perhaps—still more optimistically—they were strong enough now to counterattack and smash Hitler once and for all. It was a time of great tension and uncertainty.

It was in June or July that we heard for the first time terrible new rumors: gassings. The SS were using gas in specially equipped trucks to put thousands of Jews to death, and gas chambers for mass murder were in operation. Death factories, in towns we had never heard of before: Treblinka, Sobibór, Auschwitz. Gas chambers! It was impossible even to conceive of it: Men, women, and children screaming, gasping for air, choking, suffocating, a heap of bodies writhing on the floor in their death agony. How could this be? Why didn't the world do something? How could those great leaders Churchill and Roosevelt permit it to happen? Even if they could not prevent Hitler outright, they could at least issue a strong declaration and a warning. Drop leaflets all over Germany, blast over the airwaves: "Stop it! Stop the slaughter, or we will hold *all* Germans responsible!"

But as the summer wore on, everything became clear; there were no more doubts. Hitler had in fact ordered the systematic extermination of millions of Jewish men, women, and children. His method was simple: the entire operation was carried out by a few thousand specially trained killers, aided by ten or twenty thousand local policemen: Ukrainians, Poles, Lithuanians, and Latvians.

In city after city, the pattern was the same. The Germans ordered the Judenrat to announce a time when all Jews were to assemble at a designated place (usually the town square or the railroad station) to be deported to new "labor camps." They were permitted to take with them only a small bundle of belongings.

Since by that time almost everyone knew what "deportation" meant, usually only about half of the town's Jews would show up. They would be packed into cattle cars and shipped directly to the nearest gas chambers. In the small towns the SS would load the assembled Jews onto trucks and drive them to ditches nearby. There they would order the victims to undress and stand or lie down at the edge of a ditch and they would mow them down with machine guns. Then the killers would look for those showing signs of life and finish them off. Occasionally a few who were only wounded would pretend to be dead. The SS forced other Jews or local people to bury the bodies. The wounded would wait until the dirt had been thrown over them, then work their way to the top of the pile of dead, dig themselves out of the fresh earth, and sometimes succeed in escaping.

Those Jews who obeyed the orders to assemble were usually the weakest, the most docile, those who still refused to think the unthinkable and clung to the hope that they were indeed being sent to a labor camp, or those who had simply lost the will to fight. Many were refugees from Germany or other countries, strangers to Poland with no place to hide. The Jews who did not show up as ordered were the ones who refused to go voluntarily to the slaughter. Perhaps they had Gentile friends willing to risk their lives for them, or had hiding places of their own, or they fled into the local forests and fields and hid out there.

Once the SS had dispatched those Jews who had showed up for the roundup by sending them to the gas chambers and burying them in mass graves, they would start the hunt for those who had gone into hiding. It was a hunt the likes of which mankind had never seen. Whole families would hide out in skrytkas, as we had in Włodzimierz, and they would be hunted down inexorably, relentlessly. Street by street, house by house, inch by inch, from attic to cellar. The Germans became expert at finding these hiding places. When they searched a house, they went around tapping the walls, listening for the hollow sound that indicated a double wall. They punched holes in ceilings or floors. People stayed in these skrytkas for days, for weeks, often without food and water, and the Germans listened for the muffled cries of children, with desperate parents trying to smother their sounds with hands over the little ones' mouths.

These were no longer limited "actions"; this was total annihilation.

Teams of SS men roamed the streets, searching ditches, outhouses, bushes, barns, stables, pigsties. And they caught and killed Jews by the thousands; then by the hundreds; then by tens; and finally one by one.

Almost every day we heard new reports of the killer commandos going from town to town killing Jews. The death watch for the Jews of Uściług had begun.

The reactions of these doomed people varied. We had a neighbor who was an accountant. He and his wife were a handsome couple, both tall, with dark brown eyes and black hair. They were growing vegetables in a garden they had cultivated behind their house—tomatoes, cucumbers, peppers, radishes, even corn. They would get up every morning at sunrise and work in their garden; their little eight-year-old daughter, a beautiful child, worked alongside her parents. They all looked perfectly calm, but it was sad to see them. We wondered whether they would live long enough to harvest the vegetables.

Many were like that, quiet, resigned, apparently accepting the inevitability of their fate. Others, particularly the pretty young girls, found it hard to believe that any men, even Germans, when it came to it, could actually bring themselves to kill them in cold blood. They kept hoping, in spite of what they knew.

Late in July, to our astonishment, a messenger from the Judenrat came to tell us that Fred was in Uściług asking for us. We could scarcely believe it, but it was so. He had come with a German army officer who needed a number of Jewish tradesmen and couldn't find enough of them in Hrubieszów. Fred talked him into looking in Uściług, and the German had obtained a special pass for himself and Fred to cross the border. When we met we hugged each other and wept. We hadn't seen Fred since 1939, over three years earlier. He looked fine, as handsome as ever. For the next several hours all we did was hug and kiss and excitedly exchange stories, filling each other in on our doings since the war had started. Fred told us how Mother had gone to stay with him in Warsaw in 1940, how tough things had got there, how she had escaped by climbing the ghetto wall, and how finally they both had come back to Hrubieszów to rejoin Hanka. He even brought us a few dishes mother had cooked especially for us.

Too soon the German officer came and told Fred it was time to go back. We hugged and kissed good-bye, telling him that when the "action" started in Uściług we would try to make it to Hrubieszów. But as the car disappeared down the road, I remember thinking: "This is probably the last time I will ever see Fred."

On the Eastern front summer fighting had begun, as expected, and apparently in good weather the Germans were still stronger than the Russians. They launched a two-pronged offensive in the Ukraine, one thrust eastward, toward the Volga, the other south-east and south, toward the Caucasus, to capture the Baku oil fields, which they badly needed.

Initially the German advance was rapid. Their *panzers* cut deep behind the front lines, and the Russians were in retreat. But this time it was orderly, without hundreds of thousands of prisoners being taken, and after a few weeks, we knew the Germans had lost their punch. Their advance in the Caucasus toward Baku was slowing down; though they did capture some of the oil fields, those had been totally destroyed by the Russians. The German advance toward the Volga and Stalingrad was slow and along a narrow front. And most significant of all, no major German attacks came on the crucial Moscow front. Leningrad, although still surrounded, was holding out. Clearly the once unstoppable German army was running into difficulties. This gave us immense satisfaction; however desperate our own situation, at least Hitler was in trouble. If only we could live to see the day when he would be captured and exhibited all over the world in a cage!

Toward the end of August it became clear that the Uściług "action" would come any day now. Just at that time, as I was bending over the sink one day to wash my face, I felt a sharp pain in my back. I tried to straighten up and couldn't. My brothers had to lead me bent over to bed, and when I lay down I had to have my legs propped up because I could not straighten them out.

Sam knew a Polish engineer who worked for a company that did construction work for the Germans on both sides of the river Bug. He made arrangements with the engineer to smuggle us into Hrubieszów. Now the question was: Would I be able to move? For two days Felek and Sam massaged my legs and applied hot compresses almost around the clock. At last I was able to move my legs and to bend; it was now Monday, August 31.

That very day, the Germans ordered that all Jews were to gather in the town square the next morning, Tuesday, September 1, at nine. Sam gave the Pole half of all the money we had left, promising him the other half after he had taken us to Hrubieszów. Our lives were in his hands, Sam told him. He promised he would not let us down. He was to meet us at three in the morning. We were to wait for him in a World War I ditch not far from the Bug bridge.

After packing a few belongings we tried to get some sleep, but I couldn't even close my eyes from nervous excitement. So it had come—the final extermination action. I was worried about this Pole. He seemed altogether too reassuring, almost too friendly, but what good did it do to think about it? We had no choice but to trust him.

At one o'clock we left the house and started walking toward the ditch, watching out for the Ukrainian patrols. In a few minutes we had reached the ditch. So far, so good. Now we had only to wait.

The time crept by; we waited patiently. Three o'clock passed, and he hadn't come. Fear seized our hearts; he had betrayed us! But maybe he was just a few minutes late. By three-thirty we were losing hope. The bastard had taken our money and betrayed us. Still we tried to reassure each other. Maybe he was having trouble with the truck. Maybe he would still come. At four-thirty a woman and a little girl came into the ditch, and a few minutes later a middle-aged man and his wife joined us. So did a young man, a locksmith. A few more Jews came, all desperate people who had nowhere else to go. By five-thirty there were thirteen of us in the ditch.

Slowly the sun rose. It was going to be a glorious day, not a cloud in the sky. It was September 1, the day of the action, and we were trapped. The ditch was long and narrow, its top covered with long grass and weeds growing across it from either side, so that from a distance it was almost invisible. We decided to hide all that day and try to get to the river at night, if the Germans didn't find us first.

From time to time we heard machine-gun and rifle fire. It was hard to believe time could drag so slowly. Twelve o'clock came, then three o'clock, four o'clock. I would never have believed a day could last so long. At five minutes to five I decided to stop looking at my watch, hoping that would make the time pass more quickly. After what seemed at least an hour later I allowed myself to look again. It was just five o'clock—only five minutes had elapsed! I really thought my watch must have stopped, and checked it against Sam's. It was correct. I shall never forget that experience; it was as though we had entered some new dimension outside the normal movement of time. Five-thirty came. We began to hope. Maybe we would make it to nightfall without being discovered. At six o'clock we began a whispered discussion about the best route to take to the river.

It was six-thirty when suddenly we heard a harsh German voice bark: "*Juden—raus!*" (Jews—out!) At the sound my brain seemed to explode. This was it. They had us. Slowly we climbed out of the ditch. The sun was still very bright. There were two Germans with machine guns and a Ukrainian policeman with a rifle. Both Germans were of medium height. I still remember the eyes of one of them: they were shiny, almost glazed, like mirrors. Neither of them hit or cursed us; they were merely efficient, impersonal professionals who wanted to get their job done without delay.

Quickly they herded us into a group. The two Germans led the way, fingers on their gun triggers, and we followed. The Ukrainian, tall and lanky, his rifle at the ready, walked right behind us. We walked in silence. No one wept, no one pleaded for mercy.

Soon we turned into the main street of town. A strange calm came over me. The day was still beautiful, the sky still blue, even bluer against the orange red of the setting sun. The colors pierced me with their vividness. I remember my thoughts very clearly. I knew this was the last day of my life. I looked at the sun and thought, "I will never see the sun again." I looked at the trees, and thought, "I will never see trees again." I felt no bitterness, but there was a great sadness in my heart. I was not yet nineteen. I had never slept with a girl. My mouth felt very dry, and I couldn't swallow. My tongue seemed swollen to twice its normal size. I had to hold my mouth open.

As we walked down the street, I watched the reaction of the Ukrainian townspeople. They seemed undisturbed at the sight of Jews being led to their deaths. A few even laughed and joked about us. I can never forget a young woman who, seeing us from a window on the second floor of her house, turned and called to her little girl, whom she held up to see us as we passed. That there was a little girl among us seemed not to trouble her at all. I remember thinking: "How can these people be so merciless? Don't they have any hearts?"

We were now three or four blocks from the end of the street and only a few hundred yards from the execution pits. Father said to us, "One should not have children." He didn't care what happened to him, but he was in despair at the prospect of having to watch us die.

We were now approaching a narrow street that led to the tile shop where Felek and I had worked. Sam suggested that we shove our money and our watches into the hands of the Ukrainian policeman and run for it.

In a few feverish seconds we took off our watches, wrapped them and the paper money in a handkerchief, pushed it into his hand, and started running to our right, toward the narrow street. I expected the shooting to start immediately, so I ran the six or seven steps before we reached the corner with my head turned toward the Germans and the Ukrainian, to see what they would do. The two Germans weren't even aware of what had happened, and continued walking on in front of the group. The others Jews stopped and looked in our direction, confused. The locksmith reacted quickly enough to follow us, a step or two behind. The Ukrainian stood still, holding the handkerchief.

Everything was in a whirl. In about thirty seconds we had reached the back of the tile workshop. Through the windows we could see that there was no one inside. We tried the door, but it was locked and the windows were closed. To this day I don't know how I found the strength, but I managed to grab the window frame and pull it out with my bare hands, along with the two or three nails that held it. We climbed inside the room where Felek and I had worked before the action started. There were large windows all around it, and empty tile racks and a few pieces of equipment, but no place to hide. Behind the door was a storage room for cement and other materials, but it was locked. Several bursts of machine-gun fire erupted outside. They were shooting the rest of the people from our group.

Our position was desperate; at the moment the narrow street was empty, but anyone who happened to pass could see us. We couldn't understand why the door, which was usually open, was now locked. Suddenly we realized: There were Jews hiding in the other room, and they had locked the door from the inside. "We are Jews, open the door!" we called. No answer came, but we heard a noise like the shuffle of feet. We tried to frighten them. "We know you are there. If they catch us, we'll tell them where you are." After a few seconds we heard the click of the turning lock and the door opened. Two old Jews stood there, shivering with fear. We went into the storage room and locked the door behind us. There was an attic above with straw and bags of cement. We climbed up the ladder and lay down on the straw.

We tried to think what to do. It would be too dangerous to try to reach the river during the first day or two of the action, so we decided to stay where we were until the hunt and the shooting had slowed down. It continued sporadically for another couple of hours, until nightfall, when it stopped. Exhausted, I fell asleep at last and slept for seven or eight hours.

Early in the morning we were awakened by the renewed clatter of machine-gun and rifle fire. The action was in full swing once again, and the hunt was on. It was Wednesday morning, September 2. At about eight o'clock we heard a voice outside that we recognized. My heart was pounding hard. It was the voice of the Ukrainian supervisor of the shop, who was knocking at the storage room door. "I know you are there," he called out. "Don't worry. I'm your friend." In a quick, whispered consultation, we decided we had to take the risk and let him in. We unlocked the door. He came in and told us the Germans were shooting every Jew they could find. "You'd better stay right here," he said.

The only possession of any value that we had left was Felek's coat, a fine English brown herringbone tweed. "Give him the coat," I whispered. Maybe with such a gift he would not betray us. After hesitating a moment, Felek handed his coat to the Ukrainian, saying, "Here, take it. If we don't make it you'll have something to remember us by." The Ukrainian made a dismissive gesture, but he didn't need much persuasion. He took the coat, saying, "I will be back," and left.

New discussions ensued. "Is he going to betray us?" The Polish engineer had made us skeptical about trusting people, but we had no choice in the matter.

Machine-gun and rifle fire continued throughout the day. It would have been suicidal to go out. Once again night fell. We decided against going out as SS patrols were everywhere. I was in a state of nervous exhaustion, and that night slept fitfully.

The morning came, Thursday, September 3. Although we had eaten nothing in two days, we were not hungry. Thirst, however, was becoming hard to bear. My mouth and throat were very dry. Late in the afternoon a Russian who was a friend of our Ukrainian supervisor came to the door. He was not a local man but a Soviet citizen who had come with the Russians in 1939 and had been unwilling or unable to escape with the Russian army. He came into the storage room half drunk. His speech was slurred as he assured us that we had nothing to fear from him; he was a friend. On and on he kept assuring us of his friendly feeling. We couldn't figure out at first what he was getting at, until it occurred to us that he wanted something from us, money or a gift. But we had nothing left. Half of our money had gone to the Pole, the other half and our watches to the Ukrainian policeman. Felek now had no coat, and the coats of the rest of us were old and valueless. We didn't know what to do. Felek had a straight razor that we all used to shave with, but should we offer it to the Russian? Perhaps he would be offended by such an insignificant gift. We were reluctant, too, to give it up because we had talked about using it to cut our wrists. Better that than to be shot by the Germans. Giving the razor away would mean losing the chance to take our own lives.

The Russian kept gabbling away. Finally Felek said, "We have nothing left but this razor." He handed it to the Russian, who examined it, opened the blade, tested its sharpness, closed it, put it in his pocket, and staggered out of the room, as we tried to assure him of our sincerity. "Really, we have nothing else left. Please believe us."

It was night again, but I could scarcely sleep. My mouth was very dry and there was not a drop of water anywhere. Friday morning came, and the shooting still continued, although now it was less frequent. We decided we couldn't stay any longer where we were. At least two people knew we were there, and they might have told others. And our thirst was becoming unbearable. We decided to leave that night—if only we weren't betrayed in the meantime.

Late in the afternoon the Russian returned, even drunker, and rambling still more incoherently. He became abusive, calling us *"Na-doedlivye Yevrei."* There is no exact English equivalen for *nadoedlivye*, but it means people who are a nuisance to others. *Yevrei* means Jews. We knew it was just a matter of time before he betrayed us, and could only hope he was too drunk to do it before nightfall. When he left he was reeling, so drunk he couldn't walk without holding on to something. After he had gone, we counted the minutes.

It finally got dark outside. We decided to go first to Mietka, who had been Sam's friend and lover during the Soviet occupation. She lived in her father's house on the outskirts of Uściług, and we were hoping to get water and food from her, and then go to the river Bug.

At about midnight the locksmith wished us luck and went out. Then the four of us stepped out into the dark. (The two old Jews had decided to stay.) We dashed from one dark spot to another, hiding whenever we saw a guard until he passed. When we arrived at Mietka's house, Sam called out her name in a low voice. A wave of joy swept over me when I saw the tall blond girl come to the door. I'll never forget her face—a sweet face with a strong nose—and her long, straight blond hair. She was surprised to see us, and glad that we were alive.

Nor will I ever forget the sensation of drinking the milk she brought us. That milk was an elixir of life, filling every dry cell of my body. It was heaven. We drank and drank and drank. Only after we finished the milk did we realize how hungry we were, and we wolfed down the bread.

The girl warned us to be quiet. Her father was asleep, and she was afraid that he might not want us there. Evidently he was not so brave and humane as his daughter; I had the feeling too that he didn't approve of her friendship with a Jew. She led us out to the barn so we could get some rest. I lay down on the straw, enjoying the bliss of a full stomach, and promptly fell asleep.

Just before dawn we were awakened by a loud man's voice. It was the girl's father, and he was not in the least friendly. "Out, out you go," he ordered. We pleaded with him: "It's almost day, please let us stay here just until night. It would be very dangerous to go out in the street now." But he was adamant. "If you don't leave immediately, I will get the police."

We came out of the barn and started walking toward the river. The sun was not up yet, but soon it would be daylight. Suddenly we heard a voice say, "Stop!" There was a Ukrainian carrying a rifle but not wearing a uniform, only an armband—he was one of the auxiliary militiamen who had been enlisted for the duration of the action. We knew right away that he was no danger to us—he even showed us which way to go to avoid the SS patrols. We thanked him and walked on a few more blocks.

Soon we realized that we were near Lipińska's, whose son I used to tutor; Sam and Felek knew Mrs. Lipińska, too. It was almost daybreak. We had to find a place to hide for that day, and so we cautiously entered the Lipiński yard. The house was on the edge of a property of about two and a half acres, with vegetable and flower gardens in front. Farther down was a barn with a cow, and a stall where Mr. Lipiński kept a horse. On the opposite side of the path, facing the stall, was a haystack. Behind it was a fruit garden with raspberry bushes and other fruit trees and bushes. The hay was packed tightly between four poles about twelve or thirteen feet high, which formed a square, each side seven or eight feet long. A tile roof rested on top of the four poles, and a ladder leaning against the hay led to the top of the haystack. It had been made from the trunks of two young trees, with small branches for rungs. We climbed the ladder to the top of the stack and wearily lay down on the hay.

Soon we saw Mrs. Lipińska come out of the house and walk toward us. She was a woman of about forty with blue eyes, light brown hair, and a round, pleasant face. Cautiously I called out, "Mrs. Lipińska!" She was startled but calm. "How many of you are there?" she asked. Father, Sam, and Felek raised their heads so that she could see the four of us. She nodded and told us to be very quiet and not come down, because the SS and the Ukrainian police were searching all over town for Jews. She said she would come back later, then went into the barn.

At least she hadn't thrown us out; probably she would let us stay until nightfall. But we were worried about her husband, whom the Germans had appointed mayor of Uściług; to what extent was he cooperating with them?

In mid-morning Mrs. Lipińska left the house. A few hours later she returned, went into the house, and came out to us carrying a bag full of food: potatoes, soup, bread, butter, and milk. This we had not expected; what a wonderful woman! At least for the moment the pressure was off, and we enjoyed every bite. She came back to collect the dishes and warned us again to be very careful. Her husband and children must not see us, she said. Her children might say something to their friends, and her husband might not be willing to run the frightful risk of having Jews found on his property.

No wonder. In the afternoon a sound truck drove by, blaring out a warning: Anyone caught hiding Jews, or helping them in any way, would be summarily shot. If he or she had a family, they also would be killed. It took a very special person to run this kind of risk. Mrs. Lipińska knew very well that she was endangering not only her own life, but also the lives of her son, daughter, and husband.

Those were wild times, savage, merciless. It meant nothing to the SS to take a life, Jewish or Gentile. The order was "Kill all Jews," and anybody who stood in the way was eliminated as a matter of course. Nevertheless, Mrs. Lipińska never hesitated. It was clear to us that she was prepared to do whatever was necessary to save us, regardless of the risk.

On our second day there we heard a woman's voice humming a little tune as she approached the Lipińskis' house. We recognized the voice as that of an elderly woman known for her anti-Semitism even before the arrival of the Germans. She was always very solemn; Felek and Sam, who knew her well, had never before heard her laugh or sing. "Can you hear her now?" Sam said. "Happy as a lark. She's delighted to see Jews being killed."

Later that afternoon we suddenly heard the voices of men nearby. As they drew closer, we realized that they were Ukrainian police searching for Jews in the bushes nearby. Suddenly there was a commotion, and a female voice, pleading. Then we heard a shot, and a loud scream, a full-throated cry of terror. It was cut short by another shot. The voices of the Ukrainians grew louder, until we could hear their every word. There were two of them, and they were directly beneath us.

One of the two poles of the ladder leading to the top of the haystack was longer than the other, and from our perch we could see the end of it. Suddenly it shook a little. My heart stopped. Then one of the voices said, "Oh, there's nobody here. Let's look in the stall." We heard steps move away and the creak of a door. After a moment we heard them close the door of the stall and move off toward the house. We went limp with relief. But how much longer could we live with such tension?

Later, Mrs. Lipińska came out to the haystack. She had seen the whole thing from her window. The Ukrainians had found two elderly Jewish sisters hiding in the bushes and shot them on the spot. Then they walked over to the haystack, and she saw one of them set his foot on the first rung of the ladder, about to climb it. "This is the end," she thought. Her heart was beating so hard she was afraid of a heart attack. We could imagine her relief when she saw him change his mind. The two Ukrainians then came to the house and questioned her about the two Jewish women. She assured them that she hadn't known they were there. One of the policemen happened to know her husband, and they took her word for it. Later in the day laborers came and removed the bodies of the two women, loading them into a wagon.

We told Mrs. Lipińska that our plan was to swim across the Bug to get to Hrubieszów and join the rest of our family. She had been born in Uściług and knew the area very well. She told us that there were heavy patrols along the river near Uściług, and that in any case the current there was too strong for us, especially Father, to swim across. Two or three miles downstream it would be easier to cross, but even there we would need help, she thought. Sam suggested that Mrs. Lipińska contact his friend Mietka. Mietka was Polish and had friends in Hrubieszów. The idea was for Mietka to use her contacts and arrange for Fred and Mother to send a guide to meet us at the river Bug and take us to Hrubieszów.

We told Mrs. Lipińska it might be many days or even weeks before we received an answer; was she willing to let us stay that long? Was it possible for her to hide us for such a period of time without her family finding out? And what about the risk in getting involved with messengers? She shrugged: What else could we do?

Mrs. Lipińska contacted Mietka, who in turn agreed to help. We waited. Twice and sometimes three times a day Mrs. Lipińska would bring us food: meat, potatoes, borscht, bread, milk. As we sat on top of our haystack, we could hear people passing by in the street. Sometimes Mrs. Lipińska's children played right beneath us. Occasionally friends would come to visit. No one ever suspected our presence. The only time we left the haystack was late at night, to relieve ourselves in the nearby bushes.

The days dragged on, and we had no idea whether the message would ever reach Fred or, if it did, whether he would be able to arrange for a guide. We weren't even sure what had happened by now to the Jews in Hrubieszów. Maybe they had had an action there too, and no one was left. But even if the Hrubieszów ghetto was still in existence and we did succeed in joining our family, sooner or later an action was certain to begin there. Everything was so hopeless.

I tried to steel myself for the moment of execution. It would be scary, but short. A moment of fear, that was all. A bullet in the brain, and it would all be over. Living in this world wasn't worth it anyway. Time and again I recited this to myself, and after a while I felt I had mastered the fear and was prepared to die. I wished that it would be over quickly, and that I would die with dignity. It wasn't all that easy, though. The next day the old stubborn will to live and the terror of death would regain the upper hand and I had to start the rationalization all over again.

I was not religious in those days, but I tried praying. "Dear God, please save us. We haven't done anything wrong." But I felt only contempt for myself, making such an appeal. "You phony, who are you trying to kid?" I stopped praying.

Day after day we waited for news from Hrubieszów. At last one day Mrs. Lipińska came out to the haystack in great excitement. A messenger had come with a note, brief and unsigned, from Fred. At midnight on September 17 we were to wait for a guide to meet us at the crossing Mrs. Lipińska had suggested. He would whistle as a signal, and we were to whistle back. He would take us to Hrubieszów.

What joy! They were still alive, and where there's life, there's hope. Frantic discussions ensued; how would we find the place in the middle of the night? Could we trust that the guide would really come, and if he did, that he would not betray us? Would we actually get to see Mother, Fred, and Hanka again? Our nerves were strung tight with anxious anticipation.

When the night of the rendezvous came, Mrs. Lipińska told us how to get to the crossing, warning us to be very careful; SS patrols were still around. Then she said good-bye. We thanked her from our hearts, and she went back to the house. As we set off, tension seized us again; would we make it this time? Suddenly we saw Mrs. Lipińska coming back from the house with a coat on and a shawl over her head. She was afraid we wouldn't find the meeting place alone, and had decided to take us there herself. She would lead the way, and we were to follow her at a distance.

We could scarcely believe her courage. This lady was ready to take us to the border in the middle of the night, with guards and patrols all over the place. "Are you quite sure you want to do this?"

we asked. "If anything goes wrong, you will be killed along with us." "I'm sure," she said. "Let's hurry, we mustn't be late."

She struck out across the fields at a fast clip. We followed her for about an hour. There were no roads; we walked up hills, through woods, and across fields. We realized that we never would have made it without her; it was like following our guardian angel. As I walked I marveled at her incredible bravery and strength. What made her do it? How was it possible for the human race to produce such polar opposites—a Mrs. Lipińska and the heartless woman who lifted her little daughter up so she could watch the Jews being marched to their death? To this day, more than forty years later, I can still see in my mind's eye Mrs. Lipińska silhouette before us, leading us through the dark night. That this woman was willing to risk everything to save other human beings is still and will forever remain the greatest inspiration of my life.

Every town had a few Gentiles who were willing to hide Jews from the SS. They too were heroic, but in most cases their heroism was of a somewhat different order. When fellow human beings appealed to them, they didn't have the heart to turn them away; in some cases, they even offered to shelter their Jewish friends on their own initiative. But Mrs. Lipińska went far beyond that. She didn't even know us very well, and to walk to that river with us in the dark of night in such times of lawlessness and terror was an act of courage only the very best of the human race could perform. She was truly of God—sent by him to inspire courage in us, to counterbalance the evil that seemed universal, to hold out the hope that somehow—in ways we shall never understand on this earth—there is a reason for our being here.

The river Bug appeared in the distance. As we approached it, Mrs. Lipińska stopped and showed us the spot where we were to wait for the guide. A quick embrace, a few mumbled words of farewell, and she was gone. It was a cloudy night. We sat down to wait for the whistle. Twelve o'clock came, and no one appeared. We started to worry; maybe it would be like with the Polish truck driver again, left in the lurch. For two hours we waited, and no one came. We were heartbroken. We didn't know what to do. How could Father get across the river without a rope to help him from the other side? And even if he did, once we were across we didn't know the way. With heavy hearts we decided we had no choice but to return to Mrs. Lipińska. We knew she would help us once more.

So that was what we did. We got lost on the way back, and for a while we were wandering without knowing where we were, but luckily we encountered no patrols.

It was almost dawn before we got back to the Lipiński yard. We climbed up the ladder, and there we were, back on the haystack. I dreaded the moment when Mrs. Lipińska learned that she had risked so much and been so courageous for nothing. In the morning we heard the familiar voice calling softly, *"Panie"* (Mister), with a mixture of hope and fear. Hope that there would be no answer, fear that we might have come back, that her ordeal was not yet over. I leaned out over the edge. When she saw me, she just clasped her hands over her head, turned, and left without a word. But this great lady could not stay discouraged for long. In a little while she returned and told us not to despair. Something must have happened that couldn't be helped. "Let's wait and see."

We waited. The intensity of the hunt was slackening, so we weren't quite as anxious as we had been our first few days there. We just had to be careful not to be seen by the children or by anyone else. Mrs. Lipińska continued to feed us well. I've never understood how she managed to keep us there for so long without anyone, not even in her own family, knowing about it. God was with her, and with us.

Then one day, full of joy, she came with another message from Hrubieszów. There had been a misunderstanding—no further explanation. On the night of September 30 we were to return to the same spot. This time the guide would be waiting for us without fail.

Those last few days passed as if in a dream. Minutes dragged like hours. Our long stay on the haystack was taking its toll. We were edgy and irritable. We loved each other, but lying for so long in such close proximity, scarcely able to move, was beginning to fray our nerves. Only Father never expressed any annoyance; he was the most patient, the most forbearing of any of us.

September 30 came. Mrs. Lipińska again insisted on taking us to the crossing, and this time, remembering how lost we had gotten on the way back, we made no protest. It was drizzling lightly. Mrs. Lipińska led the way once again, and we followed. We saw no patrols. We arrived without incident at the river crossing and hugged her good-bye once more. She turned and went back as we sat down to wait.

At midnight we heard a whistle. I whistled back. It was very dark. On the other side of the river a silhouette of a man appeared. We went down to the riverbank. He waded in and pointed to the spot where he wanted us to get into the water. The Bug was not wide there, but the current was very swift. About twenty feet separated us from the man. He threw a rope and I swam out and grabbed the end of it. We started swimming, but it was difficult. Father was not a very good swimmer, and he was weak besides. He managed by holding on to us. In the middle of the river we lost the rope. The current carried us about fifty feet downstream before we got across, but we made it. We climbed up the bank on the Polish side.

The man who met us was a heavyset Polish peasant with shrewd little eyes. He led us to a horse and wagon loaded with hay. He had brought with him farmers' clothes for Felek and Sam, hats and all. Father and I buried ourselves in the hay at the bottom of the wagon. The Pole, Sam, and Felek climbed onto the wagon, and off we went.

The trip took about an hour and a half. Father's asthma made it difficult for him to breathe under the hay. But we were filled with hope; so far we had come through. Finally the wagon stopped. The Pole climbed down and told us to get out. We could see Hrubieszów in the distance. The Pole told Father and me to stay and hide among some tomato plants growing in the field around us. He would take Felek and Sam to town, and later someone would come to get us. They left us and, shivering from the cold, we lay down on the ground among the plants, which didn't provide much of a cover. Time passed, and no one came. We had to be especially careful not to be seen here, not even by other Jews, for everyone knew us in Hrubieszów, and now we were escapees from the Russian side. We were illegal even here.

Back in Hrubieszów

■

T he sun rose slowly. There were some clouds in the sky. We saw from a distance a bunch of Polish boys, teenagers. One of them spotted us. I recognized him; I had gone to public school with him. He had a red face, like the tomatoes around us, with a lot of pimples. I had never liked him. He was a rough kid, one of the town riffraff.

He looked at me for a moment, then said, "You are Orenstein." We must have looked terrible after weeks of hiding. "Please don't tell anyone you saw us," I said. "Stay here, don't move," he replied. Then he and his friends went away, heading back toward town.

I didn't trust the kid; I knew we were in danger. But we couldn't go into town by ourselves. The house we had lived in wasn't in the ghetto, and we didn't know where our family lived now. We decided to wait.

Later I learned that my suspicions had been well founded. The Polish boy had gone straight to Fred's office and told him he had seen us hiding in the fields. It was obvious that he was asking for money. Fred thought quickly. Felek and Sam were already in a safe place, but there apparently had been a mixup about retrieving Father and me and getting us there too. Fred needed time to send someone to fetch us.

One of the local Gestapo, Hans Wagner, was a patient of Fred's. Germans, and especially Gestapo, were not supposed to use Jewish doctors, but Wagner had a special problem: he had become temporarily impotent. He had no faith in the Polish doctors, but he knew Fred had had a practice in Warsaw, and he believed that of all the local doctors, Fred was best qualified to treat him.

To gain time, Fred told the boy that he would be glad to give him some money, and to please wait for him in the office while he went out to get it. He then warned the boy to be very careful in his absence, because a member of the Gestapo was coming for a treatment and was due soon. When the boy heard the word "Gestapo" he turned pale, excused himself, and disappeared. Fred never heard from him again.

Meanwhile, Father and I, growing hungry and thirsty, were still waiting in the tomato field. I had always had an aversion to tomatoes; Mother never succeeded in getting me to taste one. They reminded me of blood. Out there in the field I was willing to give them another chance. Father ate a few, and held one out to me. "They're good. Here, try one, you need to eat something." I bit into it; it wasn't bad. I then ate two or three. Then and there I overcame my aversion to tomatoes.

Finally a young man, a Jew, appeared. "Are you the Orensteins?" he asked, and told us to follow him. Soon we were in the poor Jewish section, the Wannes, where the Germans had set up the Hrubieszów ghetto. He led us to a house, and up into the attic. It belonged to the parents of a nurse Fred knew, named Fela, and

Fred had made arrangements with her for us to stay there. Sam and Felek were already there, and we all embraced. We had made it. It was October 1, 1942.

Fela soon came up to the attic, introduced herself, and greeted us warmly. Fred, Mother, and Hanka would be coming to see us soon, she told us. We could scarcely contain ourselves in our excitement.

When they came, I was shocked at the sight of Mother. It had been only three years since I had seen her, but she had aged fifteen years; she looked like an old woman. Hanka was almost sixteen. A child when I left, she had grown into a beautiful young girl. We did nothing but weep, kiss, and hug each other for a long, long time. At last the family was together once again. Then each had to tell the others of his experiences, what he'd gone through since we had separated—all the incredible events.

Mother had brought dinner for us. She was the best cook in the world; we hadn't tasted food like that since before the war: gefilte fish, chicken soup with *kneydlakh*, beef and potatoes, and a delicious cake. We enjoyed a feast that almost made it all seem worth it.

Evening came, and with it the curfew. Fred, Mother, and Hanka had to leave, but first I wanted to know what was happening on the Russian front. There had been heavy fighting in Stalingrad, they told us, but the Russians seemed to be holding. I asked them, next time they came, to bring a newspaper and some books. After they left we lay down on the cots they had set up for us. What luxury, after a full month of being hunted like animals! We knew it was only temporary, that an action in Hrubieszów was inevitable, and that we had almost no chance of surviving the war, but for the moment we were all together, we had plenty of food and warm shelter, and we were thankful for the respite.

When Fred came the next day, he brought a German newspaper and a couple of books, one of them a Polish translation of *Gone with the*

Wind. I had never heard of it. It was almost a thousand pages long, but the last twenty pages were missing. I always liked to read anything about America, and hoped it would be interesting, but first, of course, I studied the newspaper. There was indeed heavy fighting in Stalingrad. The Germans had penetrated very deep into the heartland of Russia, but it was nevertheless obvious that the momentum of the war had swung from total German superiority to what looked like their last desperate attempt to win the war. Winter was coming soon, too, and that was what the Germans on the Russian front dreaded most.

The first two weeks of October were like a holiday. We were still in hiding, but the loft was large, the cots were comfortable, Fred, Hanka, or Mother came to see us every day, and Mother cooked all kinds of delicious dishes for us. For fear of informers, of course, they had to be careful not to be seen. For the four of us, the most important thing was knowing that for the moment we were not being hunted. All through September, beginning with our escape from under the machine guns on the first day of the action, we had been in continuous and constant danger. Every footstep, every rustle of the leaves could mean a murderous search party. It felt like heaven to be relatively safe and to have the rest of the family so nearby, to be loved and pampered once again.

Mother and Hanka told us about their life under the Germans: how, when Hanka had to work outdoors in the cold, an hour's walk from their quarters, Mother would bring her a thermos of hot soup and tea every day, although she had varicose veins and it was hard for her to walk. They recounted their adventures in the Warsaw ghetto and described all their lucky escapes. We in turn told of our adventures under the Soviets and the Germans.

I found *Gone with the Wind* fascinating, and was able to immerse myself totally in the story of Scarlett O'Hara and Rhett Butler. Although my sympathies were with the North and its struggle to abolish slavery, I greatly admired the gallantry and bravery of the South. My brothers all made fun of me. "How can you get so involved in a book at a time like this?" I had no good answer. It could have been pure escapism, or perhaps my insatiable curiosity always to be learning about new things and places. My knowledge of America at that time was largely confined to Zane Grey's Wild West tales and American history books. *Gone with the Wind* presented a rich panorama of life during the Civil War and I reveled in it, despite our circumstances.

But it was impossible to ignore for long the awareness that a heavy cloud was hanging over us, spoiling the joy of our reunion; tears of happiness were mingled with tears of fear and frustration. All the signs pointed toward a final extermination action against the Jews of Hrubieszów in the very near future. Eyewitnesses who had managed to escape from death trains or execution pits confirmed that in town after town a total liquidation of Polish Jewry was well under way. There seemed to be no way out.

There were three possible avenues of escape, none offering much chance of success. Some Jews who didn't look stereotypically Jewish succeeded in blending in with the Poles, but they were very few; perhaps one in a thousand could pull it off. Poles were very quick to recognize Jews, the necessary false identity papers were not easy to obtain, family ties restrained those individuals who might have been able to "pass" on their own, and since only Jews were circumcised, any male could be found out immediately if he was suspected. "Drop your pants" were the words most dreaded by Jewish men who had succeeded in establishing themselves as Poles. Probably no more than ten or fifteen Jews from Hrubieszów survived the war as Poles, and most of them were women.

Or one could try to find a trustworthy Polish family willing to risk their lives to hide Jews. There were some who did it for money, others out of friendship, still others simply from compassion, but their number was very small. I doubt whether more than ten Jews from Hrubieszów survived by hiding out in Polish homes.

The third possibility of escape was by taking refuge in the forest or joining the partisans. But the severity of the Polish winter, the difficulty of getting food, and the hostility of the vast majority of Ukrainians and Poles (including the partisans, who fought the Germans with single-minded intensity but in most cases refused to accept Jews into their ranks)—all these considerations made this route very chancy. Perhaps fifteen or twenty Jews from Hrubieszów survived the war in the forest. As far as my family was concerned, there was almost nothing we could do.

The news from the front, however, was encouraging. The Russians were fighting for every building left standing in Stalingrad, almost brick by brick, and it seemed that the German summer offensive of 1942 had come to a standstill. The Russians had turned the German advance into a retreat in the first winter of the war, and we were full of hope and the expectation of similar good news during the second winter. But time was running out for us.

On October 18, the dreaded news came. The Gestapo ordered the Judenrat to have all the Jews in Hrubieszów assemble in the central square of the town at nine in the morning of October 20. They were to be "resettled" in an unspecified labor camp. Each person was permitted to bring with him a small bundle of belongings and food. Those who did not show up would be shot. Although we had all expected this, the actual summons came like a hammer blow. This time there were to be no exceptions; no Jews were to remain in Hrubieszów. Like all other towns of Poland, it was to be made completely *Judenrein*.

What few options we had held out little or no hope. The train was a direct trip to the gas chamber. Hiding was very difficult, because even if the search parties didn't find us, how long could we stay in a skrytka without food and water? Father approached a few of his Polish acquaintances in search of a hiding place for us, but to no avail.

Then, unexpectedly, a woman came with a message from a Polish army colonel whom Fred had met during the war through the president of the Polish Landowners Association in Hrubieszów. A liberal and a good man, he had been a friend of Father's before the war. During the summer he had fallen ill and consulted Fred, who diagnosed advanced cancer of the lung.

When the colonel heard of the impending action, he sent his housekeeper, who was also his mistress, to offer Fred a hiding place in his house. Fred knew that the colonel would not be willing to hide all seven of us, but perhaps one more might be acceptable, so he took a chance and asked Hanka to join him.

On the evening of October 19, the two of them said farewell to the rest of the family. We were all in tears, knowing that we would probably never see each other again. Then Mother joined Father, Felek, Sam, and me in the skrytka in the attic of the house in which we were hiding out. The countdown for the hunt had begun.

Early on the morning of October 20, our landlord and his entire family joined us. There were ten of them, including a three-month-old granddaughter. We had about a two-week supply of food and water. Through the little opening in the attic wall, we could see groups of Jews carrying bundles going toward the center of town. It was heartbreaking to watch them. They walked with no visible emotion other than sadness and resignation. Families kept together, mothers and fathers with their bundles on their backs or shoulders holding babies in their arms, or walking hand in hand with the older children.

Most of them knew they were going to be killed, but there was no more fight left in them. They were the descendants of many generations of Jews who had been brought up to obey orders, to do what the "authorities" told them to do, and so they obeyed these authorities now, even when the orders were to go to their own deaths. The *Sonderkommando,* who had come to town to supervise the action, and the local Gestapo and their henchmen were busy directing the Jews toward the train station, where they were loaded into waiting cattle cars.

That day about three thousand Jews were shipped to the gas chambers of Sobibór. About three thousand others remained in town, hiding in skrytkas as we did, or simply staying in their houses. The rest of the prewar Hrubieszów Jewish population had either escaped to the Russian side in 1939, had been killed in the preliminary partial actions before this main extermination action, or were scattered through the nearby fields and forests.

We spent a restless night, during which the feeling of being a hunted animal came back to me in full force. Early the next morning, October 21, an all-out house-to-house hunt began. I was able to observe through the opening in the wall what was taking place in a small section of the street directly below us.

I could see the SS and the Ukrainians entering a nearby house, from which they soon emerged, accompanied by several of their victims. Many of the Jews were easy to find. They hadn't followed orders because they didn't want to die in the gas chambers, but they had nowhere to hide, so they simply stayed at home, without attempting to conceal themselves—at most they went up to the attic or down to the cellar. Now they were roughly pushed and dragged out of their houses, beaten and kicked. Old people and children who couldn't walk fast enough to suit the Germans were struck with rifle butts; babies were crying. A few Poles were aiding the Germans in this ruthless hunt, leading them to houses they suspected of concealing skrytkas. On the street some Polish children even kicked the Jewish children as they went by, and threw stones at them. It was

Lejb Orenstein (author's father) at the age of fifty-seven.

Golda Orenstein (author's mother) at the age of thirty.

Hrubieszów, center of town. The three-story building was where the author lived until he was sixteen years old.

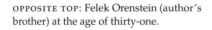

The author at the age of six and his sister Hanka at the age of four.

OPPOSITE TOP: Felek Orenstein (author's brother) at the age of thirty-one.

OPPOSITE MIDDLE: Fred Orenstein (author's brother) in U.N.N.R.A. uniform, 1945, at the age of thirty-six.

OPPOSITE BOTTOM: Sam (Shlomo) Orenstein (author's brother) at the age of thirty.

ABOVE: Photo taken in 1937 of *(left to right)* Chaim Ajzen, author, cousin Joe (Józiek) Strum, Bolek Goldstein, and cousin Józiek Peretz.   BELOW: Deportation of Jews to a death camp in the Lublin district.

Jews awaiting their fate, surrounded by guards.

Jews waiting to be deported to a death camp.

Jews before their execution, surrounded by the S.S.

Jews at the edge of a pit just prior to their execution.

BELOW LEFT: *Appel* (roll call) in the Sachsenhausen-Oranienburg Concentration Camp near Berlin. Author was a prisoner there in 1945. BELOW RIGHT: A group of S.S. men who carried out the "*Aktion*" in the Lublin district.

91	Polit. R.	Syk	Iwan	5. 5. 11	St. Rair	✝ 7. April 1945
92	S.V. Pole	Siergiejew	Peter	1. 1. 9.	Bergen-Belsen	24. Jan. 1945
93	Pole	Paprocki	Antoni	17. 1. 99	Shu	3. März 1945
94	Polit./R.	Bondartschuk	Wolodimir	1. 10. 24	Shu	3. März 1945
95	Polit./R.	Tarankow	Wiktor	18. 7. 20	Shu	3. März 1945
96	S.V. Pole	Chalasinski	Bronislaus	14. 12. 14	Mi	7. April 1945
97	Polit./R.	Lachno	Ladislaus	6. 5. 15	✝ 15. Feb. 1945	
98	Pole	Pukowski	Georg	14. 6. 21		
99	Jude	Cronheim	Arno	28. 8. 22	Shu	3. März 1945
00	Jude Polu	Eisenstadt	Pinkas	13. 10. 04	Shu	3. März 1945
01	Jude Polu	Orenstein	Mordko	13. 10. 23	Shu	3. März 1945
02	Jude Polu	Orenstein	Szloma	10. 5. 14	Shu	3. März 1945
03	Jude Polu	Kissmann	Josef	16. 12. 06	Shu	3. März 1945
04	Jude Polu	Stark	Marceli	19. 9. 08	Shu	3. März 1945
05	Jude Polu	Warszawski	Lejzor	2. 6. 02	Shu	3. März 1945
06	Jude Polu	Wortmann	Philipp	3. 12. 99	Shu	3. März 1945
07	Polit. Frz.	Petit	Jean	3. 3. 12		
08	Polit. Frz.	Fischat	Julien	10. 7. 03	✝ 13. Jan. 1945	
09	Polit. Frz.	Huiget	Paul	4. 10. 19	Shu	3. März 1945
10	Polit. Frz.	Clerget	Marcel	22. 6. 01	Mi	15. Feb. 1945
11	Polit. Frz.	Montagnon	Paul	26. 7. 24	Shu	3. März 1945
12	Polit. Frz.	Weigel	Noel	14. 12. 16	Shu	3. März 1945
13	Polit. Frz.	Chagnot	Robert	11. 6. 11	Shu	3. März 1945
14	Polit. Frz.	Thierry	Alphonse	18. 4. 16		
15	Polit. Frz.	Chagnot	André	18. 9. 14	Shu	3. März 1945
16	Polit. Frz.	Cardot	Andre	4. 9. 23	Shu	3. März 1945
17	Polit./Schü	Fuchsler	Georges	25. 12. 18	Shu	3. März 1945
18	Polit. Frz.	Caridey	Lucien	17. 12. 25	Shu	März 1945
319	Polit. Frz.	Montavon	Edmund	12. 1. 12	Shu	3. März 1945
320	Polit. Frz.	Arnold	Alfred	19. 12. 01	Shu	3. März 1945
321	Polit. Frz.	Vienot	Raymond	8. 6. 11	Shu	3. März 1945
322	Polit. Frz.	Grosclaude	Georges	28. 8. 00	Mittwoch	4. April 1945
	Pole	Ino	Frantis	11. 1. 18	Shu	3. März 1945

Der Reichsführer SS   Feld-Kommandostelle,
    38/55/44 g   den 25.5.44

An

  SS-Obergruppenführer   P o h l

      B e r l i n

      Unter den Juden, die wir jetzt aus Ungarn hereinbekommen, sowie auch sonst unter unseren Konzentrationslager-Häftlingen gibt es ohne Zweifel eine ganze Menge von Physikern, Chemik und sonstigen Wissenschaftlern.

      Ich beauftrage den SS-Obergruppenführer Pohl, in einem Konzentrationslager eine wissenschaftliche Forschungsstätte ein richten, in der das Fachwissen dieser Leute für das menschenbean spruchende und zeitraubende Ausrechnen von Formeln, Ausarbeitun von Einzelkonstruktionen, sowie aber auch zu Grundlagen-Forschu gen angesetzt wird. Das Ahnenerbe wird beauftragt in Zusammenar beit mit dem Reichssicherheitshauptamt, das unter den russische Gefangenen eine ähnliche Auswertungsstätte eingerichtet hat, di von der Wissenschaft und Rüstungsindustrie als vordringlich er achteten Aufträge einzuholen und sie zu stellen. Gesamtverantwor tung: SS-Obergruppenführer Pohl, wissenschaftliche Leitung: Ahne erbe, SS-Oberführer Wüst, in Vertretung: SS-Standartenführer S vers. Die wertvolle Anregung zu diesem Gesamtkomplex stammt von SS-Obergruppenführer Koppe.

      Als Sonderauftrag für das Ahnenerbe gebe ich die sofor tige Inangriffnahme der im Krieg von Dr.Scultetus angefangenen Rechnungen der Grundlagen für eine langfristige Wettervorhersag die im Jahre 1939 aus Kriegsgründen abgebrochen werden musste. Ich wünsche monatlichen Bericht, zum 1. Mal am 1.8.1944. - Dr Scultetus ist z.Zt.unter der Anschrift: SS-Stubaf.Oberregierun rat Dr.S., Königsberg-Devau (5b) Fliegerhorst-Wetterwarte zu reichen.

                 gez. H. Himmler

Reichcommander SS   Field Commandpost
38/55/44g   May 25, 1944

To: SS-Obergruppenfuehrer Pohl

Berlin:

Concerning the Jews, whom we now have from Hungary, as well as other prisoners in our concentration camp, there are without doubt, a lot of
physicists, chemists and other scientists.

I am assigning SS-Uppergruppen commander Pohl, to a concentration
camp that is for scientific research, to assess the knowledge of these people for the demanding and time consuming calculation of formulae, technical preparation for one time construction, for the foundation of research
work. The ancestor inheritance recovery of assets is to be considered in
cooperation with the main office of Reich security, which furnished a
similar solution among the Russian prisoners to place them in the science
and armaments industry since it was urgent from orders to catch up.
Total responsibility: SS-Obergruppenfuehrer Pohl, research leadership;
Inheritance, SS-Oberfuehrer Wuest; representing: SS-Standartenfuehrer
Sievers. The valuable suggestion of this complex issue originates from
SS-Obergruppenfuehrer Koppe.

As to the special contract for the inheritance giving immediately in the
event of outbreak of war from Dr. Scultetus has already begun for the ba-
sis of a long term prediction of war but were suspended in the year 1939
because of reasons related to war. Dr. Scultetus is at this time reachable
at the address: SS-Stubaf. Oberregierunggenrat (council) Dr. S., Koenigs-
berg-Devau (5b) Airbase-Weatherstation.

Sent H. Himmler

71

Geheim!
Dringend!

872

+ sfd hsspf ost krakau nr. 273   8.9.44   1850 --

.-- g e h e i m -- az.: 2716/44 geh --

an den

reichsfuehrer-ss

h. h i m m l e r

-- feldkommandostelle --

betr.: wissenschaftliche arbeiten im kl plaszew fuer

kriegswirtschaft

mein eichsfuehrer --

die die mir im kl plaszew in einer besonderen wissenschaftlichen

abteilung zusammenge zu zusammengefassten juedischen haeftlinge

+ juedischen haeftlinge haben in den letzten monaten unter leitung

der deutschen wissenschaftler des institutes fuer deutsche ost

wissenschaftler des institutes fuer deutsche estarbeit mit gutem

erfolg ap der leesung der verschiedensten kriegswirtschaftlich

wichtigen wissenschaftlichen aufgaben gearbeitet.

inzwischen ist das institut fuer deutsche estarbeit nach schlesz

zandt ueber cham/ bayr.ostmark verlegt worden. das institut legt

wert darauf,die gemaess den einzelnen fachgruppen der chemie,

mathematik, physik und bakteriologie in arbeitsgruppen zusammen-

gefaasten juedischen fachkraefte der weiteren fortfuehrung der

den interessen der ruestung und kriegswirtschaft dienenden

wissenschaftlichen arbeiten nutzbar zu machen.

72

ich schlage daher vor, die wissenschaftliche abteilung des kl

plaszew in das kl flossenbrueck zu verlegen, damit die deutschen

wissenschaftler des instituts fuer deutsche estarbeit dort auf

der bisherigen grundlage weiterarbeiten koennen und die bereits

geplante erweiterung des wissenschaftlichen einsatzes der juden

unter ausnuetzung der bisherigen erfahrungen des instituts fuer

deutsche estarbeit durchgefuehrt werden kann.==

gez.: k o p p e

ss-obergruppenfuehrer u. general der polizei +

+uebermittelt durch rvst bln+

9/8/44
To Reichsfuehrer-SS
H. Himmler

Field Command Quarters

Subject: Scientific Work in Concentration Camp Płaszów for War
Economy

My Reichsfüehrer:

We have in Concentration Camp Płaszów in a separate scientific section put together Jewish prisoners who have worked in recent months under the leadership of the German scientists of the Institute for the German Eastwork with good results regarding the solution of various important war economy scientific projects.

In the meantime the Institute for the German Eastwork [*Ostarbeit*] has been moved to Castle Zandt over Cham in Austria [*Ostmark*]. The Institute considers it important that the combined effort [*gemaess*] of the individual groups of experts in chemistry, mathematics, physics, and bacteriology in work groups of assembled Jewish scientists of the various specialties be made useful in furthering the continuation in the interest of arms production and war economy.

I recommend, therefore, that the scientific section in the Concentration Camp Płaszów be transferred to the Concentration Camp Flossenbrueck, so that the German scientists of the Institute for the German Eastwork can continue their efforts based on the work done to date, and the already planned expansion of the scientific tasks given to the Jews in making use of the experience to date of the Institute for the German Eastwork can be continued.

[Wilhelm] Koppe
Group Leader of SS and
General of the Police
[in Poland   ]

Dr. Lucjian Dobroszycki's comments on the Himmler letter

One of the most revealing stories in Henry Orenstein's memoirs is an account of his participation in the "Chemical Kommando" of phony scientists composed of Jewish prisoners in the concentration camps of Budzy´n, Majdanek, Płaszów, Ravensbrück, and Sachsenhausen. The existence of the "Chemical Kommando" was, until Mr. Orenstein's account, entirely unknown. Although the author's truthfulness has not been challenged by anyone, historians look for at least one document that corroborates oral history of this kind. Such a document came to my attention after Henry Orenstein's book was published.*

This document—or I should say the letter quoted opposite, in extenso—is indeed of extraordinary value, because of the man who wrote it, as well as the addressee and its subject matter. The letter, marked "Urgent!" (*Dringend!*) and "Secret!" (*Geheim!*), was written by Wilhelm Koppe, the Highest SS and Police Leader in occupied Poland, and is addressed to his immediate superior, Heinrich Himmler, the SS Reichsleader and Chief of the German Police, whom Hitler made responsible for the destruction of European Jewry. Koppe informs Himmler of three crucial facts: first, that he has established a scientific department in the concentration camp of Płaszów consisting of some of the Jewish scientists imprisoned there. Second, that those Jewish specialists, under the leadership of German scientists from the Institute for German Advancement in the East (*Institut für Deutsche Ostarbeit*) in Cracow, had achieved good results in solving various important scientific problems related to the war economy and armament. Third, Koppe asks Himmler to allow the Institute, which had already been evacuated from Poland to Austria (following the Red Army's summer 1944 offensive), to have the Jewish scientists evacuated as well since this would permit the Institute to expand its important work.

The work done by the "Chemical Kommando" was transparently phony and thinly disguised. One might wonder who really was behind this bizarre enterprise. Koppe and Himmler should be excluded from any consideration. It is extremely unlikely that either would have bothered with inventing such a cover-up. Was the "Chemical Kommando" the invention of certain German professors who, fearful of being drafted and sent to the Eastern Front, set up sinecures for themselves? If so, did they act alone, or with the consent of people in the Nazi power structure in Cracow or Berlin? These and other questions might be answered if additional documents on the subject come to light.

---

*I have to admit that I got hold of the document not as a result of laborious research but by sheer accident. Recently Dr. Gotz Aly, a fellow historian, came from West Germany to see me at YIVO and asked me to read his study on Helmut Meinhold, a former Nazi staff worker of the *Institut fur Deutsche Ostarbeit* in Cracow and author of many anti-Jewish and anti-Polish pamphlets, and who, after the war, became the main scholarly adviser both to the government and parliament of the German Federal Republic. In his study, Dr. Aly quoted a few documents, one of which immediately caught my eye. I read it and it turned out to be Koppe's letter to Himmler.

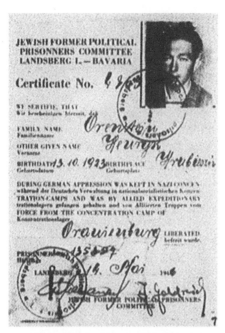

Author's concentration camp certificate card issued in Landsberg, Germany.

(*Left to right*) author, Hy Silberstein, and Bencio Fink, ca. 1975.

Author and Fred Orenstein, ca. 1977.

Respected Dear Family Orenstein:

This is to let you know that I received your letter and the photographs. I'm very grateful to you. If you only knew what a joyous day that was for me. I started to cry from joy when I looked at your photograph. You are so pleasant, nice-looking. Every day I take a look at it, put it away, the next day I look at it again, and I remember those scary, horrible times, which forged such a bond between us, made us like family. And I am grateful to God that He helped me to accomplish such a good deed to the end. I am proud of it. When I think about it, I see that with every step, God was helping us.

A few days after you left us, they took us to Germany to do forced labor. It was horrible, they took me, my husband, and my daughter who was only nine years old. Our son was not home at the time, so he stayed behind. In those times miracles happened.

But all of that is in the past, and may it never happen again. You suggested that I try to get papers to visit you. I tried to get documents so that I could come to you. I would like very much to see you but it seems impossible, because I am old, my health is poor, and I have chronic bronchitis, and also my legs hurt. That's how it is with old people. I have all kinds of problems, but one thing that is very lucky for me is that my daughter is very good. I often stay with her. My son lives far away, he visits rarely.

I am very pleased that you live well and I shall pray to God to give you health and good life. I tell you, you are such a good man. There aren't too many like that in the world. So many years went by, and you still remember me. I am very appreciative of that. You are such a good person. I wish you and your family happiness and good health. I kiss you all.

Your friend,
Lipińska

ABOVE LEFT : Author and his wife,
Susie Orenstein.

ABOVE RIGHT: Mark and Annette
Orenstein (author's children).

Edward I. Koch, mayor of New
York City, at the dedication of the
Orenstein Building.

TOP: The Lejb and Golda Orenstein Building.
ABOVE: Lejb and Golda shelter. RIGHT: Plaque
at the shelter

THIS SHELTER IS IN MEMORY OF
LEJB AND **GOLDA ORENSTEIN**
AND THEIR CHILDREN **FELIX** AND **HANKA**
ALL KILLED BY THE NAZIS IN THE HOLOCAUST

בית לייב וגולדה אורנשטיין
וילדיהם פליקס והנקה
אשר נרצחו בידי הנאצים
דיור לניצולי שואה ומרכז יום לקשיש

Author at the Lejb and Golda Orenstein Building.

From left, Mark, Henry, Susie, and Annette Orenstein.

incredible to me to see Poles, who had suffered so much themselves under the German occupation, helping their oppressors round up and kill their fellow countrymen. I couldn't bear the sight of it, and buried myself in *Gone with the Wind*, in which I became so engrossed that for a while I actually forgot where I was, mainly concerned that, with the last twenty pages missing, I'd probably never find out how the saga of Scarlett O'Hara ended.

In the afternoon the baby started crying, and with Germans and Ukrainians all around us roaming the streets, the noise could easily lead them to our hiding place. The baby's parents took turns rocking her in their arms to quiet her, but nothing helped. The mother tried to cover her with a blanket, but at this she only screamed louder. Finally the mother had to hold her hand over the baby's mouth, which made her face turn blue, but when the mother lifted her hand for even a second, the baby's shrieks cut through the air. All of us were panic-stricken. Even her own family began muttering, "This baby is going to get us all killed," and urged the mother to keep her hand over the child's mouth. Nobody said so, but the feeling was palpable that if it came to it, the baby should be sacrificed to save the rest of us. This state of things continued for a couple of hours. Each time the baby cried out I cringed; her cries were so loud it was only by a miracle that the hunters didn't hear them.

By nightfall my family had decided that it was too dangerous to stay where we were. A few blocks away was a small skrytka where an elderly couple we knew were hiding. We took with us some food and water, said good-bye to the others, and left. On the way we passed many houses with the doors standing wide open, just as the search parties had left them after dragging their unfortunate inhabitants out. We moved along very cautiously, hiding in the hallways of the empty houses whenever we heard a noise. When at last we reached our destination, we found that it was a double-wall skrytka, and, as we expected, hiding inside was the elderly couple who owned the house. They were glad to let us in even though our presence made it very uncomfortable for them. There was room for us all to lie down, but just barely. In the attic we had left, there was at least some light coming through from outside; here it was almost totally dark. We had no idea what was happening outside.

We spent the next seven days in the skrytka, and it was awful. We couldn't wash or change our clothes. We had either to stand or lie flat on the floor. At night we sneaked out one by one to relieve ourselves, but even this was difficult because to reach the outhouse we had to crawl through an open space. Usually we waited until three or four in the morning, when the searchers had stopped for the night. Our greatest fear was of running out of water, and we drank ours very sparingly. Those three days in the tile shop in Uściług had taught us a lesson.

It was heartbreaking to see my parents, who were both sixty, suffering so much, and so stoically. They had lost all hope for themselves, and were concerned only that we should not die. We talked about Fred and Hanka, and how glad we were that the old colonel had taken them in; perhaps with his help they might survive the war.

During the day we could hear the search parties out in the street, but they never entered the house while we were there. The owner told us that they had come to the house on the first day of the action, knocking on the walls, looking everywhere. Then they had left, and hadn't come back.

As the days passed, the situation grew worse. How long could we stay there, even if the Germans didn't find us? We were exhausted, dirty, hungry, and thirsty. We discussed the possibility of going out into the fields, but we knew, really, that Father and Mother were both too weak now to survive out there for long.

During our last couple of days in the skrytka conversation came to a virtual standstill. We sat or lay in silence. I was struck repeatedly by how incredible it all was—total strangers remorselessly hunting down people who had done nothing whatsoever to hurt them. The world was mad. Did I want to go on living in it? Bad as things were, though, cruel as the world around us was, the answer was still yes. The thought of being killed and watching others in my family killed petrified me.

Time dragged still more slowly. The street was quieter now, the search parties less frequent. Then, early on the morning of the 28th, we heard a commotion outside and a loud voice shouting, "Amnesty! All Jews can come out of hiding. The action is finished." We were so exhausted and sick of the skrytka that we decided to come out. We had little to lose; life in the skrytka had become unendurable. We climbed out, washed our faces, and went out into the street, where we met a few neighbors who had also succeeded in hiding from the Germans so far. The Germans and Ukrainians were going around the ghetto announcing that an amnesty had been declared, and all surviving Jews were to go to Gestapo headquarters, which were located in what before the war had been the town jail.

Suddenly, as we were standing there in the street talking to our neighbors, Fred and Hanka appeared, to our surprise and grief. We had thought they at least were safe, and here they were, in the same boat with us.

It seemed that when they arrived at the colonel's house, they found him in a very bad way and getting worse every day. He knew he was dying, and called in his mistress-housekeeper. In the presence of Fred and Hanka, he made his mistress lay her hand on a large cross hanging behind his bed and swear, by Jesus Christ, that she would continue to permit them to hide out in the house after his death. He had left her everything he possessed in his will, he told her, but only on condition that she keep her promise. A few hours later he was dead.

The next morning the mistress told Fred and Hanka that she was sorry, but she couldn't let them stay. The Germans were searching every Polish house and threatening to kill anyone caught hiding Jews. Fred begged her to let them stay at least until dark, and she reluctantly agreed. When evening came, they left.

They went to a nearby farmhouse and looked in through a window, where they saw the farmer and his family having dinner. Fred knocked on the window. The farmer came out and recognized them immediately. "You are Orenstein's children!" he exclaimed. He took Fred and Hanka to his pigsty, so his children wouldn't know that he was helping Jews, and let them stay there for two days. Then he too started to worry about the danger, and told them they would have to leave. Fred asked him to get in touch with the president of the Polish Landowners Association, hoping that he might find a place for them to hide. The president came to see them and told them of the amnesty. By then Fred and Hanka were also tired of running, and decided to go back to town.

Since the number of Jews left was too small to be sent by train to the gas chambers, we assumed that the Germans would simply shoot those who had emerged from hiding at the news of the amnesty. We were worn out, beaten. The promise of an amnesty didn't fool us, but we decided to go to the jail anyway, to put an end to our misery.

We started walking over to the jail, all seven of us, the whole family. We walked in silence, like the families I had seen going to the town square at the start of the action. My heart ached to see the grim faces of my parents, my brothers, my young sister. So this was how all our lives, my whole family's life, was going to end. Shot and then thrown into a mass grave. "What did we do?" I wanted to cry out in protest. We passed a woman who had occasionally worked for my mother, helping with the laundry. She saw us all walking voluntarily to be executed, and exclaimed, "It's the Orensteins—all of them!"

But she said nothing to us, nor we to her. She knew how prosperous we had been before the war, but that meant nothing now. We were Jews; we had to die. There were very few people in the streets, and in about ten minutes we had reached the jail. Ukrainian guards let us in through an iron gate leading to the yard behind the jail. The gate loudly clanked shut behind us.

In the yard were about a hundred other Jews, all, like us, survivors of the skrytkas who had decided that it no longer made sense to continue hiding out, that the suffering and humiliation were too much to bear. For the first time since the war began I saw some of my school friends: Nirenberg, a short boy with quick, lively eyes and a ready smile; Zajd, with whom I used to play soccer; Zalmen Regel, an earnest, very intelligent boy who was a student in the gymnasium. We sat down on top of a woodpile and talked about old times. We knew we were all going to die in a matter of hours, but no one spoke of it.

Then Hans Wagner, Fred's Gestapo patient, appeared at the fence, looked around, and noticed Fred standing in the yard. He motioned for him to come over. "What are you doing here, Doctor?" he asked, as if he didn't know. "We just got tired of running and hiding," Fred replied. "There was nowhere to go." "Is your sister here with you?" Wagner asked. "Yes, she is," Fred answered, "and so are my three brothers and my parents." "Let me see," Wagner said, and walked back into the side entrance to the jail.

An old Jew who was saying his prayers overheard the conversation. Sensing that Fred might have a chance to get out, he came over to him and surreptitiously placed a packet of money in his hand. "Here, take this money, Doctor," he said. "Use it, if you can, to feed the Jews." Then he blessed Fred, turned back, and with a serene face resumed his prayers.

Wagner evidently spoke about Fred to Ebner, the Gestapo chief executioner, for Ebner came into the yard from the back of the building and gestured to Fred with his stick, looking him over from head to foot. "Is this the elegant doctor?" he said mockingly. Even in the ghetto Fred had managed to look well dressed, but after a week of hiding he was unshaven and his clothes were rumpled. Fred motioned to Hanka, who stepped forward. Ebner remembered her too from the ghetto. ". . . and my brothers," Fred continued. Felek, myself, and then Sam, who looked very tired, moved a little closer to Ebner. When he saw Sam he made a face. "He's no good, he's sick," he said. "He just looks bad now—he is younger than I am," Fred pleaded. Ebner seemed very displeased. *"Vier Brüder"* (Four brothers), he said, as if the mere thought of letting four Jewish brothers out, however briefly, gave him pain. Poor, desperate, courageous Fred pressed the matter, well knowing that by pleading on our behalf, he was jeopardizing his own chance for life. "And my parents," he added. Mother and Father hesitated. They knew Fred was going too far, and they didn't want to endanger this unexpected opportunity for their children to get out.

The whole thing began to annoy Ebner, who didn't even look at our parents. "What do I need old Jews for?" he yelled. Now he changed his mind about letting any of us out. He pointed with his stick and shouted, *"Alles zurück zum Haufen"* (Everybody back to the crowd). Instantly Father and Mother realized that our chance was slipping away, and stepped back into the crowd. Our lives were all that mattered to them. Now Ebner spun around and went back into the building. It looked as if Fred had lost his gamble.

In the meantime, two trucks had pulled up to the fence and the Polish police started pushing the people toward them. The Gestapo chief came down the steps to see that the loading of the Jews into the trucks proceeded smoothly. We still stood in the same spot where Ebner had left us, and a Polish policeman stood nearby. He didn't understand German, and wasn't sure himself what Ebner had decided to do with us. The chief looked at us questioningly. "What are they doing here?"

Almost simultaneously Fred and the Pole said, "Ebner." The chief apparently understood this to mean that Ebner didn't want us to be killed with the others. He himself was uncomfortable with that madman, Ebner. "If Ebner said OK—go." He waved his hand at the staircase. As we turned toward the stairs, we saw Father helping Mother into the truck with the other Jews. We heard her call out, "Niuniek [Fred's nickname], *rateve di kinder!*" (Fred, save the children!). Although she almost always spoke to us in Polish, her last words to us were in Yiddish. At the last minute, the chief picked out two others, two young girls, Jentka Cohen and Tobka Beker, and told them to join us.

I felt as if my heart would explode. I was gripped by an unendurable tension. Wild emotions were raging within me, almost tearing me apart—an overpowering desire to live, to save myself, and a terrible guilt at not joining my parents, at abandoning them when they were about to die. We started walking up the steps, seven or eight of them, turned right, three more steps, walked through the Gestapo office on the second floor, and down the steps leading to the street. A policeman told us to go to Jatkowa Street, where the Gestapo were setting up a small service camp of about thirty Jews to work for them.

Our parents and the others in the prison yard were loaded onto the two trucks and driven to the execution pits in the Jewish cemetery nearby. Bencio Fink, who later became a friend of mine in the camps, and Rechtshaft, a *droshka* driver before the war, were among the burial crew. They later described to us what happened at the cemetery.

The Jews were ordered to undress and lie down in a row at the edge of the pit. Demant, a short, fat, red-faced member of the Gestapo who sometimes filled in for Ebner as executioner, went from one end of the line to the other, shooting each one in the head. Among them were the Krajzer family. Krajzer was a druggist who had rented his shop, which was next to our fabric store, from my father. They had a daughter, Hela, a pretty, buxom, blond girl. The Krajzer family lay down next to our parents. After the shooting, Demant went up to Hela's body, turned it over face-up, and rammed his fist into her vagina. The Jews in the burial crew were ordered to throw the bodies into the pit and bury them.

Meanwhile, we had arrived at Jatkowa Street, where we met the other Jews who had been selected by the Gestapo as members of the new work camp. Julek Brandt, Bluma's brother, was put in charge, and Rabinowitz, an attorney, was made his assistant. They assigned rooms to us in several of the houses on Jatkowa Street that stood empty, their inhabitants having all been gassed or shot to death.

We were in a state of extreme exhaustion and shock. We knew our parents were dead and could only weep quietly. It was growing dark. There was no conversation in the room, only an occasional sob or a new outburst of crying. The door opened and Wagner appeared, flashlight in hand. "Where is the doctor?" he asked. Fred got up, his eyes red from weeping. Wagner tried to console him: "At least you still have your brothers and sister." Then he went out. I was physically so exhausted and emotionally drained that I fell into a fitful sleep. Through the night I would wake up, remember what had happened, and cry myself back to sleep.*

In the morning Julek Brandt assigned various tasks to our group

---

*For years after the liberation, I felt guilty at not having gone with my parents. But as time passed, I came to see that it would have been a great mistake for us to remain with them. They suffered a terrible death, but they died knowing that we had gotten out and been given another chance at life. Mother's last cry to Fred, "Save the children!" showed she thought there was some hope for us. Father too, especially in the last few months of his life, had worried only about us and not at all about himself. It would have been unbearable for them to watch the murder of their five children.

of about thirty, including eight or ten women. Julek was about thirty years old, very energetic and a good organizer. He had been one of the leaders of the Judenrat in the Hrubieszów ghetto. He dealt directly with Ebner, who had led him to believe that when the final action came, in appreciation for his services Ebner would allow him and a small group of other Jews to remain in town. To his surprise, when the time came, Ebner personally made certain that Julek was put into one of the cattle cars of the train used to carry the three thousand Hrubieszów Jews to the gas chambers of Sobibór.

After the train had started, Brandt, Rechtshaft, and some others succeeded in forcing open a few of the wooden slats that formed the sides of the cars and jumping out of the moving train. Some of them were shot by the guards, but Julek, Rechtshaft, and a couple of others managed to escape. For two or three days they hid in the fields about ten miles from Hrubieszów, but eventually they were spotted by Polish peasants, who alerted the local police and helped them to capture the Jews. They were brought to the nearby village jail, where Hy Silberstein, his girlfriend Mirka, and a few others were imprisoned after they too had been captured in a nearby forest.

Hy was a few years older than I, from a good family, and had been a good student in the Hrubieszów gymnasium. We knew each other well, but each of us had his own group of friends. Hy was the best-looking boy in Hrubieszów, and girls used to chase after him. His father worked for the Judenrat, and one day he was called in to the Gestapo headquarters. He never came back; Ebner shot him dead right then and there. Hy's mother was killed by Demant in front of their house.

When the action started, Hy and Mirka had gone to hide at the home of a Polish friend of Hy's, Wanka Adamiuk. After a few days Wanka's family started hinting that they were afraid to keep them any longer, lest they themselves be shot by the Gestapo. Hy and

Mirka were forced to leave, and at night went to hide in the woods near Czerniczyn, a small village not far from Hrubieszów. There they ran into my school friend Chaim Ajzen and about a dozen other Jews. After two or three days they were surprised by a detachment of Ukrainian police. Some were killed; Chaim and a number of others escaped. Hy, Mirka, and a few others were captured and brought to the village jail.

The morning of October 28 they were all taken to the Gestapo headquarters in Hrubieszów. Ebner saw Julek and his group in the jail and was preparing to shoot them when Julek told him that he knew where a large cache of gold had been hidden by the Judenrat. He offered to show Ebner where it was on condition that he and a small group of Jews be permitted to stay in Hrubieszów. Ebner, who needed people to clean up the ghetto, agreed. Julek led him to the gold, and that was how the Jatkowa camp got started.

I was assigned to one of several small groups whose job was to go from house to house in the now-empty ghetto, remove the furniture and other belongings of the Jews who had lived there, and load it all onto wagons, which were then driven to one of the warehouses in which the Germans stored the possessions of the Jews they had killed.

I spent the next four or five weeks doing this work. It was eerie entering the empty Jewish houses. When the action had started, the Jews had been permitted to take very little with them, so almost everything in the houses was intact. Pots of food still stood on top of the stoves, clothing hung in the closets, most of the beds had been made. It was as if people had somehow felt obliged to leave everything in order.

We worked without much supervision, but no one thought of escaping; we were all too tired of running and hiding. It was unseasonably warm November weather.

Large-scale killing had now stopped. The great majority of the Hrubieszów Jews were dead. Many had gone to the Sobibór gas chambers; thousands of others, including my parents, relatives, friends, and neighbors, had been killed in and around Hrubieszów, most of them by one man, Ebner. From time to time the Gestapo still caught a few Jews in hiding and would take them to the cemetery to be shot. Sometimes they didn't even bother to do that; one day on the way to work we passed two Jewish women lying in the middle of the street. Their faces looked as if they were asleep, but their heads lay in pools of blood. They had been found in hiding by Alex, a member of the Gestapo, who had taken them out on the street and shot them on the spot.

Alex was a strange man; he spoke perfect Yiddish. He must have been raised by a Jewish family to speak the language so well. Those few people who were still in hiding were by now in desperate need of water, and Alex would walk around the empty houses calling out in a low voice in Yiddish, to make them think he too was a Jew, and they would answer him. He would then shoot those poor souls he had been able to deceive. He was in his late thirties, with curly, dark blond hair and watery blue eyes. It was obvious from his swaggering walk and patronizing manner how he relished his power over the few Jews left alive.

During this miserable time one thing kept us going: the news from all the fighting fronts was great. Everywhere the tide of the war was turning against Hitler. Some of the Poles had shortwave radios on which they listened to the BBC. One very nice man, a former teacher of mine, was providing us with information, sometimes at considerable danger to himself. And although they distorted many facts, the German war communiqués, which were published in the local newspapers, accurately reported the names of the towns where battles were taking place, so we had a pretty good idea where the fronts were.

First came the news of Montgomery's victory in the desert at El Alamein. Even the great Rommel, the Desert Fox, had been defeated. The BBC told the world of the tens of thousands of German and Italian prisoners taken. So the English had done it at last.

Then came another bolt from the blue. The Americans had landed in North Africa! Finally they were on this side of the Atlantic. Once again the New World had come to the rescue of the Old.

And then there was the incredible news from the Russian front. Stalingrad, where the remnants of the Russian army had held on for weeks in bitter house-to-house fighting, the city that had become an obsession with Hitler, now became his nemesis. While Russian soldiers sacrificed their lives among the ruins of Stalingrad, Stalin was moving fresh troops from Siberia, mostly under cover of night, to the two exposed flanks of the elite German Second Army under General Friedrich Paulus. So fanatically determined was Hitler to capture the city bearing Stalin's name that he pushed Paulus's army into the tip of a large enclave without adequately securing its flanks.

On November 19 the Russians struck. The ground was covered with snow, it was freezing, and the Germans and their allies were exhausted. The Russians broke through with tanks and infantry and poured through the gaps they had opened to the northwest and southwest of Stalingrad.

Four days later they closed the trap; three hundred thirty thousand Germans were surrounded. We could hardly believe it—invincible just a short time ago, Hitler was now actually losing the war. We assumed he would order Paulus to break out and rejoin the main German forces, saving his army, as the British had at Dunkirk. But no; the maniac's dark soul was so consumed with hatred, with his contempt and loathing of his own generals, that he ordered Paulus to make a stand and fight on in surrounded Stalingrad.

Then he made a second big mistake; he ordered Field Marshal Erich von Manstein and his army to abandon their drive on the Caucasus and try to rescue Paulus and his men. This put an end to any chance the Germans had of capturing the Baku oil fields. The Russians held off von Manstein, and that sealed the fate of the German Second Army.

All this was balm to our broken hearts, and it gave us a wonderful feeling of satisfaction to know that the greatest murderer in history would soon have to pay the price and meet the terrible fate awaiting him. But as far as our own lives were concerned, the great war news was coming too late. Our parents and most of the people we loved were dead. We were living and working in a ghost town, and Ebner and the rest would never let us come through alive to bear witness against them. And even if by some miracle we did survive, what would it mean, to go on living in this cruel, heartless world? I turned these thoughts over and over in my mind during those terrible days.

In retrospect, I can see now that what kept me alive more than anything else was my intense, almost fanatic desire to live to see Hitler destroyed. As if by osmosis I could feel how he was squirming in agony, with the agony growing worse at every defeat. I wanted him to suffer, to pay for all the evil things he had done. Now the bastard was like a rat in a trap, lying to his countrymen, deceiving them, but knowing deep down that all was lost, and there was no way out for him. I used to lie awake imagining how this devil incarnate must be feeling, having reached the pinnacle of power, having basked in the subservient adulation of his fellow Germans, having all Europe prostrate at his feet, and now the nightmares he must be suffering night after night, in terror of the retribution that awaited him.

By the end of November our work of collecting the contents of the empty houses that had belonged to Jews was coming to an end, and at the same time the population of the Jatkowa camp increased. Julek got permission from the Gestapo for other Jews in hiding to join our group. Soon the number of Jews in the camp had grown to one hundred. We carried out a variety of assignments, and in effect served as a central pool of free labor for the Gestapo and the local police to draw upon at will.

Fred had a bad scare when Ebner summoned him one day to the Gestapo building. Usually such a summons meant death, so we were all extremely apprehensive. When Fred arrived, he was directed to Ebner's office, where he found him sitting at his desk. Standing on one side of him was a Ukrainian policeman and on the other was Brenner, a Jewish lawyer from Lublin.

Brenner lived among the Poles as a *Volksdeutsche* (a German who had lived in Poland since before 1939), and Fred knew this. Ebner pointed to Brenner, and in his sharp, cutting voice asked Fred, *"Ist er Jude?"* (Is he a Jew?) Of course Fred knew that Brenner was, but to say so would have meant his death, so he tried to pretend he didn't know him. Then Ebner gestured to Fred to inspect Brenner's penis. *"Ist er Jude?"* Ebner screamed again. Fred knew that to irritate Ebner when he was in such a mood was to risk his own life as well. He became so confused and frightened that instead of Brenner he went over to the Ukrainian and said to him, "Drop your pants." The Ukrainian and Ebner burst out laughing. Realizing his mistake, Fred then turned to Brenner, who obligingly took out his penis. Fred tried to fudge, saying, "Well, it looks as if it might have been circumcised, but there are cases in which there is some question . . ."

This was too much for Ebner. *"Raus!"* (Get out!) he yelled at Fred. Now in complete panic, Fred took the wrong turn out the door and ran into the prison yard. He heard Brenner's screams, and ran back through the building and out into the street. He returned to Jatkowa completely unnerved.

Many of the Jews in Jatkowa were the only survivors in their entire families. They were very lonely, and naturally befriended others in the same situation. A few marriages were arranged, but most of these couples simply lived together. Before the war most Jewish girls in Hrubieszów were virgins when they married. That had now changed; we all knew we were living on borrowed time, and the girls were eager to make love so that when the time came to die, they would at least have experienced one of life's most talked-about pleasures.

I had always been very shy. Only twice before had I had the opportunity to make love to a girl: the first time was some months before the war, when a Polish maid let me know she wouldn't be averse to a visit from me to her bedroom behind our kitchen. I was tempted, but my room was right next to my parents' bedroom, and I was afraid of being caught. The second time was with Itka Kaufman in Włodzimierz during the Russian occupation. Now, at Jatkowa, I discovered that there were two girls interested in me. One of them was Sarah Shechter, a pretty girl of about seventeen (I was nineteen), with brown eyes, brown hair, pale skin, and a slim body. The problem was that in Jatkowa we worked all day, and at night we were not allowed to leave our quarters, where we slept two or three to a room.

But one day Sarah and I were assigned to a group loading hay for the German army. We were given twenty minutes for lunch, so we lay down on a small haystack, out of sight of the soldier who was supervising us and who had sat down to have lunch himself. Sarah and I kissed and then I lay on top of her and embraced her. The proximity of the German made us even more nervous than we would have been in any case, but we both wanted badly to make love even and were willing to take the risk. Even so, my lack of experience and Sarah's virginity made matters difficult. I was struggling with the problem when we heard someone coming. We hastily readjusted our

clothes and sat up, pretending to be talking, when a Ukrainian policeman appeared. He stared at us suspiciously and said, "Go back
to work."

I was very embarrassed and couldn't look Sarah in the eye as I offered a few clumsy excuses. She was nice about it, though. She took
my hand and whispered, "You're very sweet." That made me feel
a little better, and I swore to myself that next time I would manage
things more efficiently.

One morning the Gestapo dealt the Jatkowa camp a new blow. First
they summoned Julek and Rabinowitz to the Gestapo building.
Then, during our morning roll call, they selected about half of the
Jatkowa Jews and had the Polish and Ukrainian police load them
onto a truck, telling the rest of us to return to our quarters. When
the truck pulled out we were left in a state of shock and feared the
worst. Later in the day Fred was piling wood in the yard when a
young boy, Shepsel, came and told him that Demant was in the
camp asking for him. Fred was very frightened; any summons from
Demant was bad news. He went out into the street, where Demant
was waiting. "What are you doing, Doctor?" he asked. Fred told
him that he had been ordered to stack the wood. Demant shook his
head. "You don't work any more; you are taking over for Brandt."

Fred knew immediately what that meant: Julek, Rabinowitz, and
the others had been killed. Later we found out that they had been
driven to the Jewish cemetery and shot. Ebner had personally shot
Julek. A rumor spread that Julek had kept up his contacts with the
German civilians who had been involved in running the ghetto before the action, and the Gestapo didn't like it. After Julek was killed,
Wagner recommended that Fred be made the new head of the camp.
He was told to move into the house where Julek had lived. Each
morning he was to receive orders from the Gestapo for the day and

then assign the various jobs. He was also responsible for the distribution of food and for other administrative details. Fred had, of course, no choice but to accept this new post; to refuse would have meant instant execution. But by accepting it he placed himself and his family in greater danger; one false step, the slightest mistake, and all of us—perhaps even the entire camp—would be liquidated.

We lived in constant terror of Ebner, who was a real lunatic. He used to go to the Jewish cemetery at night and stand for hours on top of the pits containing the bodies of hundreds of the people he had killed. The very sight of him made us freeze with fear. Then suddenly, one day in the middle of December, we learned to our astonishment that Ebner had been killed. He had been shot by Baran, a Polish partisan, who had been hiding in his mother's house when someone tipped off the Gestapo. Having killed thousands of people with impunity, Ebner must have believed himself invulnerable. He went out to the house alone, accompanied only by his driver, to get Baran. Ebner entered the house while Baran was asleep in the loft and shot his mother dead. When Baran heard the shot, he looked down from his hiding place, saw what had happened, and shot Ebner with a rifle, mortally wounding him. Ebner staggered out of the house and died before he could reach his car. It wasn't until much later, after a long manhunt, that the Gestapo found Baran and killed him.

Ebner's death was a momentous event for us at Jatkowa. This cold-blooded murderer of thousands of men, women, and children had been a constant evil presence in our minds, and when we learned that he was dead, it felt as if the devil himself had died. We were exuberant, but at the same time fearful that the Gestapo would take their revenge on us. Apparently, though, at least some of them were almost as relieved as we were; Ebner had intimidated even his henchmen in the Gestapo.

Toward the end of the year, I was assigned to work with a group at the train station loading sugar beets into railway cars. It was very cold, usually below zero degrees Fahrenheit, and the work was very hard. Supervising us was a tough German army sergeant who wouldn't let us rest for even a few minutes. But I was in good physical shape and had no trouble doing the job. After work I used to stop in at Fred's office. He always kept a supply of liquor on hand for the Gestapo, so I'd have a drink of strong Polish vodka just to get warm. Fred knew I didn't really like alcohol, and he used to make a joke of my "drinking." "Here comes the big boozer," he'd say when he saw me returning from work.

The severe winter weather forced some of the Jews who were hiding out in the woods near Hrubieszów to come to Jatkowa seeking shelter and food. In some cases Fred managed, by bribing Wagner with liquor or other scarce luxuries, to persuade him to let them join the camp and become "legal," but he could not do it for old people or small children, who were not able to work. Sometimes people who had become "legal" themselves built skrytkas for their parents or small children in the cellars or attics of the houses they were quartered in, or in empty Jewish houses nearby.

Wagner was a frequent visitor to the camp. He was a tall, well-built man, an Austrian from Linz, perhaps six feet two inches, ramrod-straight. He had blue eyes, small, curved lips, and very pink cheeks—the picture of innocence and serenity. He once confided to Fred that he had been nervous and uneasy when he was ordered to shoot a Jew for the first time. He must have got used to it, because by the time we knew him in Jatkowa it didn't bother him even to kill children. It was hard to believe that this cherubic-looking man could be a cold-blooded killer of babies. He needed Fred because his medical problems persisted, and he considered Fred to be the best doctor around.

One day he was standing in the street with Fred when he spotted a young girl who seemed nervous. He ordered her to show him what she was carrying under her arm. It turned out to be some Polish *kiełbasa* (sausage), which was not part of our permitted rations. He took out his revolver and was about to shoot her. Fred, begging him not to do it, got Wagner and the girl to come to his office, and after more pleading Wagner relented and let the girl go. (She survived the war.)

But most of the time, particularly when it came to old people and children, even Fred's influence was not enough. One day I came back from work to find him completely shaken. During the day, while most of us were out working, a Polish woman had gone to the Gestapo and told them that she had heard the sound of crying babies coming from one of the empty Jewish houses. Wagner went to investigate and found a skrytka with nine small children in it, together with five old women—some of them the children's grandmothers. He took them all outside and serenely, with a half smile, shot them one by one in the head. One little girl tried to escape, but Wagner ran after her and shot her down too. Fred stood nearby, in helpless despair, knowing that throwing himself at Wagner to try to stop him would only have resulted in the annihilation of the camp.

Another time Wagner caught a pregnant girl from the camp carrying some "illegal" food and shot her on the spot. Apparently he was worried that the girl's boyfriend might seek revenge, because the next day he decided to kill the boyfriend as well, and came to Jatkowa looking for him. When the boy saw Wagner coming toward him, he tried to run to Fred's office, hoping Fred might save him. But he didn't make it; Wagner shot him on the run. He fell in the snow, where he bled to death, the red blood in sharp contrast against the stark white snow.

Alex, the Yiddish-speaking member of the Gestapo, didn't like Fred, especially Fred's occasional success in talking Wagner out of killing people. He had to be careful, though, because Wagner was higher ranking than he. One evening Alex came to the camp drunk, with a few phonograph records in one hand and a flashlight in the other. He ordered Fred out of his office. Fred thought Alex was going to kill him, but then Alex seemed to change his mind, threw down the records angrily, and walked away.

One day Wagner told Fred to go to see his Polish girlfriend, who was ill. Wagner went with him. We weren't supposed to leave the camp, but Fred assumed that on Wagner's orders it would be safe for him to go. While they were there, a messenger came running from Jatkowa and told Fred that Alex was at the camp, shouting and cursing because he couldn't find him. Fred told Wagner, "I'm afraid this time he's going to kill me. Please come with me." They walked back to Jatkowa together, and Wagner told Fred to open the door to his office. He took out his gun and stood to one side. "Don't be afraid," he said. "I'm right behind you." Fred was afraid Alex might shoot him before realizing Wagner was there too, and opened the door wide. Before he saw Wagner, Alex, waving an automatic pistol, yelled at Fred, "What were you doing outside the camp?" Fred started to explain that he had gone there on Wagner's orders, to which Alex responded with a disparaging remark about Wagner. Wagner, gun in hand, stepped into the doorway and said, "What was that you said about me, Scharführer?" Alex stood there dumbfounded, and Wagner coldly told him to get out.

Extraordinary events were a daily occurrence at Jatkowa. One day Fred witnessed an incident that as a doctor he found almost incredible. An old woman who had apparently gone mad in her skrytka ran out into the middle of the street and started screaming incoherently. She was completely disheveled, in rags. Wagner came and shot her in the head at point-blank range. The old woman continued to stand there and scream. Wagner shot her twice more, his gun only inches from her head. Still she was on her feet, shouting and cursing him. Wagner ran out of bullets, and in disbelief reloaded his gun and shot her once more. This time the woman collapsed and died. Fred told us later that he would have never believed that anyone with three bullets in the head could remain upright for so long.

Not all Gestapo men were as bad as Ebner, Alex, Demant, and Wagner. A new man came to join the Gestapo in Hrubieszów and got to know Fred, in whom he confided a bit. He told Fred that he had been drafted into the Gestapo against his will, and was unhappy about what Hitler was doing to the Jews. One day he was ordered to shoot a Jew who had been caught hiding. He killed the man, then came to Fred's office, white-faced and shaking, looking to get drunk. Shooting an innocent man made him sick to his stomach, he told Fred, but what could he do? If he disobeyed the order, he himself would be put to death.

Around this time, too, a new chief of Gestapo, Waldner, came to take over. He was a tall, erect man, who, we saw immediately, was not a bloodthirsty killer like most of the others. Under his command even the mass murderers such as Demant, Alex, and Wagner were no longer permitted to kill any member of the Jatkowa camp without a reason—which didn't, of course, stop Wagner and the rest from killing any Jews they found in hiding. Still, the new chief, although strict, seemed to want to be as just as he could, given the lawless hell in which we were living.

One of the men at Jatkowa was able to establish contact with Polish partisans, which, considering that he was a Jew, was unusual. A Pole in Hrubieszów tipped off the Gestapo, and Wagner came to Jatkowa to shoot the man. He was in a room talking to Hy Silberstein and my sister Hanka. Suddenly Wagner walked in, pointed his gun at the man, and said, "Come with me." While Wagner's attention was concentrated on the man, Hanka slowly opened the window. It took great courage for her to do that. Knowing he had nothing to lose, the man threw himself through it, fell to the ground, got to his feet, and started running toward the nearby Huczwa River. Surprised, Wagner ran after him, gun in hand, but it was too late; the Jew had escaped. Unfortunately, a few weeks later he and the Polish partisans whom he had joined in the forest were surrounded by the Germans and killed.

Unexpectedly, sometime in February, during the morning roll call, the Gestapo took forty people out of the lineup and loaded them onto a truck. Given our previous experiences, we were certain that they were going to be shot. Later we learned that they were taken instead to Majdanek, a concentration camp near Lublin. This was the first time since the liquidation action in Hrubieszów that any group of Jews was taken away and not killed.

In those times, even many of the truly religious people found it difficult to go on believing in God. Having witnessed the murder of their children, their parents, their brothers and sisters, they asked, "If there is a God, how could He have let this happen?" There were some, however, who continued to believe, their faith unshaken; they died chanting "Shma Israel, Adonoi Alohejnu, Adonoi Echad" (Hear, O Israel, the Lord is our God, the Lord is One). One man in the Jatkowa camp, Velvele, continued to pray every day, with prayer shawl and all. One day, when we were working together on the new Gestapo building, I asked him, "Velvele, they killed your wife, your children—how come you're still praying?" Velvele thought for a moment, then shrugged and said, "Tomer" (In case). Should God turn out to exist after all, Velvele wanted to make sure He was on his side. But most of the young people in that time of death and despair did not think of turning to God.*

Life in Jatkowa began to become almost routine. We were living in limbo, our moods swinging between hope and despair, depending on the events of each day.

A new young man from the Gestapo arrived in Hrubieszów. He was a simpleton, with a horse-like laugh, but at least he never harmed anyone; he was the only member of the Gestapo no one was afraid of. He was supervising our crew that was working on the new Gestapo building, and he didn't think I was a very good worker. One day he observed me for a while, then came over and said, "Orenstein, you aren't even worth the salt you eat." Pleased with his wit, he snorted with laughter. I remember thinking, "So this is a member of the Master Race." That whole concept of a Master Race was puzzling to me. I never could understand how Hitler, who himself was at best an average-looking man with dark hair, had come to promote the idea of the racial superiority of blond Nordics.

---

*I was not particularly religious before the war, still less so during the Holocaust. But many years later I came to believe in God. Nevertheless, although my Jewish identity is very strong, I still don't go to a synagogue or observe the religious holidays. However, I believe that the Creator of this Universe—so perfect in its complexity and harmony, compared with which even the greatest achievements of man seem child's play—could not be fundamentally cruel. The answer then must be that whatever happens to us on earth, however harsh our individual fate, our existence here is part of a great mystery, which we, in this lifetime at least, shall never understand. Since logic is useless here, we must take it on faith that God, who had the power to create the universe and its awe-inspiring phenomena, is also wise and just. The perfection of His Great Design is inconsistent with cruelty and murder. The answer is only to be found in the mystery that lies beyond our reach and which we shall never understand in our lifetime. All we can do is try to follow what we believe to be His will, and that is to be just to one another, and try to help our fellow man.

After the Gestapo building was finished, the chief, very pleased with our work, ordered extra food for all the people at Jatkowa. He intended to feed us all in the new building but apparently changed his mind. Perhaps he thought that the other Gestapo members would not approve of such generosity to Jews, so instead he had the food sent over to Jatkowa.

I never again had a chance to pursue my friendship with Sarah, but a second opportunity unexpectedly presented itself. There was another girl, Henia, who seemed to like me too, and one day when I didn't go to work I found out that she had also stayed in the camp for the day. She came over to the room I shared with my brothers, where for once I was alone. We started kissing, and soon lay down together on the bed. We were taking a great risk—Wagner and others of the Gestapo made frequent unannounced visits to Jatkowa—but the urge was very strong, and we started to make love. Henia was an extremely passionate girl, with beautiful deep blue eyes. We were both very excited, and this time I had no difficulty. Afterward I noticed there was blood on the bedspread. I said, "Henia, was this the first time for you too?" "Yes," she said, "and I am glad we did it." She was a sweet girl from a very good home, and I'm sure that before the war she would never have dreamed of sleeping with a man before marriage. I took the bloody bedspread off the bed and buried it deep in the bottom of the garbage can. When my brothers came back from work they were mystified—why would anyone bother to steal an old bedspread?

Henia and I made love twice more. Once we almost got caught. We were in my room in the midst of lovemaking when we heard voices. We got up quickly and looked out the window, where we saw Wagner standing right next to our house talking to David Rotenberg, Fred's assistant. I often wondered what would have happened if Wagner had surprised us. Had I not been Fred's brother, he certainly would have killed us. But even Fred's influence might not have saved us, given the seriousness of the "offense."

The news from the fighting fronts was getting better and better. On February 2 the entire German army under General Paulus surrendered to the Russians in Stalingrad. Hitler had been desperate. Rather than let the world see a German army surrender, Hitler had preferred that all his soldiers be killed, and he ordered them to fight to the last man. At the very end he made Paulus a marshal of the German Reich, supposedly because no German marshal had ever surrendered. Paulus and his men fought bravely, but chose at last not to follow the Führer's orders, and surrendered. Beside himself with rage, Hitler declared Paulus a traitor.

The Russians were also victorious on other fronts, pushing the Germans farther to the west of Moscow and breaking at last the siege of Leningrad. The Russian people—both citizens and soldiers—who defended Leningrad wrote a new chapter in the history of endurance and heroism. They had been surrounded by the Germans for a year and a half. At first they received some meager supplies across the ice of Lake Ladoga, but soon nothing at all came through. Hundreds of thousands died of starvation; toward the end cannibalism was rampant, but they did not surrender.

In the south, the Russians took Rostov in March, and were approaching Kharkov.

In Tunisia, the ring around hundreds of thousands of Germans and Italians was drawing tighter. The Allies controlled the air and the sea; no supplies were coming through. Even in the Pacific, the tide of war was now running in favor of the Allies. There were bitter air and sea battles, in which the Japanese proved themselves formidable fighters, eager to die for the Emperor. But they couldn't cope with the flood of American war matériel. After the massive early defeats, the Americans were learning how to fight the tough Japanese, and here too, in the Pacific theater, were gaining the upper hand.

At all this glorious news, our hearts sang with joy. But none of it improved our chances for survival; we knew that when the Russian front came nearer, the Germans would probably kill us all. We felt great bitterness, knowing that the whole world had witnessed the greatest massacre of innocents in history and done nothing to prevent it; but at least our murderers would be brought to account.

Winter came to an end, and spring arrived, in its full glory. I remember looking at the blooming trees and flowers and thinking how incongruous is the beauty of nature against the ugliness of man.

In the middle of May the Gestapo initiated a new and disturbing procedure. Every day after work they took us to a place where the river Huczwa widened almost into a lake. On its right bank was a large, open field surrounded by low hills. We were ordered to go into the water in our underwear, to swim and bathe. The first time we were certain it was a trap, so that they could shoot us while we were undressed and all gathered together. It was a perfect spot; all they had to do was set up a couple of machine guns on the hills, and there we were, caught between the guns and the water. It was a huge relief when the guards ordered us to get dressed and marched us back to the camp.

These "bathing" expeditions went on uneventfully for several weeks. Apparently the Gestapo were rehearsing in expectation of an order to kill us. They were afraid that this time, unlike during the first Hrubieszów action, we might resist, and they wanted us in a position where we could be mowed down with no trouble.

On May 13 the Axis armies, trapped in Tunisia, surrendered, the Allies taking a quarter of a million prisoners. Africa was free of the Nazi scourge. The big question now was when the Allies would open a second front in Europe. Suddenly it began to seem as though the Germans might collapse at any time. It was obvious that they no longer had any chance of winning the war. Hitler boasted about *Festung Europa* (Fortress Europe), but everyone knew this was mere bravado; he had lost his gamble and now was prepared to bring the whole German nation down with him if only he could delay, however briefly, the inevitable moment of defeat. And as all this was happening, our frustration could only mount. So near to rescue, and yet so far. Whatever happened, we felt that Hitler and his henchmen would kill us before their own end.

June arrived; days and even hours dragged maddeningly slowly. We were running out of work, and the Gestapo could find little for us to do. We knew our lives were in grave danger; any change in the routine was now ominous. So when they began marching us each morning to the yard of the new Gestapo building on Długa Street for the roll call, we felt they were setting us up; why had they changed the roll call from Jatkowa to the Gestapo yard?

On July 3, we got our answer. After the roll call, Waldner addressed us. Half of us were to be shipped to a labor camp called Budzyń, not far from Lublin. We shouldn't worry, he told us; conditions there were good, and there was plenty of work. Then he selected the people who were going to be sent to Budzyń; our family was among those who were to remain.

Those who had been selected to go were loaded onto trucks. We were all convinced that they were going to be shot, but we were told they would be taken to the train station, and from there sent to Budzyń. Those of us who remained went back to Jatkowa in a state of utter confusion, unable to guess who was better off.

A few days later a message came from the Budzyń group. They had indeed arrived at a labor camp, but conditions there were very bad. Still, we rejoiced at this news; against all expectations, they were at least alive.

Early in the morning of July 10, the fifty or so of us who were left in the camp were on the way to the Gestapo yard for the roll call when my former teacher, who was our source of information, walked past us. When the guard wasn't looking, he whispered, "They've landed in Sicily." The Allied forces were back in Western Europe! But now even this great news had little impact on us; our fate would be decided in a matter of days, even hours. And in fact, after we arrived in the Gestapo yard and the roll call had been taken, the chief announced that the rest of us were to be sent to Budzyń as well. We were to leave directly from there, without returning to the camp. This time we thought he might be telling the truth, but we still didn't fully trust him. Why hadn't they sent us with the others, a week ago? Maybe the first group were the lucky ones; maybe we were the ones who were going to be shot.

My brothers and I had hidden a small package of ten or fifteen gold coins and about a hundred dollars in paper money in the cellar of a house on Jatkowa Street. We had buried it in the wall, about four feet above the ground and six inches deep. We needed badly to retrieve it; without money we knew we could scarcely survive in the new camp. Fred took a big chance. He went to Waldner and asked for permission to go to a bakery shop next to Jatkowa to buy some bread for the trip. The chief nodded, and ordered two members of the Gestapo to escort him. I remember thinking that at least we'd had a bit of luck in that it was he who was the Gestapo chief on this critical day.

After buying the bread, Fred asked his escort for permission to go to the house and get some clothes for the trip. Once in the house, he asked if he could go to the cellar for just a minute to get a jar of marmalade. That too was permitted. Fred went down into the cellar, which was really only a cave under the floor, and started digging in the wall with his hands, but he couldn't find the package. The guard was yelling at him to hurry up. Fred was almost a foot into the wall, but the gold wasn't there. That money might mean the difference between life and death to us; Fred got so anxious that he dropped the marmalade. He bent over in the dark to pick it up, and suddenly felt the package with the gold. It must have slipped out from the hole in the wall while he was digging.

Before his return to the Gestapo yard Fred managed to dig a hole in a loaf of bread and hide the package in it. When he was sure no one was looking, he gave it to me. Wagner had grown suspicious at the length of time Fred had taken to buy the bread. He came over to him and asked, "Did you bring anything else with you?" Fred looked him straight in the eye and said, "Herr Obersturmbahnführer, if you don't believe me, search me." Wagner looked back at him, hesitated, and then walked away.

A wagon with seven or eight small Jewish children, whom the Gestapo had found in Jatkowa after we had left for the roll call that morning, was now brought into the yard. "Do these children belong to anyone here?" the chief asked. A couple in our group were the parents of two of the children. It was a tragic moment. They knew that if they admitted to having hidden the children from the Germans while they were living at the camp, they would be killed— and that nothing could save the children anyway. There was silence. No one claimed the children. Waldner ordered them taken away.

We were loaded onto a waiting truck. "Don't worry," the chief repeated, "you're going to Budzyń." Still, we were very frightened; with the Germans, you never knew. To our immense relief, we saw that the truck actually was heading toward the railway station. At least they were not going to shoot us in Hrubieszów. There were about fifty of us on the truck, with the nice Gestapo man, the one who was opposed to Hitler, in charge. Fred, worried that in Budzyń the SS would search us and find the gold, took a calculated risk and told him about the gold hidden in the bread. He begged him to hold on to it and give it back to us after the search. The German was sympathetic, but refused to take the chance.

At the station we were loaded into a cattle car with bars on the window. The trip took about eight hours. It was hot and uncomfortable, but most of us were young and in good physical condition, and withstood it well.

Late in the day the train pulled into a station near Budzyń. We were taken out of the car and immediately surrounded by two SS men and a number of Ukrainian guards with dogs. They ordered us to form a column and start marching.

Budzyń

■

T hey marched us toward what was obviously a prison camp; in the distance we could see guard towers and rows of barbed wire. This looked like a labor camp, not an extermination camp; so far the Gestapo chief had told us the truth. SS guards in green uniforms and Ukrainians in black uniforms were standing at the entrance gate. Over the gate was a semicircular sign reading *Arbeit Macht Frei* (Work Makes You Free).

In the yard we could see prisoners in civilian clothes. As we lined up at the gate, we came near enough to see their faces. A cold fear seized my heart. I had never seen human beings looking like that. Many of them were emaciated, with hollow eyes; their hands were covered with scabs. They didn't walk; they shuffled. They had a look of degradation, stupor, and despair.

The fear I had known before, during the hunt, was a different kind of fear from this. Then it had been the fear of getting caught and shot, of instant death. And in Jatkowa we had expected every day that they would surround and kill us; we were used to living with the fear of violence against us. This was a new kind of fear—a fear of slow death from hunger, of filth and sickness, of a life of hell on earth. "I won't last a month in this camp," I remember thinking. I had always been considered something of a "softy"; I was never one of the tough athletic types who might have a chance in such conditions.

But then I noticed that there were some prisoners who seemed to be in somewhat better shape than the others. "Maybe there's a way to buy food here," I thought. After all, we did have some money with us.

We marched through the gate in rows of five, two SS men counting us as we passed. As soon as we entered the gate we were met by several men in Polish army uniforms. They were Jews—like the other prisoners, they wore yellow patches—but they looked well fed and strong. One of them, whom the others called Szczypiacki, had a pinkish face and a big mustache. He looked us over with great interest. Compared to the Budzyń inmates, we looked good. In the Jatkowa camp food had been plentiful, and we wore decent clothing.

"You guys really had it good in Hrubieszów. We'll show you how different it is here," declared Szczypiacki sarcastically. Without warning he hit the man nearest him with a stick. "Let's do a little exercise now," he shouted. "Let's see how fast you can run. Let's go, run, run, run!"

Bewildered, we started running. "Down!" screamed Szczypiacki. Some of us followed his command and threw ourselves to the ground. Others, who had never done this sort of thing before, stopped and stood still, confused. Szczypiacki started hitting them with the stick, and soon had us all running and falling all over the camp yard.

The SS guards and the Ukrainians watched this with delight, laughing and shouting obscenities at us. The show went on for about twenty minutes. A few of the older ones couldn't continue and lay on the ground gasping for air. Some of the others who couldn't keep up were kicked and beaten. Finally a tall, handsome Jew, also in a Polish army uniform, called a halt. From Szczypiacki's demeanor we could tell that this man, Stockman, was in charge. He was about thirty, erect and calm, and seemed to be a decent person. He instructed Szczypiacki to take us to the reception barracks. As we were waiting in line to be registered, we had a chance to talk to a few of the other prisoners. They told us that the camp was run internally by a group of Jewish former Polish army prisoners of war. Some of them, such as Szczypiacki, could be genuinely brutal, but most of the time it was a show they put on for the benefit of their German masters.

One of the prisoners told us, "You guys don't know how lucky you are. Feix left Budzyń just a few days ago." "Who was Feix?" we wanted to know. "A mad killer and torturer." "And who is the commandant now?" "Axmann—he's a killer too, but nowhere near as bad as Feix—nobody could be."

In the registration office they took down our names, assigned to each of us a number, and gave us yellow patches to attach to our jackets. They searched us, but not very thoroughly; I was able to hold on to the bread that had our fortune hidden in it.

Later we learned how thoroughly they searched incoming prisoners in the "official" concentration camps, and this information turned out to be of crucial importance to us. We were very fortunate that Budzyń wasn't as yet in that category, otherwise we would have had all our money taken away from us.

After the registration, they ordered us to go to the barracks that was to be our new home. It was the last in the row of seven; only the camp latrine separated us from the barbed wire. No one had to tell us where it was; the stench was overpowering. Each barracks held about four hundred prisoners. The single women's barracks wasn't as crowded, because there were fewer than a hundred fifty women in the camp.

The barracks were of wood, and in the center of each was a small room, the "office" of the Stubenälteste (the prisoner in charge of the barracks), containing a table and chair; his bed was in there too. The rest of the barracks space was occupied by rows of three-tiered bunks. The top tier was the only one prisoners could sit on; the two lower tiers had just enough space to sleep in. We were not allowed to leave the barracks after the doors were shut for the night, so the latrine had to be used before that. In the middle of the barracks stood a large can for urinating at night.

There were many Jews from the Warsaw ghetto in our barracks. One group had arrived after a stopover at the dreaded Treblinka extermination camp. One of them, Richie Krakowski, introduced himself to me. He was very farsighted and wore glasses with thick lenses that made his eyes appear huge. Richie was of medium height and slightly stooped. One could tell immediately that the brutality of Budzyń had not affected his innate humanity, nor even his subtle sense of humor. He was very helpful, was up to date on all sorts of information, and I sensed at once that he and I would become friends.

Soon the work commandos began returning to the camp, and we were ordered to line up for the evening *Appel* (roll call). We lined up on the *Appelplatz* (the roll-call plaza) in columns, called "blocks," five deep. Each block, consisting of prisoners from one barracks, was supervised by an SS man and a couple of Ukrainians, who ran around making sure that all the prisoners were out of the barracks and the latrine. They were barking out orders to line up in precise ranks behind one another so there would be no mistake in the count.

The minute I saw the SS man in charge of our block I knew he was a sadist. I don't remember his name, but after more than forty years

I can still see his face. He was a stocky man with thin brown hair, bulging eyes, and a cruel, mad-dog expression. One of the prisoners standing two rows to my left was a tall young man with a gaunt face. The SS man came from behind and noticed that he wasn't standing exactly in line with the prisoners in front of him. He grabbed him by the shoulders, spun him around, and punched him in the face. Weakened by hunger, the young man fell to the ground with a thud. He looked up at his attacker, his eyes full of fear, afraid to get up. This seemed to enrage the German still further, and he began kicking his victim, aiming at the groin. The Jew howled with pain, trying to protect his testicles with his hands. The SS man pulled out his gun and screamed at the prisoner in a high-pitched voice, threatening to shoot him if he continued to use his hands to protect himself. Almost beside himself with pain and afraid of being shot, he took his hands away, and the SS man immediately kicked him again in the groin. On reflex, the prisoner brought his knees up, his body curled. In a frenzy the German ran around him, viciously kicking him in the back and head, continuing to kick him even after the man had stopped moving. His fury spent, the SS man walked away.

I was so mesmerized by this spectacle that I forgot all caution and kept staring at the now lifeless victim. Strangely, there was no sign of blood. Bencio Fink, who was standing next to me, whispered, "Don't look—or you'll be next." I was trembling, my fists clenched, aching to tear the beast apart limb from limb. But of course before I got anywhere near him I would be shot, and my brothers and sister would be tortured and killed. I felt utterly helpless.

Meanwhile, the SS man in charge of the roll walked from block to block carrying a pad and counting the number of prisoners. When he came to our block our SS man pointed to the prisoner lying on the ground to make sure he was counted. The numbers must have checked out, because the commandant signaled that the Appel was finished. Our *Blockälteste* ordered two other prisoners to carry the body on the ground to the camp hospital. I don't think the prisoner survived the kicking; I never saw him again.

Depressed by the incident, on the way back to the barracks some of us from Hrubieszów asked the others whether this was a common occurrence. "You think that was bad," they told us; "that was nothing compared to what went on before Feix was transferred." They said that Feix used to hang prisoners naked, head down, and beat them with bunches of barbed wire until the flesh was torn all over their bodies, while repeatedly kicking them in the head. After Feix had satisfied his sadistic urges he left, ordering the Ukrainians to stand watch and make sure no one tried to help his victims. A few begged the Ukrainians to shoot them, but the guards refused. Screams and moans were heard in the nearby barracks all through the night. Many died after a few hours; those who survived until the morning Appel were shot.

Another of Feix's amusements was to visit the hospital, where he would get the sick and weak out of bed and order them to run and dance. Those who couldn't move fast enough to suit him he would line up against the wall and shoot.

Back at the barracks after the Appel, two prisoners came in lugging between them a huge container of soup. This was our dinner. We lined up, and one of them would dip a big ladle into the can and pour its contents into our *menashka,* as we called our soup dish. Even before I got my ration I could see the soup was mostly water, but not until I tasted it did I realize why almost everyone in the camp was starving. It was nothing but salty water, with a few cabbage leaves in it and one or two little pieces of turnip. It tasted so bad I spat out the first mouthful. A *Musulman* (this was the nickname, in Yiddish, for prisoners who were in the last stages of starvation and had lost all capacity to resist and will to live) immediately came over, looked at me with sad eyes, and gestured to me to pour my soup into his empty *menashka*. Horrified, I did. After each prisoner had got his portion of soup, there was some left over. Pushing, clawing, and shoving, a line immediately formed to get seconds.

I asked one of the prisoners about the other meals. "What other meals? All you get here is a slice of bread and coffee in the morning, and once every few days a bit of margarine. If you want to eat anything during the day, you save a piece of the bread. Make sure it lasts you until supper."

Those of us from Hrubieszów had brought bread from Jatkowa, so we had some of it for supper. But it would last only for a couple of days. We had to find a way to get extra food, or we would soon become Musulmen ourselves.

My brothers and I discussed ways of exchanging our money for food. We had to be extremely careful; some of the prisoners were thieves and informers. But before long several prisoners who were "dealers" in bread and other commodities discreetly approached us; it was known that many of the survivors from the small towns had brought valuables with them. The way this worked was that every morning each Stubenälteste received one loaf of bread for every ten prisoners in his barracks, and he simply cut the bread into eleven pieces instead of ten, which gave him four extra loaves of bread. These were sold by the "dealers" for gold or other valuables. Some of the Ukrainian guards also sold food and other commodities to the prisoners.

It was a relief to know this trade existed; we realized how lucky we were to have that package of gold and money. Now we had to find a way to hide it. Thieves were especially active during the night, when the prisoners were sleeping, exhausted by beatings and hunger. We decided the safest way was to divide the money among ourselves and sew it inside our jackets and pants.

Soon they would lock the barracks door for the night, so I went to use the latrine next to it. It was a big room with two long ditches, each about four feet wide, that were filled with feces almost to the level of the floor. The prisoners had to squat down on a thin wooden plank thrown across the ditch and empty their bowels into it. But there were feces everywhere, all over the planks and the floor as well as in the ditch. Many of the prisoners couldn't control their bowels from diarrhea, and had to relieve themselves before they could reach the planks; others were just too sick to care. Beatings from the latrine supervisor had no effect.

I tried to step around the feces, but it was impossible. When I finally reached a plank I was so unnerved that my bowels clamped shut. I was about to leave when a prisoner from Warsaw who was next to me said, "Better give it another chance; you can't leave the barracks at night, and you don't want to walk around tomorrow with your pants full of shit." I tried for a few more minutes, but it was no good; I was too tense. I was afraid that one of the Musulmen nearby might lose his balance and drag me down with him into the ditch. After leaving the latrine, I rubbed my shoes in the dirt to clean them off as best I could. The visit to the latrine left me very depressed.

Before going to sleep, my brothers and I talked about our impressions of our first day in Budzyń. Things were very bad here, but we were still alive. We had some money, so at least we wouldn't starve for a while. And time was marching on. We had heard during the day that the teacher's report of the Allied landings in Sicily was true. And there was always the chance of an unexpected German collapse at the front; Hitler could be assassinated; who knew what might happen?

Many of the prisoners were being trained to work at a Heinkel factory about four kilometers from the camp. Heinkel was an airplane manufacturer, and the Budzyń plant had been set up to make wings for the planes. It looked as if this was a productive labor camp, and to that extent it was a safer place than Jatkowa, where we were living on borrowed time. Here at least our work was really needed. If we could only hang on, maybe—just maybe—we had a chance.

The barracks door was locked, the big central light put out, and I climbed up to my bunk. The remaining lights were very dim. Making sure nobody was looking, I carefully sewed two or three gold coins and a twenty-dollar bill into my jacket and pants and promptly fell asleep.

I was awakened by a sharp whistle. At first I couldn't remember where I was, then I opened my eyes and saw the bunks and prisoners. Budzyń. I put on my pants and got down from the bunk. Men were standing in a line to use two washbasins at the side of the barracks. I was near the end of the line. There was a long wait, even though many, especially the Musulmen, didn't bother to wash. Finally my turn came, and I washed my hands and face with a little piece of smelly dark soap. Then began the customary pushing and shoving to get in line for the distribution of bread and "coffee." Most prisoners wanted to be at the head of the line, fearing that there might not be enough bread for everybody. The Stubenälteste and a couple of helpers stood behind a table on which were placed about three dozen loaves of dark, presliced bread. Next to the table was a large kettle of coffee. Each prisoner was handed a slice of bread and a ladleful of the coffee. Some of the Musulmen would grab their portion of bread and devour it all at once in quick, agitated gulps, leaving themselves with nothing to eat for the rest of the day except for the evening soup. It was very depressing to be near them. For one thing, they smelled terrible, from a combination of feces, sores, and sweat. Many had a feverish look in their eyes; they seemed to see through you, without seeing you. Most were so weak they couldn't lift their feet off the ground, and walked in a shuffle. I noticed that subconsciously I was avoiding them, and that made me feel embarrassed.

At about five-thirty we started forming for the morning Appel. I made a point of getting into the center of the block in order not to attract the attention of the SS man in charge. This morning, though, he seemed in a somewhat better mood. Aside from a few random blows with his truncheon, he left us alone.

The Appel count went smoothly, and after it was finished the various work commandos started to form at the gate. I was assigned to a group that was working at a construction site, building a warehouse for the Heinkel factory.

As we marched through the gate we were counted again by two SS men. There were ten "blacks" (Ukrainian police in black uniforms) guarding us. We marched in rhythm to a black calling out, "*Eins, zwei, drei, vier* [one, two, three, four] *links, links* [left, left]. *Eins, zwei, drei, vier.*" It was funny, the way these henchmen of the SS tried so hard to emulate their masters, even in the language, which they distorted ludicrously. They were for the most part a brutal, illiterate lot who in normal times would be the dregs of society. They were happy to do the SS's dirty work for them even though the Germans were openly contemptuous of this riffraff, whom they considered, like all Slavs, as Untermenschen (subhumans). Yet we were wholly at their mercy; they could kill any one of us at any time without reason, at the slightest whim and with complete impunity. Almost all of them were big, strong, sadistic bullies who enjoyed beating and kicking us.

After we'd been marching for a while, the leader of the blacks shouted, "*Juden—singen!*" (Jews—sing!) Only a few prisoners responded, but without any coordination, not even being sure what to sing. The Ukrainian became furious and again screamed, "*Juden—*

singen!" To make his point, he started striking prisoners at random with his rifle butt. Finally one of us had the sense to call out the name of a popular Polish song, and at first thinly, with a few scattered voices, then more strongly, with many more joining in, we sang. This time it sounded much better, and the Ukrainian smiled broadly. "You see, you can sing; all you Jews need is a few good blows to the head." Some of the prisoners lagged behind the column, unable to keep pace, and the guards beat them mercilessly. Others who were in better physical shape tried to help the weak ones.

At last we arrived at the work site, and a German army engineer divided us into groups and told us what to do. Felek and Sam were with me, and so were Bencio Fink and Richie Krakowski. (Fred had been told to stay in camp and work in the hospital.) My job was to unload bags filled with cement and stack them in piles. They weighed about a hundred pounds each, but I was twenty years old and still in good physical condition, and didn't have any difficulty doing it. The German engineer was a nice fellow and didn't bother us much, but a few of the blacks "encouraged" us from time to time by hitting those they thought were moving too slowly.

Then it was lunchtime. I gave a piece of my bread to Bencio, and we sat down to eat it. Many of the prisoners had no bread left, and watched with hungry eyes those of us who were eating. After fifteen minutes or so the guards ordered us back to work. Time dragged. My back started to hurt, but soon I had finished unloading the cement. I spent the rest of the day doing odds and ends.

At the end of the day the Ukrainians ordered us to form a column, and we started marching back to the camp. This time they didn't make us sing, and I wished they had; it was easier to march to a tune. When we arrived back at the camp, they counted us again at the gate. Other work details were arriving from the other sites, and we all lined up again on the Appelplatz.

This time, when they finished counting us they were one short. They began the count again from scratch, block by block, and at the end there was still one missing. By now we had been standing in our ranks for an hour and a half. The SS men and the Ukrainians fanned out, searching the whole camp. Finally word came that they had found a prisoner dead in the hospital latrine, and they let us go.

I was tired and didn't want that terrible soup anyway, so I went to the barracks and lay down on my bunk. Fred came in and told us that he had been able to arrange a deal with a prisoner who worked in the hospital: We were to get a few loaves of bread and a piece of lard in exchange for a gold coin, the bread to be delivered over a period of several weeks. Fred had brought the first loaf with him, and we divided it into five pieces. (Hanka was in the women's barracks, but we were still in contact with her; at that time the men and the women were not totally separated.) We were worried about whether the man would actually deliver the bread after he got the gold, but we had to trust him. At any rate, we felt a little more secure now.

Before going to sleep, I went to the latrine, again without success. Not only was it filthy, but one was in constant danger of falling into the ditch full of feces. Prisoners who had lost control of their bowels rushed in, often unable to make it to the plank in time, and a stream of liquid feces would shoot out of their bowels with force, splashing the people near them. Every visit to the latrine was so upsetting that even with the help of a laxative Fred got for me from the hospital, it was almost a week before I could empty my bowels.

Soon we became used to the camp routine. Danger was every-where, but so far we had been luckier than most. Bencio Fink had no money, so each time we divided our extra bread I asked my broth-ers to cut a piece for him. We all liked Bencio and didn't have the heart to see him turn into a Musulman, although we were worried about what would happen when our money ran out. Much later,

Richie Krakowski told me that Bencio would often share with him the bread he received from us.

Richie too was liked by everyone. I never saw him lose his composure or become unpleasant or even irritable. He came from a town near Warsaw, from a very well-off and assimilated family; they wanted to be considered Poles rather than Jews. All of them spoke perfect Polish and no longer even understood Yiddish. When the Germans occupied Poland, they began moving Jews from the smaller towns into large ghettos in the cities. Richie and his family were forced to move to the Warsaw Ghetto, where they remained almost to the end, to the final uprising.

Richie's father had bought cyanide tablets for the whole family before they were taken to the Umschlagplatz, where the SS was loading Jews into cattle cars. When it became certain that the train was going to the gas chambers of Treblinka, and with his father and dozens of others lying dead from suffocation in the cattle car, Richie decided to take his cyanide pill. He found that he couldn't do it with a dry mouth, so he urinated into his cupped hand and used that to swallow the pill with. And nothing happened. Apparently some of the Warsaw Jews, desperate for money, were selling phony cyanide pills.

When the train finally arrived at Treblinka and those Jews still alive were ordered out of the cattle cars, an SS officer asked mechanics and other people with technical training to step forward. Seventy or eighty people did, Richie among them. They were loaded into another cattle car and shipped to Budzyń. All the rest, including Richie's mother and sister, were killed in the gas chambers. Treblinka was solely an extermination camp; that was the first time any Jews had arrived there and not not been killed, but had been shipped out.

After a few weeks, Felek, Sam, and I were assigned to work in the Heinkel factory. This was a stroke of luck; working in the plant would offer some protection from a selection or an evacuation.

Occasionally we were able to get hold of German or local Polish newspapers, and it was now obvious that Hitler was losing the war. Things were going badly for him on all fronts. In previous years the summer, with its warm weather and dry ground, had favored the Germans. In the summer of 1941 they had smashed the Russians, taken millions of prisoners, pushed deep into Soviet territory, and had brought the Red Army close to collapse. In the summer of 1942, even though Hitler was apparently running short of men and maté-riel, he still managed to push on to Stalingrad and into the Caucasus Mountains. But now, in 1943, the summer battles did not start until the first week in July. The Germans massed their best troops and tank units near Kursk, hoping to open a great hole in the center of the Russian front with one tremendous blow, pour thousands of tanks through the breach, and envelop the Russian armies to the north and south. But this time the Russians were prepared for them, with thousands of their own tanks ready to do battle. In fact, the greatest tank battle of World War II was fought at Kursk. German war communiqués told of tremendous tank engagements near that city. In the first few days they spoke of progress on the Kursk front, then only of "heavy battles," without mentioning any progress, and finally, about two weeks later, they started referring to the "heavy defensive battles." "Heavy defensive battles" were mentioned too as occurring at Orel and a few other places.

I had learned by then how to interpret German communiqués. "Defensive battles" was the euphemism for retreat, in this case on a wide front between Orel and Kursk. And this in the summer! What would the Russians do to them in wintertime! Meanwhile, the Al-lies were advancing rapidly in Sicily. I was delirious with happiness. Words cannot describe the feeling of triumph, of joy with which I read these scraps of newspapers that reached us sporadically. Oh, how sweet was the feeling of revenge, to know how Hitler must be suffering from these blows. I would lie awake on my bunk at night visualizing and relishing the agony that this cruel, maniacal murderer was enduring every day, every minute. Now there was no more hope for him. We were very realistic about our own situation; we knew that our lives were not worth much, that we would need a miracle to survive. So for us it was a strange mixture of feelings, exuberance and sadness, knowing that our chances of actually tasting the final fruits of victory and living in freedom were slim indeed.

Meanwhile, at the Heinkel factory, we were learning how to produce metal parts for the assembly of airplane wings. The plant was under civilian management, and a number of technicians were brought in from Heinkel's plants in Germany to teach us. My *Meister* (master), as we used to call him, was on the short side and bald, and always carried a big ruler. We were given metal parts to fabricate as a test of our skill. Our training took a couple of weeks, and whenever my humorless Meister was dissatisfied with my work, he would hit my hands with his ruler. This reminded me so much of my early school years that it was sometimes hard to keep from laughing.

One day they asked whether there were any draftsmen among us, and I decided to take a chance and volunteer. I was no draftsman, but I had always been good at geometry. I was given a drawing to do, and with a little help from a prisoner who really was a draftsman, I passed the test. I was put at a drawing board in a small room next to the workshops. Some of the work was complicated, but luckily I had a graduate engineer working next to me, and whenever I ran into difficulty he would help me out.

I was very happy with this new job; the plant was clean, we were supervised by civilians, and most of us were still in fairly good health. It was a lot better than lugging cement, and, after spending the day in a decent, orderly plant, under working conditions that were almost normal, it felt like reentering a nightmare to go back at night to that filthy camp and all its brutality.

One day in August, after we had returned to the camp and the Appel was finished, the guards selected about five hundred prisoners and lined them up in two rows three feet apart. I was one of them, scared and confused and not knowing what to expect. The Ukrainian guards positioned themselves behind us, and we were told that a prisoner would be running between the two rows and that we must slap him as he passed. Anyone who didn't slap him hard enough would be killed. There was a general hubbub and nobody could make out what was going on, except that one of our supervisors, a Jewish prisoner of war, told us money had been found on the man.

The Ukrainians brought him to the head of the line and made him run the gauntlet, the prisoners slapping his face as he passed between the two rows. Some of us, afraid of being shot, hit him pretty hard. The guards kicked and beat the prisoners who they thought weren't slapping the man hard enough. The lines were close together, and the man stumbled and fell several times. Right behind me was a Ukrainian and I wanted to make sure he didn't shoot me, so I took a big swing as the man ran past, but checked it just before my hand made contact with his face. The Ukrainian didn't notice it—at least he didn't react. Past me the line curved slightly, and I couldn't see what happened to the man. Later I heard that he had collapsed before the end of the run, and been hanged.

More and more of the prisoners were dying from malnutrition, from the beatings, and from disease. We were all covered with lice. At first this drove me crazy, but later I got used to it and, like everyone else, became an expert at finding and killing the little beasts— which didn't help much, because no matter how many you killed there were always more. Occasionally there was an *Entlausung* (delousing) when they sprayed the bunks, but that didn't help much either. The camp hospital was always overflowing; increasing numbers of us were becoming Musulmen. More and more my brothers and sister and I appreciated our great good fortune in being able to buy extra food for ourselves and a few friends.

September came, and then October, and the good news from the fighting fronts continued to arrive in a steady stream. Early in September Italy surrendered. The Russian armies were rolling westward, occupying such key cities as Kharkov, Kiev, and Smolensk. There was a smell of victory in the air. The invincible Master Race was being brought to its knees by the "subhuman" Russians, whom they had planned to exterminate on a gigantic scale.

The mood of the camp lightened somewhat; those of us who were still fairly healthy even indulged in a few pranks. We heard increasing talk of evacuation. The Russians were still hundreds of miles away, but they were pushing the Germans steadily westward, and the German army seemed unable to stop them. The big question for us of course was, what would they do with us when the Russians were approaching?

Early in November came spine-chilling reports that large Jewish labor camps not far from us were being totally liquidated, the inmates killed en masse. Our Ukrainian guards cheerfully informed us that twenty thousand Jews in the Majdanek concentration camp, less than two hours away, had been herded into a field and mowed down by machine guns. The Trawniki and Poniatowa labor camps, which made German army uniforms, had been liquidated as well, the Jewish workers either killed on the spot or shipped to the Sobibór and Treblinka gas chambers.

The mood of the camp blackened. Everyone was depressed. So our turn would come any day now. To have survived so much, and yet be killed in the end! But it came as no real surprise; we had always known it would be senseless for Hitler and his SS killers to leave any Jews alive as witnesses. Some optimists among us thought they might spare us, at least for the time being, because we were working at the Heinkel plant, but that seemed doubtful because the plant wasn't yet in full production, and the front was moving closer every day. Rumors flew wildly. Then one day late in November we heard that the extermination crew had arrived from Majdanek to "take care of us," that cattle cars were waiting on a nearby railroad track to take us to Treblinka.

The next day we were told after the Appel to go back to barracks; no one was going to work that day. So this was it. Our turn had finally come. Once again the deathwatch had begun.

I looked at my brothers, my sister, my friends, and my heart silently wept. So it had all been in vain! The running, the hiding, the suffering. We tried to face our approaching end bravely, but a terrible sadness descended on us. The old fear of dying a brutal death returned to me in full force. Some of the other prisoners were discussing the possibility of escape or a mass breakout, but we were surrounded by three rows of high-voltage barbed wire with machine guns mounted on top of the guard towers.

Herbst, a tall young fellow from Hrubieszów, took me aside during the day, swore me to secrecy, and told me that he, his younger brother, and a few others were planning to make a break for it that night. They had stolen a pair of heavy shears from the factory and were going to cut the wires near the latrine. Their chances, I knew, were just about zero. Besides, I had my brothers and sister to consider. Herbst tried to persuade me to join them, but I refused even to think of it.

When it got dark my brothers and I embraced each other farewell, in case the liquidation should start before daybreak. Just before the doors were locked for the night, we heard the clatter of machine and hand guns outside the barracks. Guards came running and blocked the door, and we heard Germans and Ukrainians shouting outside. We couldn't tell what was going on, and everyone was very frightened. But it didn't seem to be an organized liquidation of the camp; the guards were running around aimlessly, unsure themselves of what to do. Then I remembered Herbst.

The guards bolted the door, and we spent the night in sleepless anxiety. There was a lot of traffic back and forth from the urine can as everyone tried to catch the latest rumors. The Stubenälteste, himself unnerved, began hitting people with his strap and screaming, "Go back to your bunks, you Musulmen!"

When the morning whistle sounded, we went outside to see what had happened. Dead prisoners were lying outside the barracks, with a trail of bodies leading to the latrine. There were fifteen or twenty bodies in the latrine itself. It was still dark and very cold, only about 10 degrees Fahrenheit. One of the bodies was still sitting crouched, and I was surprised that it hadn't tipped over. Perhaps it had frozen there during the night. There were also three or four bodies lying near the barbed wire. It was impossible to see their faces, and I wondered whether the Herbst brothers were among them.

I went back to the barracks, where no one seemed to know for sure what had happened. We got our morning rations of bread, ersatz coffee, and marmalade, and went outside for the Appel, which took much longer than usual, more than two hours. The guards ran back and forth from the latrine, lining up the bodies to be counted along with us.

Again it was announced that no one would be leaving the camp that day, and we were warned that if anyone else tried to escape, all the prisoners from his barracks would be killed—which seemed a pointless threat, since obviously the entire camp was about to be liquidated in any case. We were then ordered to go back to the barracks, and I learned that the two Herbst brothers were indeed among the dead. I felt bad for the brave boys, but perhaps their quick death was preferable to what was awaiting us.

Tension in the camp was running very high, and the guards were walking around in groups, which was unusual. Prisoners were standing around, discussing the situation and speculating about what was happening. Some thought that this was the end, that the SS was preparing for the kill. Others saw hope in the fact that this was the second day we were confined to the camp, and yet nothing had happened so far. If the Germans intended to kill us, they reasoned, why should they wait? It was nothing to them to exterminate three thousand people—look at what they'd done at Majdanek and the other big camps.

Evening came at last, and again I couldn't sleep. I talked for a while with Richie, who was philosophical about it all, which calmed me down a little. Finally I closed my eyes and slept restlessly for a couple of hours.

In the morning they chased us outside again for the Appel. It occurred to me that perhaps their plan was to shoot us while we were conveniently lined up on the Appelplatz. I looked around for any ominous new signs, such as extra machine-gun emplacements, but everything seemed the same as always. This time the Appel didn't take long, and after it was over they told us that again no one would be going out to work that day. All prisoners were to return to barracks.

It was crazy; the third day with no work, and still they kept us alive. Speculations ran wild, and as the day wore on many of the prisoners grew more optimistic: "If they wanted to kill us, why would they wait so long?" I felt a little more optimistic myself, and so weary from anxiety and all the arguments and discussions that when night came I lay down on my bunk and fell into a heavy sleep, awakened only by the morning call. Again we got our rations and went out for the Appel. Something had to happen soon, I felt; this could not go on indefinitely.

After the Appel they told us to form work commandos. A great sigh of relief swept through the ranks of prisoners. It was going to be okay; they weren't planning to kill us just yet. A few thought it was a trick, and that they just wanted to get us outside and kill us there. But somehow I sensed that, for the moment, everything was returning to normal. The routine had been restored; the SS and the Ukrainians were acting as they had before the crisis. We were almost lighthearted as we marched out of the camp. A crazy game of "now you live, now you die" was being played with our lives, but for now it was "you live." This time the Ukrainians didn't have to force us to sing; we broke into song spontaneously, and it felt good.

In the ensuing days, information started to seep through to us about what had happened. It seemed that orders had come from Gestapo headquarters in Lublin to liquidate Budzy´n, like all the other camps in the Lublin area. But the German management of the Heinkel plant pleaded with the Gestapo to spare Budzy´n for the time being: the plant was about to start production of the airplane wings that were vital to the war effort. Their pleas had no effect, until finally the head of Heinkel aircraft reached someone at the very top of the Gestapo hierarchy in Berlin, and the Lublin Gestapo received orders from higher up countermanding their orders to kill us. The factory was too important—or perhaps someone up there owed the Heinkel people a favor. In any case, Budzy´n was the only camp in the whole area to be spared.

A key reason for Heinkel to fight so hard to save the camp, I feel sure, was the fear that if the Budzyń factory were to be shut down, the German civilians themselves would be inducted at once into the

Wehrmacht. The Russians were beating the hell out of the Germans, whose greatest fear now was being sent to fight on the Russian front, particularly in the cruel Russian winter. Hitler had lost three hundred thousand of his best troops in Stalingrad alone, and he was expecting the Allies to soon open a second front in the West. In consequence, there was a tremendous shortage of manpower. Students were being drafted, and the only civilians to escape military service were those who were directly involved in arms production. As the fortunes of war shifted, so did the patriotism of many Germans. The *Vaterland* suddenly looked a lot less important to them than saving their own skins. It was interesting to see the change in the attitude of the Germans toward Hitler himself. Those who had originally been opposed to him before the war were basically decent people, who used to make fun of him and deplored the excesses of his Nazi henchmen. But when he had reached the peak of his triumphs, when he was master of virtually the whole continent of Europe, they were convinced that this was their man of destiny. They chose not to see what was going on before their eyes, or listen to what was told them by eyewitnesses to the unprecedented slaughter of innocent men, women, and children. Now, when it was becoming obvious that Germany was going to lose the war, and the "Master Race" was not destined to rule the world after all, their old doubts about Hitler returned. Most were still afraid to criticize their Führer, but some, like the managers of the Heinkel plant who had become friendly with some of their Jewish workers, were beginning to complain about him in private.

That winter was very severe, and many of the prisoners who worked outside suffered from frostbite. This often meant death, since those who couldn't work were entirely expendable. Our indoor jobs were a blessing during the day, but they didn't save us from SS sadism within the camp. Just before the end of 1943 our barracks had another Entlausung, and this time the SS decided to have some fun. Before we took hot showers we took off our clothes in an adjoining room. Usually after the shower we went back in that room to get dressed again. That day, after our showers, with the temperature about 10 degrees Fahrenheit and snow on the ground, when we tried to get back into the room where we had left our clothes we found the door locked. There were about four hundred of us, and the guards chased us outside into the snow and ordered us to get back into the room through a single small window, which only one man at a time could climb through. We were standing in the snow naked, wet, and shivering. An incredible melee followed as most prisoners tried to get through the window at once. There was so much fighting, pulling, and shoving that it took almost a half hour before all of us were inside. The SS and the Ukrainians stood about having fun, hitting some of the naked men as they fought to get inside. I was frozen stiff.

When we got back to our barracks, my brothers and I massaged each other to get warm and drank some hot tea Fred was able to get for us from the hospital. Many of the prisoners caught pneumonia from this little exercise, and a number of them died. Luckily the four of us had no ill effects. It seemed miraculous; before the war I had frequently caught colds. But this sort of thing was not unusual in the camp; we discussed it often, and came to the conclusion that under unusual stress the human body sometimes develops unique defenses that are not normally there.

Once more life became routine. Hanka was sent out with a girls' commando. She had a good, strong voice, and became the "soloist" of the group as they marched out to work. Sometimes when I had returned from work in the evening before her, I could hear her beautiful voice rising over the rest as they approached the camp. She and Dunek Jakubowski, a curly-haired blond doctor from Warsaw, fell in love, and in spite of all the hardships she was aglow with happiness. They were not permitted to visit each other's barracks, and could meet only for a few minutes a day outside the barracks.

January 1, 1944, arrived, and the plight of the prisoners who had no source of extra food became more and more desperate; the rations were so meager that they were wasting away. Those who had no more strength to work were sent to the camp hospital, where they died almost at once. We stretched our own extra rations as far as possible, not knowing how long our few remaining gold coins would have to last.

After the advances of 1943, action on the war fronts seemed to have slowed down. The Russians and the Western Allies were preparing for their next offensives. After their triumphs in the second half of 1943, it was clear that the Russians had mastered the art of mobile warfare, and now had a clear superiority in men and matériel. We expected their winter offensive to start anytime. Although the German war communiqués kept boasting of their "victories" in sinking Allied convoys on the way to Russia, we knew that many were getting through.

Everyone was full of admiration for the Russians. With so many millions of their soldiers killed or taken prisoner and 75 percent of their industrial capacity lost, with Hitler's armies occupying most of their industrial centers, they had nevertheless managed to evacuate, reorganize, and reassemble some of their factories deep inside Russia, to learn from the enemy the art of Blitzkrieg, even improving on it, and to begin dealing body blows to the invader. At first intimidated by the legendary German war machine, they had since learned how to handle modern weapons more efficiently, and with ever-increasing confidence discovered that they were more than a match for the Germans. And the mass murder of hundreds of thousands of Russian prisoners of war, the inhuman treatment of the populations in the conquered territories, and the daily spectacle of hangings and shooting transformed the stolid average Russian into a ferocious fighter, a defender to the death of his motherland. It was a great joy to us to hear that these "subhumans" were beating the hell out of Hitler's elite divisions.

The Allies seemed to be making slow progress in Italy, but they were expected to open the second front sometime in the spring of 1944. Every night I tried to guess where that second front would come. I didn't think it would be in the Mediterranean; the supply lines from the main Allied base in England would be too long. Northern Europe seemed the likeliest place.

The Germans repeatedly used the expression "Festung [Bastion] Europa". I loved it—here was clear proof of how the whole German mentality had changed. Before, they had been the conquerors, their armies driving across Europe, capturing city after city, country after country. Now, like a pack of cornered rats, they were desperately trying to hold back the Allied and Russian armies. There was despair in the souls of the Germans because they well knew what crimes they had committed. Now they were trembling in anticipation of the coming punishment.

Still, all our excitement and pleasure at the great news from the fighting fronts was overshadowed by the knowledge that our own outlook was very bleak. For the moment we were relatively safe, working on the start-up of a new and essential plant. But what would happen to us with the launching of a new Russian offensive, when the Germans were forced to retreat from Poland? Victory for our liberators could mean our death warrant. Lying on my bunk at night I examined the possibilities. They might evacuate the plant, and us with it. But it was not yet in full production, and evacuation would be more trouble than it was worth. In that case, they would probably kill us, as they had the Jews in the other nearby camps.

Or they might ship us to camps farther west. But why bother? They didn't really need us. Liquidation seemed the only sensible solution, from their point of view. Rationally, we had very little hope. But the will to live was strong, and I felt, against all the odds, that we had a chance to survive. Now, with the good news from all the fighting fronts, the desire to witness Hitler's end, to taste victory, to have a good life, good food, freedom, was so strong that the thought of being killed was hard to bear.

One day in January, just after returning from work, I was outside the barracks when I heard the following announcement: "All Jewish scientists, engineers, inventors, chemists, and mathematicians must register immediately." It was repeated several times, and had an immediate and tremendous impact on me. I sensed that it could be of the greatest importance to us, perhaps decisive for our survival. But what would it mean? Why would they want such highly trained specialists? Had they decided in fact to liquidate the camp and evacuate only certain technicians whom they might need later? This was not the customary list of "intelligentsia" they had used to select educated Jews for "special treatment" in the ghetto. And if they did intend to evacuate only those on this list, was there any way we could become part of such a specialized group? Not one of us belonged to any of those professions. Fred was a doctor, Sam an attorney, Felek had studied medicine for a couple of years, I hadn't even finished high school, and Hanka had been only thirteen when the war started.

My mind was in turmoil. Perhaps the reason they had repeated the announcement so many times was that everyone else was to be immediately liquidated. If so, being in that group could save our lives. On the other hand, what would they do to us when they discovered our deception? I didn't know where any of my brothers were at the moment, and I was afraid we might miss getting on the list. I was torn between the advantages and disadvantages of registering. Finally I decided that being in this group couldn't represent any immediate danger. The Germans were losing the war, so why not gamble on living now, and worry later about the consequences of having lied? When in danger, I always felt that almost any action was preferable to inaction.

I went into the barracks where the *Lagerälteste* (the prisoner in charge of camp administration) had his office, and with fear in my heart registered all five of us: Fred, Felek, and Hanka as chemists, and Sam and me as mathematicians. Then I thought of Bencio Fink, and added him to the list as well. If questioned, I was prepared with the names of certain Polish universities where we supposedly had been educated. Since Hanka would only be eighteen in February and I was only twenty, I was going to tell them that we hadn't yet graduated, but were still students. Fortunately, all the clerk wanted then was our names, prisoner numbers, and professions.

Afterward I had qualms about what I had done, being all too conscious of the enormity of the risk I had taken with the lives of my brothers, my sister, and Bencio. Had I the right to do this? Ought I to have waited until I had at least talked it over with them? But was there time to do that? I knew that I had acted too quickly, on impulse, but my intuition had told me it was now or never.

I was wandering around in a daze when I finally found my brothers and told them what I had done. They were terribly upset, as I had feared. What right did I have to register them without their permission? And Hanka—not even eighteen! I tried to explain that this might be our only chance, but it did no good. Their anger was all the greater since it was now too late to do anything about it; had they tried to get off the list, I would almost certainly have been killed for lying. Bencio was more philosophical about it and tried to defend me. In any case, the die was cast. Over the next few days we found out that while a number of legitimate engineers and a couple of mathematicians had registered, about forty or so others had also registered without being qualified.

In the following days and weeks, nothing further happened about the registration. My intuition that the camp was to be liquidated immediately had been wrong, and that registration now loomed as a potential time bomb. Had the Germans questioned any of us in detail, we all would have been in mortal danger. But surely the Germans were too methodical to take the trouble to register such specialized professionals without some definite purpose; I could only hope that I had not doomed us prematurely.

At the end of January we were told that we were to be moved to a new camp near the Heinkel plant. This didn't seem to be an SS trick; we knew that the Germans were building a new camp, with guard towers. We had seen the site. The German civilians in the Heinkel plant knew about it too. This new camp was supposed to be an "official" concentration camp, like the ones in Germany. While no concentration camp could be worse than ours, there was still a great deal of anxiety among the prisoners over this new development. For one thing, we heard rumors that only the prisoners in good physical condition would be selected to go to the new camp; the weak and sick would be killed.

Someone got the idea to put on a show for the whole camp before the move. To our surprise, Stockman was able to get approval from the commandant. Hanka was one of the performers, and she and a number of other talented prisoners treated us to a show in Yiddish, featuring songs and humorous skits. The writers had the challenging task of producing material that truthfully depicted Jewish life in the ghettos and camps, yet did not offend the Germans—and somehow they pulled it off. A number of the skits were funny, and despite everything we were able to laugh and have a good time. Hanka sang a very sad song that had come out during the war and made many of us cry. She sang it beautifully, and we were very proud of her.

A few days later, there was an announcement ordering the prisoners who had registered as specialists to assemble in the Lagerälteste's barracks after the evening Appel. So the moment of truth had arrived. We all rehearsed the claims I had made about our education and experience, and even tried to memorize the answers to some elementary technical questions they might ask. After the Appel we lined up in front of the Lagerälteste's office. I was shaking with fear. What would happen when they found out we were frauds?

When my turn came and I was brought into the office, I saw two German civilians sitting behind the table. I was so nervous that I don't remember what they asked me, except that it was very easy. They were very polite and friendly, and asked little more than to confirm verbally what I had written down on the questionnaire. The whole thing took only a couple of minutes.

On my way out I felt enormously relieved, and also very puzzled. What was going on? I had just turned twenty in October. They had seen the form I filled out, a tissue of lies about my "mathematical education." How could they have believed it? My head was spinning.

Suddenly an extraordinary thought struck me. Could it be that these civilians were creating a phony commando? That somehow they themselves were covering up for us? But why, and for what purpose? Was it possible that they were part of some group that might be trying to help save a few Jews? But why would they do that? To protect themselves, perhaps; to give themselves an alibi to use after the war, as proof that they had not been Nazis. Or was it that they were organizing a commando of phony scientists to save themselves from being drafted into the army? By that time, many Germans would go to almost any lengths to avoid being sent to fight on the Russian front. This made more sense than any "humanitarian" theory. Still, to organize such a fraud would require a conspiracy on a large scale, involving a great many people, including receiving authorization from the highest echelon of the SS. Or perhaps the whole thing was legitimate after all, the people who interviewed us only low-level functionaries, and at some later time we would be interrogated by experts.

We discussed this business endlessly and futilely—everyone was completely confused. When nothing further happened, we shifted our attention elsewhere. We had plenty of more immediate things to worry about.

Early in February most of us were moved to the new camp, but hundreds of sick and very weak prisoners were left behind. (Later we heard that they were sent to the gas chambers.) The new camp was on the whole much better than the old, the most important improvement, much to our surprise, being our food rations. We hadn't expected it, but we got a larger piece of bread with a pat of margarine every day, and the soup was thicker, with a couple of pieces of potato in it. These increased rations still weren't nearly enough to sustain life, but they prolonged the lives of many, increasing their chances of survival.

The barracks and the latrine were much cleaner too, which made me happy. On the other hand, the SS distributed to each of us a pair of striped pants, a jacket, and a coat, all made of very thin material, and not nearly so warm as our old clothes had been. Sometimes, when the Appel lasted longer than usual, we would arrive at the plant half frozen, especially if the temperature was low and the wind was blowing hard. Those of us who worked inside the plant were very lucky; the ones with outside jobs suffered severely. Our new camp was only a few hundred yards from the plant, and that too was a help; its proximity gave our Ukrainian guards less opportunity to beat and kick us.

The Heinkel plant had actually begun the assembly of three airplane wings, and seemed about to go into full production. Then one morning in March after the Appel came the bombshell: prisoners on the specialist list were ordered to remain in the camp. Only a few—including Hanka—were excluded. (Hanka was just eighteen, obviously too young to be a chemist.)

So it had come. Were we going to be sent to another camp? Perhaps in Germany? Now my rash decision to register us would prove critical, but in which direction? Again, I agonized over what I had done. Apparently the new Budzyń camp was going to be too useful for the Germans to liquidate; my earlier judgment had proven wrong. But if they did take us to Germany, we might still have a better chance of surviving than we would in Budzyń, because sometime in the near future the Germans were going to have to evacuate the Budzyń camp, and its prisoners would once again be endangered.

To give my brothers their due, despite their alarm, which was at least as great as mine, they did not reproach me anymore for what I had done. In any case, we scarcely had time to do more than kiss Hanka a tearful good-bye.

If we were being sent to another concentration camp, upon arrival we would have to undress before taking a shower and would not have access again to our old clothes, in which our money was sewn. We still had two gold coins and some paper money left. We didn't have much time, so we quickly rolled up the paper money into little tubes, wrapped them in cigarette paper, and pushed them up into our rectums. Gold presented more of a problem, but we got hold of a piece of tape and I taped the coins to the bottom of my right foot.

Within minutes after this was done our new commando was ordered to assemble at the gate, where a large truck was waiting. There were about forty of us, including only one woman, Hela Fürst. Quite a few people from Warsaw were in the group, and a few German Jews. The guards ordered us to get in the truck, the doors were closed, and it drove off. A number of SS and Ukrainian guards followed in a smaller truck.

We had no idea whatsoever where we were going, but we knew it wasn't far, because the truck didn't stop at the railroad station. The only camp nearby was Majdanek, but it was supposed to be empty; it had been liquidated the previous November. Besides, why would such a specialized commando be going to Majdanek? After a couple of hours the truck stopped. The guards opened the doors and told us to get out. There was a big gate, with the familiar *Arbeit Macht Frei* sign over it. We were in the infamous Majdanek concentration camp.

Majdanek

■

The guards led us through the gates, then ordered us to stop. We were standing between rows of electrified barbed wire. An SS officer came over with a list of our names, which he read out, then waited for each prisoner to answer, "Here." When his name was called, Felek didn't respond immediately, and Fred, afraid he might be punished, answered for him. Then when Fred's own name was called, he again responded, "Here." Noticing that Fred had spoken up twice, the SS officer walked over to him and said, "Didn't you answer before?" Fred tried to explain, but the German punched him in the face before he could speak. His nose started bleeding heavily, but we were standing at attention and he was afraid even to try to stop the bleeding, so blood dripped over the whole front of his jacket. We had to stand facing straight ahead, but I looked at Fred out of the corner of my eye, and my heart was crying.

"What the devil are you Jews doing here anyway?" the officer screamed at us. "We are finished with you here." A man in the front row said, "We all belong to the chemical commando." "What commando?" The man tried to explain, but the officer waved his hand in dismissal. *"Sie sind alle verrückt."* (You're all crazy.) He barked out an order to an SS Oberscharführer, "Take them to Field Three. Make sure they go to Entlausung first."

We were led by the Oberscharführer and a few guards to the reception barracks. What were we doing in Majdanek? Why didn't the SS officer even know who we were? Evidently they hadn't expected us. I was very unhappy at having got my brothers into this mess.

Soon we arrived at the delousing room, where they ordered us to strip and place all our clothing to one side. There were relatively few of us, and I had to be very careful with the gold coins taped to the bottom of my foot. I was less worried about the paper money in my rectum, although in Budzyń I had heard that in some concentration camps they X-rayed all the prisoners on arrival.

I was at the end of the line and could see what the guards were doing with the men ahead of me. They were checking everyone's hands, armpits, and genitals, looking for hidden valuables. Sometimes they looked under their feet, or made them bend over and examined their rectums. I decided to play it safe and get rid of the gold. We were standing on two-inch wooden slats on top of a cement floor. The wood was wet, and so were my feet. There were only a few people ahead of me to be searched; I had only a few seconds left. With difficulty, using the big toe of my other foot, I managed to detach the tape holding the coins in place, just before the guard got to me. I pushed the gold down through the opening between the wooden slats. I doubt if anyone had ever been so happy to get rid of gold as I was at that moment.

After the search we went into the adjoining room, where we took hot showers. They gave each of us a new set of striped outfits with a number, a red triangle, and a yellow triangle sewn on the jacket. The red triangle meant that we were political prisoners (all Jews were considered Communists), and the yellow triangle signified that we were Jewish.

Then we were assigned to a barracks. The camp was divided into six sections, called "fields." Fields One to Five contained many barracks; the sixth field was almost empty. The fields were very large, each one as large as or larger than the entire Budzyń camp. Like Budzyń, the whole of Majdanek was surrounded by fences of electrified barbed wire, and the guards in the towers bore machine guns.

None of the other prisoners we met were Jewish, a new experience for us; in Budzyń, everyone had been Jewish. Our Stubenälteste, a Russian prisoner of war, was surprised to see us. He had thought all the Jews in the Lublin region had been killed, and couldn't understand why we had been brought to Majdanek. This Stubenälteste seemed to be quite well read. I discovered that like me he was fond of Gogol, Dostoyevski, and other nineteenth-century Russian authors, and I hoped that we would become acquainted. Perhaps he might be able to help us. Our new barracks were not very different from the one in Budzyń; the bunks were full of the usual lice and fleas. We felt lost; nothing made sense. Why were we here?

The evening Appel was called, and we lined up on the Appelplatz of Field Three. A separate Appel was held on each field; on ours, we were the only Jews, the others being mostly Poles and Russian prisoners of war. During the Appel the SS man doing the count noticed our yellow triangles. He stopped in surprise and asked the SS man in charge of our block about us. Our guard shook his head; he didn't know what we were doing there either. After the Appel we went back to our barracks and they brought the container with the evening soup. As in Budzyń, it was practically nothing but water.

The latrine was filthy too, as it had been in Budzyń. On my first visit there I had to be careful not to lose the tube with the paper money in my rectum. Crouching, I felt every bit of feces with my fingers, searching for the tube. I had to be very careful not to arouse suspicion, and yet make sure not to miss it. Finally I found it—a happy moment. That money could well mean the difference between life and death. I cleaned the tube off and put it in my pocket. Later I was able to borrow a needle and thread and sew it into my uniform.

I lay down on my bunk that night with a heavy heart. It was very cold, but I managed a few hours of fitful sleep. They got us out of our bunks at four in the morning, even earlier than in Budzyń. The morning bread ration was small, with a little marmalade and some ersatz coffee. After the Appel they kept our group on Field Three and gave us clean-up work to do. Having become used to working indoors in Budzyń, it was tough working outside all day in the sub-zero cold, with a wind that penetrated to our bones, which by now were covered with little more than the thin fabric of our striped uniforms.

Fred was sent to work in the camp hospital. Most of the beds were empty after the November massacre, but the temperature charts were still attached to the beds. Many of them showed fevers as high as a hundred and five, and Fred was sure there were a great many cases of typhus in Majdanek. With such heavy infestations of lice everywhere in the camp, it was inevitable that typhus would spread among us, which could mean death to our whole commando.

The days that followed brought little change. We were very hungry, but afraid to try to buy bread with the paper money we had left, being unable yet to trust anyone in Majdanek. The bitter cold continued, and our group suffered severely. We all regretted having registered for this chemical commando. Work in the Heinkel factory in Budzyń had been comparatively light, and even though we had been in constant danger, there was still enough spirit for an occasional joke or reminiscing about the past. Here everything was gray and hopeless.

Most of our group changed markedly in their appearance and attitude. Fred in particular became depressed over the typhus. Within a few days he began to look like a Musulman, walking around in a stupor, his head hanging low and tilted to one side. He even stopped shaving. This was particularly upsetting to my brothers and me, because Fred had always kept himself neat and clean, and had usually been optimistic. We tried hard to cheer him up, but without success.

One evening I asked the Russian Stubenälteste to tell me about the massacre of the Jews in November. He shook his head. "You don't want to know." But I persisted. He had been in Majdanek for about a year. The hunger was so bad, the beatings so severe, and shootings so continuous that the life span of a new arrival averaged only about three months. Over one hundred thousand people, most of them Jews, had died in Majdanek even before the November massacre.

Then, in the first two days of November 1943, there were signs of increased SS activity, with hundreds of new guards and dogs arriving. On November 3 there were eighteen thousand Jews in Majdanek, including a couple of thousand in two small satellite camps. Most were Polish, but there were a number of Slovakian and Dutch Jews, and a few hundred German Jews. After the morning Appel that day, instead of the usual *"Arbeit Kommandos formieren"* (Work commandos, assemble), the SS ordered the Jews to be separated from the Gentiles. The latter from Field Five were taken to Field Four, and the Jews from Fields One through Four were ordered to run to Field Five. On the way they were beaten and kicked by hundreds of the SS special commandos, who used trained dogs to attack the prisoners who weren't moving quickly enough.

Once in Field Five, the Jews were driven into a large L-shaped barracks and ordered to strip. In the middle of the barracks the SS had placed large boxes, into which they ordered the Jews to throw all their valuables. The fence between Fields Five and Six was cut to provide an opening, and the naked Jews from the L-shaped barracks were driven toward long ditches, which had been dug on Field Six. It all happened very fast. The SS ordered the first ten Jews to lie down next to each other on the bottom of the first ditch, machine-gunned them, ordered the next ten to lie down on top of the freshly killed bodies, machine-gunned them in turn, and continued this procedure until the last layer of bodies reached the top of the ditch. Then they started farther down the ditch on a new layer of ten. Women and men were shot in separate ditches. The massacre took place to the sound of dance music—waltzes, fox trots, and tangos—which was played through loudspeakers.

The shooting started at six in the morning and ended about seven that night—thirteen hours. The SS men from the *Sonderkommando* who were doing the shooting changed shifts every three or four hours. Before the action started, they had selected three hundred Jewish men and three hundred Jewish women and locked them in a barracks. After they had killed eighteen thousand people, the SS walked alongside the ditches, looking for signs of life and finishing off any who were still moving or moaning. The six hundred Jewish men and women were then brought out from the barracks and made to search the clothing and other belongings left behind for valuables. After they finished doing this, the SS killed them as well.

On November 5 the Russian prisoners of war began the job of disposing of the bodies. First they extracted the gold teeth, then piled up the bodies, poured gasoline over them, and burned them. Afterward they sifted the ashes and shards of bone through sieves, looking for stones or gold they had missed before. Finally the remains, now powder, were poured into bags and taken to a nearby SS farm, where they were used as fertilizer.

Disposing of the bodies took almost two months. A few days be-fore Christmas 1943, the SS had any depressions in the ditches filled with earth to make them level with the rest of the field; a Russian friend of the Stubenälteste was in the commando that did this work.

By this time I was used to atrocities, but this chilling account of the Majdanek massacre upset me terribly. I was scarcely able to sleep that night. A few days later, when our work commando was assigned to do clean-up work on Field Five, I couldn't keep my eyes off Field Six, on the other side of the fence. There was no sign what-soever of the mass killings that had taken place only a few months before and that haunted my mind. I couldn't escape the vision of those thousands upon thousands of naked men and women being driven and beaten by the SS, forced to lie down, riddled by machine-gun bullets, and dying to the tune of music blaring from the loud-speakers. It made me almost ill. What was the use of fighting, of struggling so hard against all odds to survive? And if by some mir-acle we succeeded, was it worth it, to go on living in such an evil world? In spite of everything, however, deep inside me there was that strong instinctive desire to live, an intense curiosity about the outcome of it all, and a yearning to see these beasts punished.

About ten days after our arrival in Majdanek, several hundred more Jews, men and a few women, arrived from Radom, a town about a hundred kilometers from Majdanek. We couldn't figure out what the Germans were up to. They'd killed tens of thousands of Jews in November, then they brought our little chemical commando from Budzyń, and here they were importing Jews from Radom for no ap-parent reason. What did it mean? While working in the aircraft plant in Budzyń, we felt the Germans had a reason for keeping us alive; they needed us for the war effort. When we left Budzyń, we had assumed they were sending us on some special assignment. So far, though, there seemed no rhyme or reason to our presence in Majdanek.

Rumors reached us that a new and successful Russian offensive had been launched, that the siege of Leningrad had lifted, and that Russian troops were victorious everywhere and were approaching the pre-1939 Polish border. There was no definite confirmation of these stories, however, not even a scrap of newspaper. Security in Majdanek was very tight, and we never left the camp. We were hungry, covered with lice, totally without contact with the outside world. I could scarcely bear even to look at Fred, he was so depressed and apathetic.

Early in April, after the morning Appel, we were told that all Jews (our group, together with the Radom Jews) were being shipped out. Once again, we tried to guess what was happening. Where were they taking us now? Had they intended to kill us, they could have done so easily in Majdanek, so probably that was not their immediate plan. Maybe they were going to make some use of the chemical commando after all. But in that case, why were they combining us with the Radom Jews? Once again, too, my brothers and I had to go through the process of inserting the tubes with our money inside our bodies; wherever they were taking us, we would have to undergo another search when we got there.

We were marched to the railway station, where a train with cattle cars waited on the siding. The SS opened the doors and started beating and shoving us inside. Our group tried to stay together. They packed us in so tightly that there was no room to lie down; we had to either sit or stand. After warning us that anyone attempting to escape would be shot by the guards stationed on the roof, they shut the doors and bolted them. It was dark inside the car, the only light coming in through the crack in the doors. Everyone was pushing and shoving, trying to make room for himself. Despite it all, though, I felt somewhat relieved. There was no knowing where they might be taking us and what was going to happen, but almost anything would be preferable to the night-mare of Majdanek.

It was at least two hours before the train even started to move. We couldn't tell in which direction it was going, but at the first station where we stopped we heard the name of a town that one of the local people knew to be to the west of Majdanek. Where could we be going? Some thought to Germany, others perhaps to Auschwitz, which we knew was a huge extermination camp as well as a labor camp.

Those who couldn't control their bladders and bowels started re-lieving themselves on the floor, and the smell of urine, feces, and sweat became overpowering. Some people had trouble breathing and cried out for help. No help came, because nobody could move. It was almost airless in there—but at least it wasn't hot, otherwise few would have survived the trip. The train made frequent stops, but the guards kept us locked in the entire time. Some of the younger Jews from Radom who happened to be sitting a few feet away from me were trying to pry open a loose board in order to escape, but they didn't succeed. Surprisingly, despite the frightful conditions, there were relatively few arguments or fights. Richie Krakowski, who was sitting near me, told me that this trip was a bed of roses compared to the one he had taken in the cattle car from Warsaw to Treblinka. At least our destination was unknown; they had known they were on their way to be gassed.

As the hours went by, my body began to ache from being squeezed so hard on all sides. A man next to me fell asleep on me, a dead weight. I tried to wake him, but he was too exhausted to respond. Someone next to me urinated on the floor, and my pants got wet. Night fell, and the air became heavier still. I had no trouble breathing, but some people began to gasp and choke. Somebody died—I heard weeping and sobbing. My brothers and I were fairly near each other, and from time to time we called each other's names to reassure ourselves we were all alive. And the train rolled on.

At last daylight came, which cheered me a little. I tried to calculate the speed of the train and the distance to the German border, and figured it would take us about twenty-four hours to get there from Majdanek. By now the smell was so bad I was sick. Sometime late in the morning the train stopped again, and this time we heard the guards opening the doors. When our doors swung open and the light struck my eyes, I blinked at the shock. We had been in the dark for a long time.

The guards drove us out, screaming, *"Juden—raus, raus, mach schnell!"* I jumped out of the car, and we saw each other in the light of day. We were all filthy and tired. My pants were soaked from sitting in the urine and feces that covered the floor, and I was hoping that they would take us to a shower soon.

The SS ordered us to form a column, and we started marching. I saw a sign reading "Płaszów," which was a Polish place name. I would have preferred to be in Germany, where we probably would have a better chance to survive. Someone said we were near Krakow, a major Polish city in the southwest, and that Płaszów was a big concentration camp. Soon we saw in the distance the familiar barbed wire, guard towers, and entrance gate. Well, at least we were still alive. They hadn't killed us yet, and as long as there's life, there's hope.

Płaszów

■

U pon entering the camp grounds, we were taken in tow by Jewish Kapos (group bosses), who showed us no mercy, pushing and kicking us as brutally as had the Ukrainians. After we were inside the reception barracks one of them actually jumped deliberately through an open window and crashed into us, feet first, knocking some of us down.

Here the search was not as thorough as it had been in Majdanek, but it didn't matter, because our money was safe in the paper tubes inside our rectums. Once again, on our first visit to the latrine we had to search through our feces to extract the tubes.

People from our transport were exhausted from the long trip in the cattle cars, and the next day a few of them developed a high fever. Fred's fears of a typhus epidemic spread by the lice in Majdanek had materialized. He went to the doctor in charge of the hospital—a Jew, a Dr. Gross—and informed him of this dangerous development, suggesting that he order an immediate quarantine to

PŁASZÓW

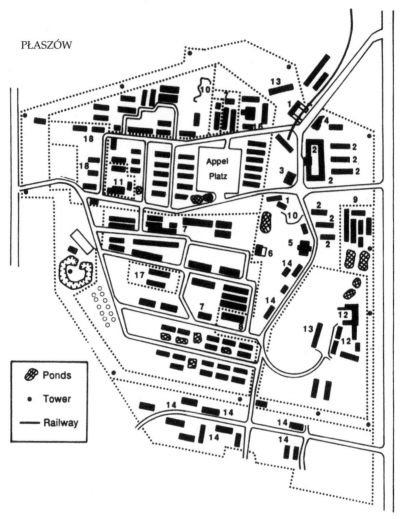

1	Offices	10	Quarry
2	SS Barracks	11	Kitchen
3	The Gray House	12	Stable
4	The Red House	13	Garage
5	Goethe's Villa	14	House for the Germans
6	Barrack for the dogs	15	Hospital
7	Cesspool	16	Bathhouse
8	Warehouse	17	Construction square
9	Warehouse	18	Camp hospital

J. Bau (in: *Proces ludobójcy Amona Goetha*, Cracow, 1947, p. 375) prevent the spread of the typhus to the rest of the camp. Dr. Gross agreed, and we were placed in separate barracks and isolated from the rest of the camp. Fred was the only person permitted to leave the quarantine area.

Over the next few days more and more people came down with the fever, among them Felek. At first we hoped that it was just a cold, but his temperature quickly shot up like the rest. He soon reached the crisis, his fever hovering around 104–105 degrees, and for a day or two it was touch and go, but then the fever started to drop. He was one of the last to fall ill; the spread of the disease seemed to have been arrested, and no new cases were reported. Miraculously not one of the thirty or forty who came down with typhus died, but those who recovered were very weak for a long time.

One day Dr. Gross came to visit our barracks. He ordered the convalescents to line up and started making notes in a book he was carrying. Fred saw that he was listing the prisoners' numbers of the people who were the weakest; these included some who had never recovered from the journey in the cattle cars. He became suspicious and asked Gross about it. Gross replied that he needed the information to obtain extra rations for them, but it made Fred very uneasy; he didn't trust Gross. However, after it was clear that the epidemic was over, our quarantine was lifted and we were moved to a regular barracks.

The first Appel in Płaszów was quite an experience. The entire camp, more than twenty thousand, lined up on the Appelplatz to be counted. The Jewish Kapos were running around helping the SS do the count, and often beating up the prisoners. The Appel took an hour and a half, and I was told that it sometimes went on for as long as three hours.

After the Appel we were marched out to work. Part of our group was taken to a construction site, a hospital for Wehrmacht officers.

Bencio Fink, myself, and about thirty others were assigned to a work detail that was excavating the foundation of the hospital. The earth was heavy with clay, which made the work difficult. Other prisoners loaded the earth we had dug into trucks, and it moved along fast.

In the middle of the day they gave us about fifteen minutes to rest. My job in the Budzyń factory had made me soft, and I developed a large blister on my right hand.

When the workday was over, we formed a column and marched back to camp. At the gate they counted us twice before we were permitted to pass through. Supper consisted of a *menashka* of soup, which I forced myself to eat just to have something warm in my stomach. After supper was our first opportunity to learn about conditions in Płaszów. It was run internally by Chilowicz, a Jewish Lageralteste, with the help of an aide, Finkelstein, and a number of Jewish Blockälteste and Kapos. All of them were brutal and corrupt, living well at the expense of their fellow Jews.

The camp commandant, Amon Goeth, was a demented sadist who hanged or shot people utterly at whim. From his house on the other side of the barbed wire he would observe prisoners inside the camp through a pair of binoculars, and if he didn't like the look of a man, the way he walked, for instance, he would shoot him with his telescopic-sighted rifle. Goeth went around the camp accompanied by a dog, Rolf, who was trained to attack when Goeth cried, "Jude!" After Rolf had done his job, Goeth would finish the prisoner off by beating him to death with his large knout, or simply shooting him.

Whenever there had been an escape attempt, Goeth would select ten prisoners at random and either shoot them himself or have them shot on a nearby hill, called Hujowa Górka. Goeth was completely unpredictable. He ignored the strict Gestapo rules and kept a Jewish woman in his apartment as his mistress. He was brazen in his demands for constant payoffs from Chilowicz and his underlings.

Under Goeth's leadership, frequent selections were conducted in the camp hospital, and those too sick or weak to work were taken to Hujowa Górka and shot. The mere mention of the name Hujowa Górka was enough to send a shiver through the ranks of prisoners. Many thousands of Jews had been killed there and buried in mass graves.

None of this information made us feel any better, but despite the hazards of life in a camp in which there were continual selections and shooting, it still seemed preferable to Majdanek, with its eerie emptiness and with no apparent reason for existing.

For the first time since we had left Budzyń, we heard reliable news from the front. The Russians were indeed continuing their offensive and had invaded the prewar Polish territories. The Allies were making progress in Italy. To our disappointment, though, there was still no word about the expected second front in the West. Again I felt that familiar mixture of exhilaration at the German defeats and despair over our infinitesimal chance of living to see the final Allied victory. Hitler and the SS had marked us down for death, we were in their hands, and nothing less than a miracle would save us.

We soon discovered that Płaszów was a much more commercialized place than the other camps. Here one could buy many things, not only food but other commodities as well. The Jews at the top of the hierarchy lived luxuriously, with the best food and even many conveniences and services. They exercised their power through a hundred or so Jewish policemen, Kapos, and Stubenälteste, who were also relatively comfortable. Apart from them, there were two classes of prisoners: those who had some money, and those who didn't. The first group readily obtained extra bread and other food; the second group were starving to death on the camp rations—which were much smaller even than they were supposed to be. Trade with the outside world was brisk, and corruption rampant and highly organized: the prisoners' rations were cut so that those in positions of power could divide the remainder among themselves and sell it.

In our barracks, in addition to a Jewish Stubenälteste, was a Kapo, a German prisoner named Fehringer. He wore a green triangle, signifying that he was a criminal. He had been sent to Płaszów for the murder of his parents, and was sarcastically referred to as "the orphan." Fehringer was of medium height, with smooth blond, almost white hair and gray-blue eyes. He was wiry and very alert, and spoke with great precision. He was cruel, always looking for the slightest pretext to attack the prisoners, and when he did, he was very methodical, like someone performing a mechanical task. He would hit his victim like a trained fighter, his fists so quick that it was impossible to protect oneself. Almost every day Fehringer would pick someone out for this treatment, and when he was finished with him, the man was ready for the hospital.

I tried hard to avoid Fehringer as far as possible, making sure not to break any rules. Fred had been given permission by Dr. Gross to send the prisoners who were too weak to work to the hospital, but he was warned that if he did this too freely, he would be punished. Fehringer's victims pleaded with Fred to give them an admission pass to the hospital. They knew that it was a dangerous place, but many preferred to run the risk of the frequent selections so that they could stay in bed for a few days and recover. Fred found it difficult to refuse them.

After a few days Fehringer began to notice the absence of the people he had recently beaten up, and found out that it was Fred who was sending them to the hospital. One day he approached Fred and said in his cutting voice, "I hear, Dr. Orenstein, that you are a very good-hearted man. You better watch out. This is a concentration camp, not a resort." When Fred told me of this, my heart sank and I begged him to be very careful. Fehringer was an extremely dangerous man to have as an enemy. Fred lifted his hands helplessly. "What can I do? When people come to me in such terrible shape, how can I refuse to help them?" It was an impossible dilemma.

One of the prisoners who knew Fehringer well told us that there was another reason besides sadistic pleasure for his systematic attacks on the prisoners: he was deliberately terrorizing them so that nobody dared complain about the smaller rations of bread. Fehringer was in charge of cutting up the bread for the four hundred or so inmates of our barracks, and every day he kept for himself four or five of the forty to fifty loaves he received. He was doing the same thing with the margarine and marmalade; what he withheld from us he sold on the black market for diamonds and gold. Fehringer, it was said, was sharing his loot with the Stubenälteste and some of the SS guards as well. He was very self-confident and cocky, and apparently believed that Fred's passes to the hospital were undermining his reign of terror. I lived in constant fear of Fehringer and of what he might do to us, particularly to Fred.

We decided to sell one of our two remaining twenty-dollar bills for bread. Fearful that Fehringer would find out about it if we were to do it in our barracks, we went to another barracks to make the deal. Fehringer shrewdly suspected us, because on one occasion he told Fred that if he had any money he had better hand it over. Fred denied having any, but Fehringer seemed unconvinced. We now had only one twenty-dollar bill left, and we doled out these last additional portions of bread to stretch them as far as possible. For the first time in the camps, I was constantly hungry.

In Budzyń I had sometimes urinated in my sleep. Here I had a bunk on the bottom tier—luckily, because the same thing happened again. But this time I didn't have to worry that a prisoner would scream and curse me, as one had done in Budzyń, which would have been dangerous with Fehringer nearby. Sleep was our only release from the dark reality of our waking lives. Sometimes I dreamed of happy times with my family, and of having plenty of food and love and hope. Every morning, upon waking and realizing with a jolt where I was, I experienced a strange sensation, as if a stone were slowly moving down from my heart to the pit of my stomach.

One day, late in April, Fred's suspicions of Dr. Gross were confirmed. The prisoners whose numbers he had written down in the hospital were summoned out of the ranks at the morning Appel, and together with Musulmen from other barracks were taken to Hujowa Górka for execution. It was disheartening to see a Jewish doctor selecting the SS's victims for them. Fred, who had recovered from the depression he had suffered at Majdanek, said, "I hope we survive the war just so I can testify against Gross at his trial."

Work on the construction site continued for a couple of weeks, and the excavation was almost finished. The pit, at the bottom of a tree-lined hill, was about eight feet deep, two hundred feet long, and forty feet wide. One day while we were working I spotted on the ground a torn piece of German army newspaper, perhaps a quarter of a page. I noticed the bold type that was always used for the German military communiqués. I was always intensely curious about what was happening on the war fronts, but usually had to rely on secondhand reports from other prisoners. Here was a chance to read it for myself. I looked around to make sure no one saw me, then quickly picked up the piece of newspaper and stuck it in my pocket.

Suddenly I heard a voice behind me: *"Jude, zeige mir was du hast in deine Tasche."* (Jew, show me what you have in your pocket.) I felt as if I had been struck by a bolt of lightning. I turned around, and there was an SS man, his hand stretched out toward me. I took the piece of newspaper out of my pocket and handed it over. He glanced at it and said, "You can't wait for us to lose the war, can you, Jew?" I was so scared I couldn't think. He took out his revolver and pointed it toward the excavation pit. This was the end, then.

I didn't understand that he wanted me to jump into the pit, and I just stood there at the edge of it. He kicked me in the stomach, and I fell in. He then pointed the gun at me, and I waited to be struck by a bullet. I had no last thoughts that I can remember, only terror. Then I heard the SS man say, "*Jude, raus.*" (Jew, get out.) The pit was very deep, and I had to jump up to catch hold of the edge with my fingertips. He stomped on my fingers with his boots, and I fell back into the pit. "*Jude, raus,*" he said again. Again I jumped up and again he stomped on my fingers. Now the skin was coming off. I couldn't hold on any longer, and fell back into the pit. The third time he waited until I had lifted myself chest high, and then he kicked me. I fell back in again.

This was repeated seven or eight times. My fingers were hurting badly. With great courage and at grave risk to himself, Bencio, who had been working next to me, whispered in Polish, "Ask him for forgiveness." That seemed like a very good idea, and I tried to say something apologetic to the SS man, but somehow no sound came out of my throat. To this day, I don't know why. After a couple more rounds of my jumping and his stomping, the SS man turned and walked away. When I realized he wasn't going to kill me after all, a wild joy surged through me. My fingers were a bloody pulp and I needed Bencio's help to climb out of the pit. "I thought you were a goner," he said. I was so happy to be alive I wasn't even bothered by the pain. I even joked about it: "At least he should have let me keep the newspaper." One of the other prisoners had a piece of cloth and bandaged my fingers with it.

When Bencio and I got back to the barracks and told my brothers about my close call, they couldn't believe my carelessness. "There aren't enough dangers—you have to create your own?" Fred brought some fresh bandages from the hospital, cut off the pieces of skin that were hanging loose, and cleaned the wounds. This was painful, but within a couple of days the torn flesh had dried out and started to heal.

It was the beginning of May, but unseasonably chilly. One especially cold morning we were standing on the Appelplatz when I saw a tall German in a white fur coat standing in the center of the square. The whispered words "Dr. Blanke" and "selection" ran through the ranks of prisoners. We were ordered to strip completely, all of us, and from barracks after barracks the prisoners were made to run in single file a few steps apart past a small raised platform on which Dr. Blanke was standing to get a better view. He held a thin stick in his hand, and as each prisoner ran past him, he would make a tiny movement of the stick to one side or the other.

Those he directed to the left had to stop at a table where a clerk was sitting and give him their prisoner and barracks numbers. They were then kept in a group apart. Those who ran to the right rejoined the others from their barracks who had already passed the selection. The SS and the Jewish Kapos made sure everybody went according to Dr. Blanke's direction. We all knew that the group on the left had been selected to die; those who looked sick or were too weak to run fast were sent there. Some of them, knowing what it meant, made believe they had misunderstood Dr. Blanke and tried to sneak over to the "healthy" group on the right, but the SS and the Kapos drove them back.

I stood and watched this scene with a grim fascination, thinking, "What an unbelievable spectacle: Dr. Blanke in his big white fur coat, standing there like an impresario conducting an audition, and twenty thousand naked prisoners running past him so he can choose in the blink of an eye who will live and who will die." I was very conscious of the fact that I was eyewitness to a unique event. Here we were in the twentieth century, and a supposedly civilized nation was doing this. I thought, "This makes Nero, the Roman Colosseum, the Christians, and the wild beasts look like a dull show." It's hard to convey the visual impact of twenty thousand naked men, and a single person the master of all these lives.

When they saw me naked, my brothers were afraid I wouldn't pass the selection. At the best of times my legs are long and thin; now I weighed only about a hundred ten pounds, and my legs looked alarmingly skinny. My brothers urged me to keep an upright posture, run fast, and try to impress Dr. Blanke with my physical condition. In spite of their fears I wasn't scared, because I felt physically well. When my turn came, I ran fast, like a sprinter, my chest out, and I passed the life-and-death test. It was a huge relief, though, because one could never be sure. The spectacle went on for hours. About fifteen hundred prisoners were selected to die. A few among the "survivors" had family who were sent to the left, and some of the survivors asked to join them, a request the SS generously granted. Those selected to die sometimes tried to dissuade their loved ones from sacrificing their lives, but usually failed.

After the selection, the rest of us were ordered to get dressed and form our work commandos; the selected group stayed behind. At the end of the day we learned that they had been shipped in cattle cars to the gas chambers of Auschwitz.

A few days later we finished work at the hospital construction site, and I was assigned to a work detail that was planting vegetables on a nearby SS farm. To my distress Fehringer was the Kapo of our group, but except for an occasional outburst he wasn't as bad as when he was in the barracks. From time to time he would disappear with his girlfriend, an SS woman who was one of our supervisors, and perhaps this put him in a better mood. It was early June now, and the weather was pleasant. Even though we were forced to work nonstop, I preferred the field work to the construction job.

During the lunch break on June 6, I noticed our SS supervisors talking excitedly. In the afternoon one of the truck drivers making deliveries to the farm told one of the prisoners that the Allies had landed in France. The word spread quickly, and I could scarcely contain my joy. We talked of nothing else through the rest of the day, and all evening after the Appel. At last, after so many years of suffering, Western civilization was coming to our rescue.

Now Hitler and his armies were doomed, trapped between the jaws of a gigantic nutcracker, the victorious Russians driving from the east, the fresh Allied armies pushing through from the west. We tried to estimate how long it would take them to crush the Nazis. I was the optimist, and thought perhaps it would be only a matter of weeks, but even the most pessimistic among us expected the war to be over before the end of 1944. We also debated the possibility that the Wehrmacht itself might get rid of Hitler and sue for peace. About that the pessimists were dubious: "The stupid Germans will follow Hitler right down to the bitter end. And anyway, how would that help us? Do you think they'd just hand us over to the Allies to be witnesses against them?" It was hard to dispute their logic, but somehow they couldn't shake my faith. There was always room for the unpredictable, a stroke of luck; hadn't my brothers and I already defied the most incredible odds against us? I felt that there was a chance that somehow, under the pressure of events, things might get out of control to create the kind of conditions that would enable us to survive.

I was so excited I couldn't get to sleep for hours that night. I tried to remember the map of France and visualize where the landings were taking place. Dunkirk would be ideal, perfect poetic justice! But probably the coastline so close to England would be too heavily fortified for the Allies to effect a landing. Yet perhaps, with the bulk of Hitler's armies occupied in trying to stem the Russian advance, they wouldn't offer much resistance anywhere in the west. And once the Allies landed, their overwhelming superiority in the air would protect them. Thus happily engaged in playing commander in chief of the Allied armies, I finally fell asleep.

The very next morning, June 7, we were standing on the Appelplatz when there was an announcement that all prisoners who belonged to the "chemist and scientist group" were to report immediately to the main office of the camp. This of course aroused both excitement and dread among us. By then we had become convinced that even if the Germans had indeed at one time been planning to make some use of a special scientific commando, they had been forced to abandon the plan, whatever it was, in the face of the onrushing Russians and the new threat from the west. What other explanation could there be for their actions, first singling us out as a special group in Budzyń, then sending us to Majdanek for no discernible purpose, mingling with us hundreds of Jews from Radom, then shipping us by cattle car to Płaszów, where for almost two months they had used us in a variety of unimportant labor commandos?

As we assembled outside the camp office, we tried to prepare ourselves for what they might ask, and rehearsed the information we had originally given the SS concerning our "education" and "experience." I was eager to get the impending interrogation behind us so that the commando could start functioning. I was weary of physical labor, for I was steadily losing weight and growing weaker. If we were assigned to something less physical, our chances for survival would improve.

Soon they started summoning people from the head of the line into the office. A few really were specialists, and obviously they were the least apprehensive about the interview. For the rest of us, the moment of truth was near. There were fifteen or twenty new people among us in addition to the original Budzyń group,

I noticed; apparently the SS had recruited "specialists" from other camps as well. I stood almost at the end of the line, hoping to gather clues as to what was going on from the people ahead of me after they had finished their interviews. To my enormous relief, most of them were coming out of the office smiling. Fred was ahead of me in the line, and when he came back he told me that after reviewing his "education in chemistry," they asked him only one question: "How many legs does a fly have?" Fortunately he knew the answer: six. I had always thought it was eight, but then I had never claimed to be a chemist; I was a mathematician. Felek and Sam returned to say they had had only to repeat the details of their "educational background," and were asked no other questions.

When my turn came, I went in and saw three civilians seated behind a table. They were very polite. One of them asked me whether I was familiar with calculators. "Oh yes, I used them a lot at school," I lied. "I'm sure I would have no trouble handling them." I had conditioned myself beforehand to speak confidently, no matter what they asked me. The interviewer smiled at me and made a note of my reply. "Is that all?" I asked. He nodded and I left. I felt tremendously relieved: I had passed!

After they had questioned us all, we compared notes. They had told some of us that soon they would have a place ready for us to work in. We didn't go out to work that morning, and spent the rest of the day in endless discussions about the significance of it all. The critical thing was that we seemed to have passed the screening—if indeed one could call it that. Had the Germans questioned us in any depth, they would have immediately discovered that virtually all of us were frauds. Talking among themselves, they had referred to each other as "Herr Professor," so apparently they were genuinely educated men with degrees in the fields in which we claimed to be expert. Had they wanted to find out what we did or did not know, they could easily have done so; it was clear that they didn't want to know. They wanted the "Chemiker" group (as we began to call it) to start functioning regardless of what our qualifications were.

Now, why were they so interested in creating this commando, and how would it affect our future? They had offered few clues as to what kind of work we would be doing, or where. But it was now obvious that this Chemiker Kommando would indeed play a decisive role in our struggle to survive. It was beginning to look as if my rash act of registering my family for it might turn out to have been the right decision after all—which was a load off my mind.

The next couple of days were filled with anxious anticipation, with one distracting event. About that time a transport of thousands of young Hungarian Jewish women arrived in Budzyń. Some were kept in a barracks next to ours, separated by a single row of barbed wire. After the Appel people on our side of the fence were talking to the women, who were all young, with shaven heads. They wore weird, shapeless garments made of what looked like flour sacks, with slits for the head and arms. But even without hair and in that getup, many of them still looked comely. They were very frightened, and anxious for any information as to what they could expect.

This was the first time I had ever heard Hungarian spoken. Since I knew several languages, I thought I might be able to understand a little of what they were saying, but I soon found that Hungarian bore no resemblance whatsoever to any other language I was familiar with. One of the girls spoke a few words of French, so I tried to communicate with her. Even bald, she was stunningly beautiful, with large dark eyes, perfect skin the color of a peach, and the loveliest facial features I had ever seen. I asked her about her family, and she told me her younger sister was with her, indicating the girl standing next to her. I then inquired about her parents. She said something I couldn't understand, but she looked sad and two large tears rolled down her cheeks. It was very frustrating not to be able to understand each other, but I tried to sound as encouraging as possible. Then suddenly an SS woman carrying a whip appeared and started hitting the girls, and the two sisters ran away with the others.

Seeing these women made me very sad. They all looked so young and healthy, and many of them were extraordinarily pretty; now I could appreciate how well deserved was the reputation of Hungarian women for beauty. But it was heartbreaking to see these innocent young girls so frightened, lost in a strange country, humiliated, beaten, and completely at the mercy of the brutal SS. For many days and nights I was haunted by the image of that girl with the tears rolling down her cheeks and animal terror in her eyes. Over the next few days I kept looking for her through the barbed wire, but I never saw her again. A week or so later they were gone. We were told they had all been shipped to Auschwitz.

About June 10 the Chemiker Kommando finally became a reality. After the Appel that morning we were ordered to form a separate group and were marched out through the gate, full of curiosity and anticipation. Our curiosity was soon satisfied. We were taken to a barracks very near the camp. Inside waiting for us were the German civilians who had interviewed us. They separated us into three groups. Sam, myself, and six others were "mathematicians"; Felek, Fred, Bencio, Richie, and perhaps twenty or so others were in the "chemist" group, and the rest were the "engineers and inventors."

A young German professor led the eight of us "mathematicians" to a table in the corner of the barracks. He was a slender man of about thirty, of medium height, with straight dark blond hair, pale skin, and blue eyes. He appointed Stark, who had taught mathematics, to be our leader. On the table were seven machines that looked like old-fashioned cash registers, with rows of keys for addition, subtraction, multiplication, and division. Around the table were benches for us to sit on. The professor, who didn't introduce himself, spoke to Stark for a few minutes, handed him a thick manila envelope, said good-bye to us, and left. We all gathered around Stark as he opened the envelope. Inside were hundreds of sheets covered with columns of typed numbers, for example: 3146.45 × 260.13 =; 52354.05 ÷ 1.263 =; and so forth. A few were addition or subtraction, but most were multiplication and division: elementary school arithmetic. I picked up the manila envelope. It was stamped *Oberkommando der Kriegsmarine* (Supreme Command of the German Navy). On the bottom was another stamp, *Geheime Reichssache* (Highest State Secrets). Stark saw me looking at the envelope and with annoyance asked me to hand it over. Already he was behaving like a boss. I made a crack about this "top secret" work that any kid could do, and he didn't like that either. He was full of his new importance, and pulled rank on us as the only legitimate mathematician in the group. Stark was close to forty, and with his bald head looked a bit like Mussolini. Every few minutes he would suck in air through his teeth, a mannerism that drove me crazy.

The others in the group besides Sam and me were Zysman and Wortman, who were real engineers but had registered as mathematicians; Arno Kronheim, a young German Jew who was a student from Berlin; and Eisenstadt, a teacher. Zysman was rather tall and thin, with a long nose and sad eyes. He was a living encyclopedia, very intelligent and with an analytical mind, and was the only one among us whom Stark really respected. Wortman was in his fifties, a pleasant, civilized man with graying hair. He was a compulsive smoker and used to trade some of his bread rations for cigarettes, although he knew he was shortening his life by doing so. He was a pessimist, and didn't think we would live long enough anyway for it to matter. Eisenstadt was a very level-headed, even-tempered, agreeable man of about forty-five. His hair was completely silver-gray, an odd contrast with his smooth pink cheeks. Arno was an exceptionally nice young man, perhaps a year older than I, with dark, slightly wavy hair, brown eyes, and a roundish face. He knew no Polish, which all the rest of us spoke. Although he generally kept to himself, he was scrupulously polite to everyone. I liked Arno and tried to strike up a friendship with him, but he didn't respond, so I left him alone. Perhaps he, like many other German Jews, was uncomfortable with the more outgoing manners of the Polish Jews. Finally there was Warshawski, a pale-faced man, in very poor physical condition, who was close to becoming a Musalman. His health improved markedly after he joined our group.

Sam and I needed to learn how to work the machine, and Zysman volunteered to help us. I started multiplying and dividing the numbers and writing down the answers. This was heaven. We got to sit at the table all day, and there was no one around to supervise us. After a while I went over to visit Felek and Fred. The "chemists" were all sitting at tables too, and what they were doing was translating Polish textbooks on insects into German. I could scarcely believe my eyes. This was what they had brought us here for? Felek said that their professor had given them the books to translate because, he said, to do their real, supposedly vital work they needed material that had not yet arrived. He appointed Bencio Fink, who couldn't read or write German, to be the librarian for these Polish insect books.

Incredulous, I went to have a look at what the "engineers and inventors" were up to. There it was total chaos. Their professor had told them that they would be working on a vitally important scientific invention, a gas that would have the capacity to bring all motors to a standstill. This gas was intended to be used primarily against planes, tanks, and trucks, effectively immobilizing the opposing army. Their professor too had explained to them that unfortunately the materials they needed had not yet arrived. In the meantime, he had brought them an automobile engine to get started on, together with some fuel. They spent the whole day turning the engine on and off.

The whole business was mind-boggling. Those who had said from the very beginning that this commando was some kind of cover-up for the professors were obviously right. It was a fake, a fraud! I went back to our table unable to contain my hilarity. Stark gave me a baleful look, and even Sam took me aside to warn me, "You have to be careful. Someone might inform on you, and we'll all be in trouble." Of course he was right, and I promised him I would stop. But after the evening Appel, all we could talk about was our new situation. We weren't complaining, of course; our new commando might well save our lives. And obviously there was a big difference between hard labor in an ordinary camp commando—which in itself could kill, on our starvation diet, not to mention the violence routinely inflicted on us—and the peaceful, even agreeable atmosphere in our Chemiker barracks.

Next morning I could scarcely wait for the Appel to be over so I could get to our new workplace. An SS guard was stationed outside the barracks, but he seldom came inside. The SS were well aware that our commando was unusual, to say the least. Some of them were suspicious, and occasionally would pass a remark expressing doubt that our work could have any value, and displeasure that Jews should have it so easy, but they had to follow orders, and they left us alone.

As the weeks passed, our life in the Chemiker Kommando became fairly routine. Once a week or so our professor would stop by, collect the finished work from Stark, and give him more sheets. It was boring, but that was the worst you could say about it. I was still losing weight, but not so fast as when I was doing hard labor. All of us were more relaxed, and sometimes told jokes and teased each other. One of the chemical group, Jurek Topaz, a young fellow about my age, was especially full of life and loved to play practical jokes on his fellow "chemists."

We "mathematicians" soon got to know each other well, sitting together at the same table day after day, and we found various ways of diverting ourselves from our utterly boring work. Someone challenged Stark with a very difficult riddle in logic, and Stark, Zysman, and I occupied ourselves for several days trying to solve it. Stark was the first to come up with a solution, but no one could understand it. Zysman was next, and his explanation was easy to understand. I didn't like Stark, and enjoyed his tortuous attempts to prove the validity of his own solution, which Zysman didn't agree with, nor did anyone else.

Stark wasn't crazy about me either, and often dropped sarcastic remarks about my interest in analyzing the situation on the war fronts. Once I overheard him telling Zysman that it had become an obsession with me, adding, "I wonder, if we should happen to get lucky and survive, what he will do with himself after the war, without any more battles to follow." This made me ask myself whether Stark wasn't right; perhaps never again would anything capture my interest to such an extent. Then it occurred to me that business was another big game, much like war. Maybe I'd go to America and become a big businessman. That made me feel better. One day, unexpectedly, another "mathematician" was added to our group—a woman from the women's barracks. So now there were nine of us.*

---

*My memory of this woman is hazy, and I don't remember the circumstances under which she joined our commando.

From day to day in the meantime I literally lived for news from the battlefield. I had always enjoyed competition, and the struggle between the Russians and the Western Allies on one side and the monstrous Third Reich on the other could be seen as a gigantic contest between the forces of good and evil. For the moment it didn't matter that Stalin was something less than a saint, that he had killed millions of his own people. What was important was the Russian people themselves, their epic struggle and their heroic ability to rise from almost total defeat to great victories, giving lessons in modern warfare to their erstwhile invaders and torturers. My heart went out to the dauntless English, who, abandoned to their fate, fought on alone, their backs to the wall, to defend their freedom against the odds. I was overflowing with gratitude to the gum-chewing, wisecracking Yanks who had come to the rescue from across the ocean. My head was spinning with joy the day one of the "chemists" brought news from the BBC that America was now producing hundreds of thousands of tanks and planes to fight Hitler. We all shook our heads in amazement. "Only in America."

The news from the fronts was exhilarating. The Russians had started their summer offensive and broken through the German lines on the central front. Early in July they captured Minsk, and a few days later Kovno and Grodno. Clearly the Germans were in a rout; in July we heard the names, one after the other, of the newly liberated Polish cities: Lwów, Przemyśl, Stanisławów.

The news from the West made us no less jubilant. About the middle of July, after a prolonged buildup of forces, the Americans broke through in Normandy, and the Germans were in full retreat across France. I could scarcely believe this uninterrupted string of victories. And why were the stupid Germans continuing to resist? It was now certain that they had no chance whatsoever. These were no temporary setbacks; everything was going irreversibly against them. Not only were their armies in full retreat, their factories were being destroyed by incessant bombing, relentless pounding by day and night, and there was no possible way of rebuilding them— while America, the arsenal of the free world, was gearing up to an unprecedented scale of production. The soldiers of the Wehrmacht were getting slaughtered by the tens of thousands, and losing their will to continue the fight. They all knew the war was lost. All that kept Germany in the war was the Nazis' terror and the ingrained German habit of unquestioning obedience.

None of this, of course, altered the fact that there was a sword dangling over us Jews. For us the question was: What kind of scenario would it take to rescue us?

The question was almost answered on July 20. When we got back to camp that evening, we heard that an attempt had been made on Hitler's life. Many conflicting stories were making the rounds: Hitler was dead. . . . Hitler was alive, but dying. . . . Hitler had survived, and addressed the Germans over the radio. . . . Hitler was really dead, but to gain time the Gestapo had someone impersonating him.

We were in a daze. We realized immediately that if it was true that Hitler was dead, the now leaderless SS might be afraid to continue mass killings of Jews, at least until it became clear who was in charge. Perhaps the Wehrmacht might seize power and ask for a cease-fire. There was even a possibility that the German soldiers would simply throw down their weapons and return home. If the assassination had really taken place, it probably was for us the gift of life. The pessimists, of course, had their say as well: "With that son of a bitch's luck, nothing could happen to him."

Unfortunately, they were proven right. After an almost sleepless night, we learned in the morning that there had indeed been an attempt on Hitler's life, but that he had miraculously survived. In a radio speech to the German people, he promised to wreak vengeance on the "traitors." The SS guards themselves were eager to inform us of the good news. During the brief march to our Chemiker Kommando barracks that morning they taunted us, "So you damned Jews thought the Führer was dead, eh? Don't worry, he'll kill the lot of you before anything happens to him."

As more details of the assassination attempt became known over the next few days, we realized how close we had been to an answer to our prayers. So near, and yet so far—it was very depressing. Now the bastard was going to be so furious, he might just give an order to kill all the Jews that were left. I was worried that this might well happen, and felt relieved every time they shouted *"Arbeit Kommandos formieren!"* (work commandos, assemble) after the Appel. Even the continuing good news from the fighting fronts failed to provide the usual lift to our spirits. At the end of July we heard that the Russians had reached the Vistula River and established a bridgehead across this largest and most important of all Polish rivers. So the Russians were now deep inside Poland. They had not only retaken most of the territory conquered by the Germans, they were pushing far beyond it, apparently hell-bent on utterly destroying the enemy.

Tension among us increased. We knew that had the rapid advance of the Russians continued, they would soon have been approaching Płaszów, and the question loomed: What would they do with us? Evacuate us? Liquidate the camp, killing all the inmates as they had done around Lublin, in Majdanek and the others? I felt somewhat hopeful that this would not happen; our German professors probably needed us now more than ever. Where would they be without us? Hitler was running short of cannon fodder, and even middle-aged men were being drafted. Surely our professors didn't want to fight Hitler's war, especially now, when things were going so badly for him. I only hoped that whatever pull they had with the

Gestapo or the German War Production Office was strong enough to keep us going.

News came of the Warsaw uprising. The Polish leaders of the underground *Armia Krajowa* (Home Army), apparently believing that the Russians, who were only a few miles away on the other side of the Vistula, would enter Warsaw in a matter of days, ordered a general uprising. Hitler, fearing that a successful rebellion in Warsaw might lead to a general revolt throughout Poland, and worried about his lines of communications, ordered an attack on Warsaw with tanks and planes, which destroyed everything that remained of the city after five years of bombardments and the burning of the Ghetto. There was justice in this, I felt: the Poles, with a few rare exceptions, had cheered the destruction of Warsaw Jewry, and now they were getting a taste of the same medicine. The victorious Russian army, however, needing time to move supplies up to the front and prepare for their next push, halted their advance in the middle of Poland. For the time being this put an end to talk of any immediate evacuation of Płaszów.

Over the next week or two things calmed down a little. The Allied armies landed in the south of France, opening yet another front against the Germans, and were rapidly moving north along the Rhine Valley. The Allied forces in northern France had spread out after the breakthrough in Normandy and were advancing toward Paris. It was now obvious that the Germans were incapable of stemming or even slowing the Allied drive, and that the liberation of all of France was imminent. But these dramatic victories no longer aroused the same joy in us as had the earlier ones. The Wehrmacht was so weak now that it was no longer a contest; furthermore, this was completely overshadowed by the question of what would happen to us.

One hot, clear day in August, when we formed ranks after returning from work for the evening Appel, we were met by a gruesome sight. In the middle of the Appelplatz, propped up on tables, were several bodies. I couldn't see the faces from where I stood, but soon a whisper swept the prisoner ranks: Chilowicz! the corrupt and brutal Jewish Lagerälteste. Indeed it was Chilowicz, with his wife, Finkelstein, and a few other of their closest collaborators. So this cunning, cruel man and his gang had finally reaped what they had sown. I had never been able to understand how even the most savage conditions could turn Jews into accessories of the SS, so that they collaborated in the torture and murder of their own people. I could understand and even forgive some of the prisoners of weak character who, when under the gun, committed offenses against their fellow Jews, but Chilowicz and the others like him went out of their way to be cruel even when the Germans weren't around. The bodies were a chilling sight, but I felt no pity for Chilowicz and company.*

This episode caused some uneasiness, but soon the camp calmed down again. We learned of the liberation of Paris, but that had long been expected. Of more immediate concern to us was whether the Germans would be able to stabilize the front on their own frontiers. From my experience observing the course of the earlier great offensives, it was apparent to me that first the Germans, and now the Russians and the Western Allies, after an advance of several hundred miles, needed time to bring supplies up to the front and prepare for a new attack.

---

*Amon Goeth had used Chilowicz and his underlings to accumulate enormous amounts of diamonds, gold, and other valuables. Chilowicz was using these valuables, which he obtained by searches of the new prisoner arrivals and other means, to secure his position as the Lagerälteste. Goeth was anxious to get rid of Chilowicz before Płaszów was liquidated, by setting him up, as well as his wife and Finkelstein, in a phony "escape plan," and then making sure that the group was caught and killed. Goeth himself was captured by the Polish authorities, sentenced to death on September 5, 1946, and hanged on September 13, 1946.

The rhythm of war was such that after every rapid advance there was a pause before another one could begin. I hoped of course that the Germans would throw down their arms and refuse to fight any longer, but I suspected, especially after the brutal killings of the leaders of the July 20 assassination attempt, that they were more frightened of Hitler and his Nazi henchmen than of the enemy.

September 1, 1944, came: the fifth anniversary of the German invasion of Poland and the second anniversary of our miraculous escape from under the SS machine guns in Uściług. I was in the barracks working on our professor's meaningless numbers when I heard shouting outside. The window nearest our table was open, so I went over to see what was happening. I looked out the window, and what I saw made me feel as though my head would explode. Just a few steps away was an SS woman holding Fred in a head-lock, while Fehringer was hitting him viciously all over his head and body. I was later told that I jumped out the window, which was six or seven feet above the ground, and ran over to Fred, but I don't remember it; one moment I was looking out the window, and the next I was grabbing the SS woman's arm and freeing Fred's head.

He was in a daze. Fehringer, always so cocky and self-assured, was looking at me in disbelief. An SS guard ran toward us, gun in hand, shouting, *"Was ist los?"* (What's going on?) Fehringer told him that he had seen Fred trying to conceal money, and that when he attempted to search him, Fred had resisted. The SS woman, whom I now recognized as Fehringer's girlfriend, accused me of pushing her and interfering with the search. I was afraid the SS guard would shoot us both—Fred and me—on the spot, but he calmed down and asked Fehringer what had become of the money. Fehringer told him that he had seen Fred with it in his hand but didn't know what had happened to it in the struggle, perhaps Fred or I swallowed it. The guard then looked at me and said, "Resisting an SS guard, eh? How interesting." He wrote down both Fred's and my prisoner numbers and ordered us to go back to work, saying, "We'll deal with you later."

Of the money we had brought with us to the camp, there was only one twenty-dollar bill left, and Fred had had it, sewn into his trouser fly. What had aroused Fehringer's suspicions was unclear. We returned to the barracks in despair. Fred was especially upset that I had gotten myself involved, since there was no way I could have helped him. Sam and Felek were devastated. So many years of suffering, and now it looked like the end for Fred and me. It cast a pall on the whole Chemiker Kommando. They felt sorry for us, but they were also gravely concerned about the effect this would have on them, even though none of them had been involved in the incident.

Fred told us what had happened; Fehringer had suddenly come into the barracks and ordered him outside, demanding that he hand over "the money." Fred told him he didn't have any. Fehringer knew where people usually hid money. He ran his hands over Fred's striped jacket and pants, felt the bill sewn in the pants fly, cut a slit in it with a razor blade, and took out the money, all in a few seconds. Then he handed the twenty dollars to his girlfriend, and they both started beating Fred up. Just taking the money wasn't enough for Fehringer; he wanted to kill Fred. Now, thanks to my interference, we were both in a hopeless position.

I sat down at the table and tried to do some work, but I couldn't bring myself even to push the buttons. "So this is the end," I was thinking. "After all we've gone through." Felek and Sam were heartbroken and kept hugging us, Sam shaking his head despondently. Everyone knew that resisting an SS guard meant almost certain death. They would probably display our bodies on the Appelplatz like Chilowicz.

We didn't have to wait long to find out. On the way back to camp, after they had counted us at the gate, one of the guards called out: "Prisoners numbers so and so—step out." They were our numbers. I tried to prepare myself for the worst, but still my heart was pounding like a jackhammer. Sam and Felek didn't even get a chance to say good-bye; all I saw was their ashen faces as we were led away.

The guards took us to the SS camp headquarters, which were not far away. Before leaving the work barracks, Fred and I had agreed that no matter what they did to us, we would stick to the same story: we had no money, and Fehringer had been mistaken. We figured that if we told the truth and said that Fehringer had taken it, it would be worse for us. First, because we would be admitting to the illegal possession of money, a capital offense in itself, and second, we knew that they wouldn't believe us anyway, not with the SS woman backing up Fehringer's story. My intervention made it all look even worse.

When we arrived at the SS headquarters, several SS guards were standing about in the anteroom. One of them said, "Wait here. I will tell Obersturmbahnführer Müller they are here," and went into the adjoining office. In a moment he came back and ordered Fred to follow him. They went in, and from the inner room I heard a loud voice questioning Fred. I couldn't hear Fred's reply, but there came a series of thuds, which I assumed meant someone was hitting or kicking him. This went on for a long time. I winced every time I heard a new thud. Of all the many things that had happened to me, I had so far been spared the sight or sound of anyone I was close to, let alone a brother, being methodically and brutally beaten up: the feeling was almost indescribable—a mixture of pain, bewilderment, helplessness, despair. But this time there was no possibility of intervening to stop it; the guards were standing right next to me, their guns at the ready. At last the sounds of the beating stopped, but soon they began again. Then I heard an especially heavy thud, as of a body falling to the floor. The door opened and I heard Müller shouting to the guards to bring me in. I entered the office, where for the first time I saw Müller close up. I had seen him often on the Appelplatz, but always from a distance. He was tall and thin, with cold gray eyes. Another SS officer stood next to him. I looked around and saw Fred on the floor in the corner. His head and face were covered with blood and he was lying on his side perfectly still, all crumpled up.

Suddenly he stirred and let out a moan. A wave of happiness rushed through me—he was alive! Müller made sure I had taken it all in, then said, "Get a good look at your brother, because that's what will happen to you too if you don't tell me where you hid the money." "We didn't have any money," I said. Müller came over to me and hit me in the head with a heavy rubber truncheon. I saw stars. Müller continued to hit me in the head, blow after heavy blow. The first four or five blows hurt a lot, but after that I felt each blow less and less. After a while it was as if someone were hitting a big, soft pillow on top of my head.

I have a slight depression at about the center of my skull that I have always believed was its weakest spot, and my only thought was that if Müller hit me there with the force he was using elsewhere on my head, he would crush my skull. As I saw the blows coming, I moved my head slightly so they would miss that spot. Müller continued hitting me and I felt no pain, but I sensed that if it went on much longer, he would probably kill me. I was quite calm now, and after about twenty or thirty blows I decided to pretend I had fainted, so I slipped down to the floor and lay there with my eyes closed. Someone threw water in my face and I opened my eyes. I heard Müller's voice saying, "Get up." I got up, expecting him to resume hitting me, but he must have been tired. On the floor Fred opened his eyes and looked at me in pain. "Throw the two pigs in the *Stehbunker* [standing bunker] and keep them there until they start talking," Müller told his assistant. The assistant ordered Fred to get up. He tried but couldn't, and motioned to me to help him. I went over to the corner where Fred was lying, helped him to his feet, and we embraced for an instant. Then the guards came in and led us away.

They took us to a barracks and pushed us into two adjacent cells, locked the doors, and left. So this was the Stehbunker. It was almost completely dark inside, but there was a small opening in the door through which I could see a tiny ray of daylight. The bunker was about two feet by a foot and a half, so it was possible only to stand up in it—one could neither lie, sit, nor crouch. It smelled foul, and the floor was covered with feces and urine. Next door Fred kept wailing, "Why did you do it? You couldn't have helped me. Now they'll kill us both!" I had no very intelligent answer to give him, and there wasn't much I could say to cheer him up. After he calmed down a little we compared notes and reaffirmed our decision not to change our story no matter what they did to us. As the only occupants of the entire row of the Stehbunkers, at least we could talk freely.

Fred was in much worse shape than I, for his beating had been more severe than mine, and from time to time he moaned with pain. I just had a bad headache; when I touched my head it still felt like a big, soft pillow.

When the ray of light disappeared, we knew it was evening and wondered whether we would get any food, or at least some water; my mouth was very dry. I tried to change position, but the Stehbunker was too small. I couldn't even lean against the wall; there wasn't enough floor space to allow an angle.

Time dragged on endlessly. I was reminded of the first day of the Uściług action, when we were hiding in the ditch. I tried some uplifting thoughts, about German defeats and how Hitler must be suffering, knowing that his end was near, but that didn't work for long. My knees started to hurt, and Fred told me to rub my legs, which helped a little. Finally I dozed off, but only for a moment; it was hard to sleep in a standing position. It seemed as though the night would never end. Fred and I spoke from time to time. We both felt that since they were almost certainly going to kill us, it would be better if they did it soon. We worried too about Sam and Felek, who probably thought we were dead by now. We hoped that the SS would not punish them for being our brothers.

When the little ray of light appeared again, we knew the long night was over. It was probably our last day, and we tried to prepare ourselves for whatever might come. It was getting very painful standing in the Stehbunker, and again we wondered if they were going to bring us any food, or at least a little water. Thirst was becoming unbearable, worse than the pain. Hunger was the least of our discomforts. Time crawled. I watched the movement of the ray of light, trying to calculate what time it was, wishing for somebody, almost anyone, to come, for something to happen. The ray of light grew fainter, then disappeared. It was night again. We couldn't understand why they hadn't taken us out during the day, either for more interrogation or to kill us. Probably they were trying to soften us up in the Stehbunker so that we would "confess." The mere thought of staying there much longer was terrifying. I felt that I was gradually sinking into a stupor. I had read about medieval prisons in which prisoners were kept in conditions similar to this, and now I knew what it was like.

The swelling on my head went down and I could feel my skull again. It hurt when I touched it. Thirst was becoming worse every moment, and now I was having trouble breathing. I urinated against the wall, and wondered how I would be able to move my bowels standing up. The night dragged on and on, and now and then I sank into a kind of sleep.

The ray of light appeared once more. Fred and I were exhausted and aching in every joint. We could scarcely talk, our throats were so dry; we managed only to exchange a few words from time to time. Nothing happened; no one came. My tongue started to swell and my lips cracked. I was losing all sense of time. The light disappeared again; we were into our third night. Occasionally I called out to Fred to make sure he was still conscious. Once when I called out he didn't answer. "Fred! Fred!" I screamed, and finally he responded. He must have fainted. My tongue was so big it almost blocked my throat, and I could hardly breathe. The light came once again, and I thought that if this continued for one more day I would probably choke to death. My tongue was so swollen that scarcely any air was getting through my mouth or nose. I wheezed every time I took a breath.

Suddenly I heard the door to the bunker open. Two SS guards came in talking loudly. Then I heard a key turn in the lock to my door. "Raus!" the guard yelled. I tried to walk, but my legs were so stiff I could hardly move. They let Fred out too, and when he emerged he had to lean against the wall of the corridor. The guards gave us a few seconds to straighten our legs, then pushed us out through the barracks door. The daylight blinded me at first, and I kept blinking, trying to adjust to it. As we stumbled along I took a look at Fred's face. It was awful, swollen and covered with purple bruises and dried blood. I saw that they were taking us back to the SS office. "Here comes another beating," I thought. I reminded Fred of our decision to stick to our story no matter what.

When we arrived at the SS headquarters, Müller and another officer were standing outside. When Müller saw us, he said to the other, "Diese sind die zwei Verbrecher." (These are the two criminals.)

To us he said, "You better tell me right now where that money is, or you're going back to the bunker." We told him again that we didn't have any money. Müller looked at Fred and said to his companion, "Look at this Jew. He would like to kill me right now; I can see it in his eyes." He then kicked Fred in the shin as hard as he could and said to us, "You can be sure that both of you will be hanged as soon as I get approval from Berlin." He turned to the guards and ordered: "Take these two to the *Strafkommando* [the penalty commando]."

As the guards marched us off, I felt confused and relieved. Müller hadn't beaten us up again, but what had he meant about approval from Berlin? Why couldn't he just hang us right away? It was unheard of, the SS needing authorization from higher up to kill Jews. Was it because we belonged to the Chemiker Kommando? That seemed unlikely. And how long would it take for him to get "approval"?

We arrived at the quarry where the Strafkommando was working and joined the fifty or so other prisoners on the detail. On the run we had to pick up and carry big stones to a waiting truck. Compared to the Stehbunker, this was a picnic; even the blows we were dealt by the SS as we were running didn't bother us much. A fifteen-minute lunch break came soon after we arrived. The first thing we did was get a drink of water. We had gone seventy-two hours without water, and the feel of it running over my swollen tongue and cracked lips was bliss. Fred's leg had been badly damaged by Müller's kick, the flesh torn and bloody. Fortunately, though, the bone wasn't broken, and he was able to carry and run with the stones.

At the end of the day we marched back to the camp, and soon all four of us were reunited; we kept hugging and kissing one another. Felek and Sam were overjoyed; they'd been certain they would never see us alive again, although their pleasure at our return was dampened by Müller's threat to hang us. Everyone was puzzled by what he had said about approval from Berlin. But despite this new cloud hanging over us, we could rejoice at being together again. It felt wonderful too to lie down on my bunk after the evening Appel; compared with the Stehbunker the bare wooden slats felt like a feather bed. I was so exhausted that I fell asleep at once and didn't wake up all night.

The next morning Fred and I were afraid they would send us out to work again in the Strafkommando, but our names weren't called during the Appel, so we happily returned to our Chemiker Kommando barracks. My fellow mathematicians were glad to see me back; they too were amazed that we were still alive. No one had ever heard of a prisoner physically resisting an SS guard and not being immediately executed. They were also mystified by the "approval from Berlin." We speculated that perhaps the SS was running short of Jews; there were jokes about what a precious commodity we had become.*

A few days later we heard the news that our crazed camp commandant, Amon Goeth, had been arrested. We didn't believe it at first, but it was soon confirmed by the prisoners who worked in the main office of the camp. Evidently, in the wake of the Chilowicz affair, the Gestapo had found out about the rake-off in money, gold, and jewelry he had been getting from Chilowicz and his gang. Everyone was happy to hear about Goeth's downfall, especially those who had been in Płaszów the longest and had often witnessed his killings and torture.

When we assembled for the evening Appel a few days after that, we were greeted by the sight of three Jews hanging from the gallows, and

---

*Not until after the war did I learn that in fact sometime late in the summer of 1944 all the concentration camps had been notified that the execution of any prisoner had to be approved by Gestapo headquarters in Berlin. The reason for this we never learned; the most likely explanation is that the Gestapo and SS camp personnel, in order to avoid being sent to the front themselves, needed to keep the camps filled with prisoners.

an announcement that they had been sentenced to death for planning an escape. This was the first time we had heard the words "sentenced to death," another innovation, like "approval from Berlin." Never before had the Gestapo or SS found it necessary to justify the killing of Jews with any explanation whatsoever. Fred and I wondered how long it would be before we were hanging there ourselves. At every morning and evening Appel I was waiting tensely for our names to be called; I knew that Müller would get the approval to hang us, and unless something unexpected happened we were going to die soon. It didn't cheer me up any when one evening after supper, Fehringer came over to me and said, "Don't think your crime has been forgotten. The doctor and you too will be hanging soon."

Over the past couple of weeks the situation on the fronts had not changed much. In the West the Allies had paused on the borders of Germany, and the Russian front in Poland was not very active. The Red Army was busy clearing the Balkans. Romania and Bulgaria had turned against their former allies, and in fact declared war on Germany, but this seemed unlikely to make any difference to us. Something drastic had to happen, and soon, if Fred and I were to be saved.

One morning in the second week in September, after the count on the Appelplatz was finished, the guards separated some of the prisoners in our barracks from the rest, Sam, Richie, and me among them. They started marching us toward the gate. I tried to explain to one of the guards that we belonged to the special Chemiker Kommando, but he just hit me over the head with his club and threatened to do it again if I said another word.

They were taking us toward Hujowa Górka, we soon realized, for there was a very unpleasant odor of burning. When we arrived at the Górka we were overwhelmed by a sickening sight. The ditches in which the thousands of Jews who had been killed on the Górka were buried had been opened and the earth removed from the top, exposing hundreds of naked, rotting corpses. The SS were going wild, frenziedly hitting and cursing the prisoners, some of whom were taking the corpses out of the ditches, others carrying them to a clearing a few hundred feet away, and still others stacking them up, pouring gasoline over them, and setting them on fire.

I threw up at the sight. Sam, Richie, and I were assigned to be corpse carriers. With one person holding a corpse's legs and the other the arms, we carried it on the run to the clearing, the SS hitting us and yelling at us all the while to run faster. I was literally in shock, in a daze; I didn't look at the bodies as I was carrying them, sometimes with Sam, sometimes with Richie. The feel of the cold, decomposing flesh was sickening. I moved as if in a dream, a terrible nightmare. The stench of the rotting and burning flesh was worse than anything I had ever known; I threw up several more times. My back hurt terribly, and Sam and Richie let me carry the legs of the corpses, which made it easier.

When at the end of the day they ordered us back to camp, I was so upset I couldn't speak. Fred and Felek had been lucky; they and most of the others in the Chemiker Kommando had gone to work as usual. It was impossible to even think of eating that evening. After the Appel I went to my bunk in a stupor and lay awake most of the night in dread of the morning's Appel and having to return to that place. As it turned out, though, I was lucky; our entire commando was sent to our usual workplace. But I couldn't concentrate on my work all day, and from then on I worried more about being taken back to Hujowa Górka than about being hanged.

After the Appel one morning toward the end of September they ordered the nine mathematicians from our commando to step out of the ranks. Three SS guards surrounded us and led us to the gate. It was so unexpected and happened so fast that Sam and I had only enough time to shout "Good-bye!" to Fred and Felek, who remained behind with the rest of the prisoners.

At the gate each of us was given a fairly large portion of bread and margarine; then we were loaded onto a waiting truck. One of the guards sat with the driver, the other two in the back with us. I was unhappy at being separated from Fred and Felek, but I was glad to be leaving Płaszów, where the order to hang us could come at any time. Fred, of course, was still in grave danger, and I was hoping they would evacuate the rest of the Chemiker Kommando soon. It was a good sign that the mathematicians were being moved out as a unit. That meant we were going to continue our work; it was an extension of our lease on life. Perhaps this time they would take us deep into Germany so that we wouldn't have to be evacuated again. I also felt that a group of only nine Jews was not very conspicuous, and might get lost in the shuffle at the end of the war. We had no idea if there were any Jews at all left in Germany, in concentration camps or anywhere else.

The truck pulled into the Krakow railway station, and the guards ordered us out. We had never seen them before; the three of them were very young and treated us well, although they seemed to have had orders to guard us very closely. We tried to find out where they were taking us, but they were not forthcoming. They led us through the station to a track with a sign over it that read *"Nach Berlin."* Was it possible? Berlin!

The other travelers stared at us, three armed SS guarding nine Jews in striped suits. I felt like an exotic animal on the way to the circus. Our guards took us into a waiting train, also marked "Berlin." It was a Pullman car, with separate compartments joined by a long, narrow corridor. Standing in the corridor were German women with children—Volksdeutsche, apparently, who were afraid of being caught by the Russians in their next big thrust to the west—and a lot of German soldiers, some wounded, others probably on leave from the Russian front. There was a feeling of evacuation, of crowds on the move, but not of panic. To make way for us our guards pushed slowly through the mass of people, who whispered and pointed at us. Every compartment we passed was jammed, with not even standing room left. In the middle of a car our guards stopped at a compartment that was empty—reserved for us, it seemed. They let us in and stationed themselves at the door.

What a farce! In this train, for a change, the Germans were packed in like sardines, while nine Jewish prisoners rode in comfort in a private compartment! We took out our bread and margarine, but were careful to eat only part of it, not knowing how long it would have to last. Through the window we saw a mob of frantic people trying to force their way in. Some were screaming at the conductors because they had tickets for the trip but couldn't get on the train.

Just outside our compartment was a colonel of the Wehrmacht sitting on his trunk. His leg was all bandaged, and the bandage was soaked with blood. Prominent on his chest was the Iron Cross, which was awarded only for exceptional bravery. He politely asked our guards to let him into our compartment so that he could lie down, but they told him they had orders to keep us separated from everyone else. The colonel tried to reason with them, but they insisted they could make no exceptions. He grew more and more angry, and finally burst into a tirade against the SS, literally foaming at the mouth, screaming that here he was, a colonel of the Wehrmacht who had shed his blood for the Fatherland, having to defer to a bunch of lazy cowards who were using the damned Jews as an excuse not to fight. At first our guards didn't answer him; one of them tried to explain again that they were just follow- ing orders, but the colonel would have none of it. Now the other Germans on the train entered the fray, one woman screaming that her children were worn out and the dirty Jews were keeping them from their sleep.

All this was making me nervous. If it continued, some higher-up in the Gestapo or the SS might come and take our compartment away from us. Fortunately, just then the train started to pull out of the station. We were surprised to see anybody, even a colonel, daring to rebuke the SS in public. Either the legendary German discipline was breaking down, or the SS was losing its power to terrorize. The whole scene was very funny, but of course we didn't dare laugh or even crack a smile.

The train rolled northward, making frequent stops, and at every station crowds of people were frantically trying to board it. Soon we arrived at the German frontier, where frontier inspectors came on board to check everyone's papers. They too were surprised to see us all alone in the compartment, and had a prolonged discussion about it with our guards. Finally the train pulled out again, and there we were—inside Germany. Where on earth could they be taking us? Our professor was from Berlin, so perhaps we were going to a big concentration camp in Oranienburg, which was not far from Berlin. We all felt more hopeful than we had permitted ourselves to be in a long time, although it was still hard to believe that the SS would ever let us survive, unless the war ended so suddenly that they had no chance to kill us first.

We passed Breslau, a major German city, and were still heading north, toward Berlin. We had now been on the train for several hours, and some of us had to go to the toilet—a major undertaking. We had to go singly, always with a guard accompanying us. When my turn came, I realized that I had almost forgotten that there was such a thing as a normal toilet, with a seat. What a fantastic luxury!

Night fell, and the guards warned us against any attempt to escape—unnecessarily, for what would we do in the middle of

Germany with nothing but our striped prison suits? We lay down on the benches to get some sleep. There was plenty of room for us all to stretch out comfortably, which gave the colonel another fit when he saw us do it.

When we woke up in the morning, we saw signs saying that Berlin was only a hundred kilometers away. We were deep inside Germany. It was the first time in my life that I had been outside Poland, and the villages and farms looked cleaner and more prosperous than those I had known. Soon we were approaching the suburbs of Berlin. I felt joy in my heart at the sight of the great tracts of rubble caused by the pounding the outskirts of the city had been getting from the Allied bombers.

We pulled into the Berlin station a little before noon. Our guards waited until all the passengers left the train before ordering us out. The station was very busy and crowded, and as we walked through it with our SS escort we attracted a lot more attention. They led us downstairs to the subway. We were once again anxious to know where they were taking us, but they refused to give us any clues. One thing was obvious; neither of them knew the city, because they had to keep stopping people to ask for directions. We arrived at the subway platform eventually, and waited for our train. It arrived and the doors opened, disgorging a crowd of passengers. The guards waited until everyone else had boarded the train, then let us in. Apparently they had never ridden the subway before, because after the nine of us were inside the car the doors suddenly closed in front of their noses, and they were left standing outside as the train pulled out. They ran after it along the platform, but it was too late. For a few seconds we could see them running alongside us in dismay, helplessly waving their arms.

The other passengers didn't know what had happened; all they saw was nine people they assumed to be criminals, and no one guarding them. Most of them fled to the ends of the car, getting as far away from us as possible, leaving us standing alone in the middle. We too were shocked and confused by this bizarre turn of events. To those few who hadn't run away, we tried to explain what had happened, in order to have witnesses that we hadn't attempted to escape.

When the train pulled into the next station, we decided to stay on it. We found we were on a line that circled Berlin, and the train would soon return to the stop where we had lost our guards; we could only hope that they would be smart enough to wait for us at the station where we had become separated. In the meantime, as new passengers kept getting in at the stations along the way, we kept repeating our explanation to anyone who would listen. It was like a scene from a comedy skit, but we were too scared to see the humor of it. After half an hour or so, we had come back to the station where we had lost our guards. There was no sign of them. Our safest course, we decided, was to stay in the car. Arno was especially helpful, since he spoke perfect German and was able to explain the situation to each new batch of passengers that entered the car. We kept circling Berlin; when we returned to our original station for the second or third time, there were our three hapless guards waiting on the platform. They were simple country boys who had become so unnerved at losing us that they had jumped on the next train. They had been following us as we circled around Berlin, until someone advised them to go back to the station where we became separated and wait for us there. We were all very happy to see one another, and I practically had to restrain myself from embracing them.

This time we all got on the train together, and after a few stops we got off and into another railway station, where after about a half-hour wait we boarded a train marked *"Nach Hamburg."* This one wasn't full, and our separate compartment caused no commotion.

Once again we were traveling through the German countryside, the North German plain. It was very flat and not as densely populated as the area south of Berlin. We still had no idea where they were taking us.

When it was almost evening, the train pulled into a small railway station, where, to our surprise and disappointment, we saw a sign *"To Ravensbrück."* We had hoped that perhaps they were taking us someplace other than another concentration camp. Ravensbrück, we knew, was the largest women's concentration camp in Germany; we hadn't known there were any men there.

Our guards led us out of the train and marched us toward the huge barbed wire enclosure, which had dozens of guard towers. We walked past several separate sections of the camp, and finally stopped in front of a small one that had only seven or eight buildings. Our guards showed their papers to the SS guards at the gate, who let us in. They separated the female "mathematician" from the rest of us and took her away, apparently to the women's camp. Inside we were met by an SS officer accompanied by a German Lagerälteste wearing the green triangle that meant he was a criminal. He was a large man who looked a little like Lionel Barrymore. Our guards turned our papers over to the officer, saluted, and left. At the sight of our yellow triangles the Lagerälteste exclaimed, "Juden! What are you doing here? I thought there were no more Jews left!" Stark tried to tell him about our mathematics commando, which only irritated him. "What kind of shit is this?" he yelled. "We'll soon take care of you!"

Ravensbrück

■

We went through the reception routine (shower, search, and so forth) and were given our new prisoner numbers. This time Sam and I didn't have to worry about hiding our money; we had none left. Compared with the camps in Poland, the latrine was clean, which made me very happy. Everywhere we went we created a sensation among the other prisoners, who couldn't believe that the SS were bringing Jews *back* to concentration camps inside Germany. They asked us many questions, and when we told them that we were a special mathematics commando, most were surprised and skeptical. The barracks we were assigned to were similar to the ones in Poland, but not nearly so crowded.

Our Stubenälteste, Karl, was very curious about the details of our mathematical work. We told him that it was top secret, and that we had received strict orders not to discuss it with anyone. Karl, a blue-eyed blond, was very quick and alert, a street-smart Berliner, and he wasn't about to buy our story. He and the other prisoners in key positions seemed to treat the inmates decently, and the atmosphere in Ravensbrück was not as tense as in the other camps.

After having known only camps where prisoners were almost entirely Jewish (except for our short stay in Majdanek), it felt strange to be surrounded by Gentiles. Here the outlook for surviving the war was much more hopeful; there was no pervasive feeling that all prisoners would be killed before the end of the war. I still had a piece of bread left from our trip, and I ate it with the soup they dished out for dinner. It was a little thicker than the soup in Płaszów and had a few pieces of potato and turnip in it. After supper I lay down on my new bunk, thinking of Fred, Felek, and Hanka. I hoped they were all still alive and well.

My neighbor in the tier of bunks was a French prisoner of war whose name I don't recall, a very nice and friendly man who was delighted that I spoke a little French. He was an electrician, and worked most of the time doing repairs in the adjoining huge women's concentration camp. I was glad to have someone to practice my French on, and soon was able to understand him. He told me some interesting things about the women's camp. It held about forty thousand women, and it was nightmarish. The SS female guards were exceptionally cruel, and tens of thousands of the women prisoners from all over Europe—many of them sent there after the Warsaw uprising of 1944—were dying from the continual beatings, not to mention the hunger. On top of that, German doctors were using the prisoners to conduct medical experiments. One of the barracks was called the "rabbit block," where hundreds of women were being injected with various chemicals, subjected to surgical operations, and generally treated as if they were rabbits. Ravensbrück also had a gas chamber where the sick and weak were gassed and then burned in ovens.

The prisoners who held positions of power, the Blockälteste and the Kapos, were mostly Polish women, who had developed a highly organized system of extortion and bribery. Food and many other things were obtainable in exchange for gold and precious stones. In Ravensbrück too the prisoners received smaller rations of bread and margarine than they were supposed to, because the Kapos and Block-älteste were holding some of it back to sell. They had become utterly dehumanized; many of them had become lesbians, and whenever a new transport of prisoners arrived in the camp, they would select the prettiest among them and force them to become their lovers. Others, who had remained "straight," were always on the lookout for the chance for some quick sex with the male prisoners who were occasionally brought in from the male camp to do specialized jobs. For this privilege they paid off the SS guards with gold and jewelry that they extorted from the newly arrived prisoners. The Frenchman's graphic account of the brutality of these women made a deep impression on me. I had somehow expected women to be less savage than men.

I was tired after our long trip, and despite our confusion and uncertainty I fell sound asleep that night and didn't wake up until morning, when we each got our piece of bread and bit of marmalade, and went out for the Appel. It was cold, but fortunately the count didn't take long. After the various work commandos left, only the eight of us remained standing. The Lagerälteste asked the SS officer in charge what to do with us, but apparently didn't get any help from him. Frustrated, he came back and after some hesitation told us to go to the yard behind his barracks and chop wood. We were very disappointed; something must have gone wrong. Again we had been sent as a group to a new camp, where they had received no instructions as to what to do with us.

The eight of us spent the day chopping wood with no supervision. Just before the evening Appel the Lagerälteste came back, accused us of laziness, and cursed us out. But he was clearly as confused as we were, and didn't know what to make of us.

This went on for about a week. To keep us busy we were given various work assignments within the camp, such as cleaning the latrine, chopping wood, and unloading supplies. The other prisoners didn't bother us, and we became friendly with a few of them. The population of the camp consisted of a motley mixture of French and Russian prisoners of war, Gypsies, German political prisoners, criminals, homosexuals, and *Bibelforschers* (Jehovah's Witnesses and conscientious objectors). Bibelforschers wore lavender triangles and were wonderful, decent people. They were very idealistic, very serene, and even though some of the guards and the Kapos treated them with contempt, they never replied, defended themselves, or complained in any way. I deeply admired these people for their courage and moral strength.

Some of the political prisoners were also exceptional human beings. They too were singled out by the SS guards for harsh treatment. I got to know one of them. His name was Willie, and he was one of the bravest men I have ever met. He was of medium build, with piercing, intelligent eyes and a ready smile. Willie always seemed to have a cold and kept blowing his nose all the time. He had been active in the German Communist party and had been in and out of concentration camps ever since Hitler had come to power, when Willie was still a teenager. He was very outspoken in his scorn for the Nazis, and when a guard hit a prisoner in his presence he would protest loudly, sometimes even placing himself between the guard and his victim. He would often get beaten up himself, but that never discouraged him. I was fascinated by Willie's bravery and his willingness to absorb punishment, even risking his life sometimes for complete strangers. Such extraordinary courage was in stark contrast to the behavior of the rest of the prisoners.

Since Ravensbrück was my fourth concentration camp, I had observed certain behavioral patterns in prisoners, and in my mind I had divided them into four basic categories. A small number were simply brutal by nature; many of these became Kapos or Stubenälteste. A fairly large number of the others were people of low character. Within days of their arrival in the camps they would start stealing, begging, pushing themselves in front of the others, with total indifference to everyone else. The third group consisted of people who were honest and wouldn't hurt anybody, but never went out of their way to help others. Their attitude was "Don't bother me, and I won't bother you."

Finally, there was a rather small number of people like Richie or Bencio, always kind to others, trying to be helpful as far as they could, never taking advantage of other prisoners. They were the moral elite, and always behaved in a way that showed their "class" no matter how terrible the circumstances; something within them refused to become dehumanized and demoralized. In the brutal atmosphere of concentration camps, there could be no pretense, no concealing one's true nature; it was there for anyone to see.

I felt sorry for the Gypsies, who were there simply because they had been born Gypsies, and for no other reason. They were not being exterminated en masse like the Jews, but they had all been herded into camps, where they were at the mercy of the SS, who often made fun of them.

The homosexuals, who wore pink triangles, were another group who had been singled out by the Nazis and sent to camps without having committed any offense. They not only had to endure harsh treatment from the guards, but were constantly ridiculed by the other prisoners as well. One of them, "Mona," managed to get hold of some lipstick and rouge and walked around defiantly swinging his hips like a woman. Mona seemed to enjoy the attention, even when it took the form of ribbing and abuse.

It was about October 7 when our professor finally showed up. We greeted him, needless to say, with great joy. He brought with him our machines and a new batch of sheets, and told Stark that he had worked out an arrangement for us with the SS Lagerkommandant. Since no suitable space was available outside the camp, a table would be set up in our sleeping barracks where we could do our work after the morning Appel was over and the other prisoners had left with their work commandos.

What a break! We didn't even have to leave the camp to go to work! Stark was effusive in his thanks to the professor, who permitted himself a small, enigmatic smile. He wished us good day and left. Exultant, we slapped each other on the backs. The saga of our commando was still continuing, and we had just entered another chapter of it. There could no longer be the slightest doubt: the professor and his colleagues were putting one over on Hitler. What imagination and guts it must have taken, to invent this preposterous scheme and sell it to the SS! Or perhaps one or more of the key leaders of the SS were willing accomplices to it because one never could tell when it might prove advantageous to be part of a plan to save Jewish superbrains. It was mind-boggling: a ragtag crew of Jewish prisoners trying to save their lives by pretending to be scientists were saving a few Germans from having to fight on the battlefront in the eleventh hour of the war. I was full of admiration for the professor and his bunch. "You did it again, you bastards!" They must have had nerves of steel to continue this charade, considering the consequences of someone exposing their "sting."*

---

*Speaking of real scientists, had Hitler's attitude toward Jews been different, it's conceivable that the course and outcome of World War II might have been affected. Jewish scientists in Germany, Austria, Hungary, and other European countries that had fallen into Hitler's hands happened to be in the forefront of nuclear research, which eventually led to the development of the atom bomb. People like Leó Szilárd, Enrico Fermi, Lise Meitner, Edward Teller, and Albert Einstein fled to escape the Nazis' racial policies, and later

The next morning after the Appel, the machines and a table were brought into our barracks, and soon we were back to punching the keys again. The female member of our commando had not rejoined us though. Apparently it was against the SS rules to have a woman work inside an all-male concentration camp. Karl, the Stubenälteste, and the other prisoners stared at us in disbelief. Our farfetched story was true after all. Even the SS camp commandant came to see what was going on. When Stark showed him the envelope marked "High Command of the German Navy—Top Secret," he just shook his head in wonder and left. At first Karl and the other prisoners regarded us with amusement, but after a few days we began to sense some resentment.

Hunger was now a serious problem. Ever since Fehringer had taken our last twenty-dollar bill in Płaszów, Sam and I had had nothing but the camp rations, which had a nutritional value of about five hundred calories a day. As the weeks went by I felt a constant gnawing in my stomach. My entire body yearned for food. There was a sensation in my mouth of wanting to taste bread, and every minute or so I would wet my lips and swallow. In the mornings when I received my daily ration of bread, I made sure to divide it carefully into three or four parts, in order to have at least a small supply of energy throughout the day. For some reason, the only food I longed for was bread. Bread was on my mind all the time. It was a great stroke of good fortune, which probably saved my life, that our

were very instrumental in the United States becoming the world's first power to make atomic weapons. It's entirely possible that had these very same scientists been working on behalf of Germany, it and not the United States could have been the first nation to have atomic weapons at its disposal. This in turn could have changed history. It's hard to imagine England not seeking some accommodation with Hitler had London and other English cities been destroyed by atomic bombs during the 1941–1945 period.

working hours were spent sitting on the bench and punching keys, which didn't consume much energy; I cannot imagine that I would have survived if I had had to do hard physical labor on the rations we received. As it was, I was steadily losing weight. In Ravensbrück I estimated my weight to be between a hundred and a hundred and five pounds; Sam was probably well below a hundred.

Food was the central topic of our conversations, and we all urged Stark to ask the professor to try to get us additional rations. After all, how could he expect seven experts, using all that brain power, to continue to give their best to the Third Reich while suffering from chronic hunger? On the professor's next visit he seemed to be in a good mood, and Stark boldly brought up the subject of extra rations. Immediately the professor's face fell; he was clearly troubled by the suggestion. It wasn't that he didn't want to help us, but he was probably too frightened of doing anything that might rock the boat. He promised to try, but with no conviction, and in fact nothing happened. Our only relief came from a Stubenälteste from another barracks who wanted someone to wash his socks. Sam was happy to oblige, and for this service every few days he was given a small slice of bread, which he shared with me. It wasn't much, but every extra bite made a difference.

In our barracks was a former Polish army sergeant who entertained us in the evenings with tales of his prewar gastronomic exploits. His favorite story was about his Sunday breakfasts. Every Sunday morning, no matter where he was, the sergeant's breakfast was the same: a large Jewish challah (white bread made with eggs and sugar) and a quart of milk. But it wasn't so much what he ate, but the way he ate it. He would break off bite-size pieces of the challah with his fingers (he made a point of stressing that he never used a knife or fork for this purpose), dip the pieces in a large glass of warm milk, and slowly swallow them, allowing plenty of time between bites to digest them properly. His vivid descriptions of these Sunday breakfasts were works of art, mesmerizing, sensual. I used to follow his story bite by bite, eyes closed, experiencing in my mind this supreme event in all its deliciousness. We all admired this fellow: "Look at this. Here is a Polish sergeant, whom many people might perhaps unthinkingly assume to be not too bright— now see how smart he really is. He was clever enough to know, in good times, just how to eat such wholesome and delicious food." I promised myself that should I by some miracle survive the war, I would follow the sergeant's menu for the rest of my life and never deviate from it.*

Week after week went by during this period without anything decisive happening in the progress of the war. It was early December, and the Russians were fighting the Germans in the streets of Budapest. It was only a matter of time before the Allies launched their next big offensive. To us, of course, timing was crucial. The best thing for us would have been Hitler's sudden fall from power. He would never surrender, I knew, no matter how hopeless his situation, not after such crimes as he had committed. But short of Hitler's assassination or sudden toppling from power by a coup, it was hard to imagine a scenario where we would survive. Sometimes we discussed the chances of the eight of us becoming lost in the shuffle during the final stages of the war, but that was unlikely. Our chances were better now, of course, than they had been during the mass killings of 1942, but it was the difference between one chance in a million then and perhaps one in a hundred now. Still, having made it so far, we kept hoping. We spent so much time together that except for Stark, who was not friendly with anyone, and Arno, who

---

*I'm sorry to say that when I tried it after liberation, the old magic just wasn't there.

was always withdrawn, I grew to know the others quite well. We talked a lot about the good life before the war, our favorite books and actors, and so on, but it was all escapism. The moment of decision was fast approaching.

One day in December there was a great commotion among the Gypsies. It seemed they had been given the chance to be released from the camp if they would agree to be sterilized. We had heard stories from other camps where Gypsies were being sterilized whether they liked it or not. After much vociferous discussion, most of them decided not to be sterilized and to remain in the camp. Talking over what we would do in their place, without exception we agreed that we would jump at the chance. We even debated the theoretical question of trading our chances of survival for a definite limited period of freedom. Again we all thought we would agree to the exchange, the only variation being in the length of time each of us would demand; it ranged from two weeks to one year of good life, with plenty of food. I was so consumed with the desire to see Hitler's end that I would gladly have traded my chance of survival for just a few months of life in the postwar period.

But despite the hunger and the hardships and the bleakness of our prospects, Ravensbrück was not so bad as the other camps we had been in. The relative tranquility of our existence there, and the lack of any imminent daily threat to our lives, gave our nerves some badly needed rest.

On the evening of December 16, I overheard Karl talking about a German offensive in the West. This seemed ridiculous, impossible. To begin with, Hitler had nothing left with which to launch any attack; and whatever strength he might have had, he would certainly prefer to use against the Russians, his most hated enemy. Since by now I considered myself an expert military analyst, I presented this authoritative view to my mathematician colleagues, and then went to sleep. Over the next few days we all learned how mistaken I had been. The German offensive was indeed taking place; the Allies had been taken by surprise, and the Germans were on the move. They claimed to have penetrated about fifty miles along the Allied front. Although a prisoner himself, Karl was a German patriot, and predicted that the Germans would soon retake Aachen, Liège, and even Brussels—and should that happen, the entire Western front would collapse. I never took this seriously because I knew that as soon as the weather improved the Germans would have no chance whatsoever against the Allied command of the air. I thought of the first days of the German attack on the Soviets, when their Stukas roamed the skies of the Ukraine at will, putting an end to all Soviet ground troop movement. However, the mere fact that the Germans were still capable of a large-scale attack was disquieting; it showed that they had stabilized the Western front after all, which meant there was little chance of any imminent collapse.

As the days went by, it became clear that the Allied reverse was short-lived. About January 10 I got hold of a German newspaper containing a military communiqué, and when I saw the familiar "heavy defensive battles in the West," I knew that everything was fine. It was also in January that we heard the news of the start of a new Russian offensive in Poland. On January 17 Warsaw fell, the Russians driving back the defeated Germans in western Poland. By the end of January virtually all of Poland was in Russian hands, and the Russians were approaching the Oder River; they were only about a hundred miles away from us. The speed of the Russian advance was surprising; apparently the Germans were completely unable now to stem the Russian tide. It was very exciting, but also very dangerous. What would happen to us as the Russians got still closer? Would the SS evacuate us again? Despite the risks to us, I could not contain my joy at the German rout. There was great historic justice in all this, and my heart was full of admiration for the Russians. I hoped fervently that it would be they who captured Hitler, not the Allies, who would be too humane. I wanted to see Hitler in a cage. In the meantime I rejoiced at the thought of him squirming like a trapped rat, knowing that soon he would have to pay for his sins against his fellow men.

Meanwhile, a transport of about eight hundred Hungarian Jews unexpectedly arrived from Auschwitz. It was good to see that so many Jews were still alive, and it also touched us more directly as an indication that at least some Jewish prisoners were being evacuated from Poland; perhaps Fred, Felek, and Hanka would be among the evacuees. On the other hand, hope dimmed for the eight of us somehow being able to mingle with non-Jews in the confusion at the end of the war. A critical factor was whether the Russians would continue their drive, which meant they would reach us soon, or halt again before the final assault. So far in the war, after every advance of a hundred kilometers or so they stopped to bring up supplies, and such a pause now would delay the liberation of the camp. A new evacuation now dominated all our conversations, especially the question of whether the SS might decide to kill us rather than go to the trouble of evacuating us. After all, how important could our commando be, no matter how persuasive our professor had been? The end of the war, of the whole German Reich, was near. There was great turmoil and fear in our hearts and minds.

One day in the first week of February 1945, after the morning Appel the SS ordered all Jews to line up at the gate. We desperately searched for someone who would ascertain whether there actually were orders that the eight of us were to be included, but no one would bother to check. The Lagerälteste personally made sure we were in the group that was assembling at the gate. The fact that only Jews were being sent away looked extremely grim for us.

What an incredible relief it was to see boxes of bread at the gate! As the first rows of the Hungarian Jews were marched out, each received a piece of bread and margarine. Our lease on life was being extended, however briefly. We went to the railway station, where the SS reenacted its familiar ritual of shoving us into the waiting cattle cars while beating and kicking us for good measure. This time we were not as crowded as during the trip from Majdanek to Płaszów. At least some of us could sit, and we weren't pressed so tight against each other. We of the mathematicians Kommando kept together, still hopeful that whatever our destination, our work would continue.

After the SS locked us inside the cattle car, we remained at the station for several more hours. When the train started rolling at last, we had no idea where it was taking us, but after a while Zysman calculated from the change in the direction of the few rays of light coming in through the doors that we were moving south. This was a surprise—why would they evacuate us south and not west, away from the front?

The train progressed slowly, making frequent stops, and soon people started relieving themselves on the floor, but it was very cold and the smell wasn't as bad as on the trip to Płaszów. At each stop a conductor called out the names of the towns to come; the last one was Berlin. We *were* moving south, and we couldn't be far now, because the total distance between Ravensbrück and Berlin was only a hundred kilometers. It was growing dark, and soon we pulled into a station where the train stopped and didn't resume its journey. Many hours passed.

Sometime late in the evening we heard the droning of planes. Then came the thunder of hundreds of antiaircraft guns and thousands of bomb explosions, first from a distance, then coming closer. Wave after wave of planes flew by, and soon the entire sky was lit up; the light coming in through the crack of the door was almost as bright as in daytime. Bombs were exploding all around us. We had heard of massive Allied bombings, but hadn't expected anything like this. The rain of bombs went on for hours. It seemed as if hundreds of planes, maybe even several thousand, were pounding Berlin. How ironic, to be killed in the end by an Allied bomb! Somehow I wasn't scared at all; in fact, I enjoyed it, knowing that Germany's capital was being destroyed. At least if death came now, it would not be at the hands of the Germans.

The bombing stopped abruptly, but we spent the rest of the night at the station nevertheless. The train didn't start rolling again until early morning, and it was only minutes before we reached our destination. The voices of the guards could be heard, and the door of our car was opened. We jumped out and saw a sign: "Oranienburg." So they were taking us to the infamous Sachsenhausen-Oranienburg concentration camp. I had heard that this was the largest one of all. It was not a good omen. Why would they be taking us to a camp even closer than Ravensbrück was to the Oder River and the Russians?

The guards ordered us to form a column, and we marched out of the station. All about us was devastation from the bombing. To our surprise, the guards marched us right through the town of Oranienburg, not around it; windows opened as we passed through the streets, and people peered out at us. We marched for close to an hour, until a huge camp appeared in the distance. Soon we were standing at the gate, which bore the familiar sign over it: *Arbeit Macht Frei.*

Sachsenhausen

■

T he gigantic Sachsenhausen concentration camp was built in an enormous semicircle, each of its numerous sections surrounded by high stone walls with guard towers, searchlights, and machine guns. We were led by the guards to the reception area, made to take hot showers, and given new striped uniforms, shoes, and prisoner numbers. Again we had to attach red and yellow triangles to our jackets. Our transport was divided among only a few barracks, and the seven of us in the mathematicians Kommando managed to stay together. Since all the work commandos had already gone out before we arrived, we spent the rest of the day in our new barracks. Our Stubenälteste was a German criminal, like Karl, but he wasn't as pleasant as Karl. We told him about our Kommando in the hope that he might know something about it, but he just brushed us off.

At the end of the day, after the work commandos had returned to the camp, we went out with the rest of the prisoners to be counted on the Appelplatz. It was so vast that it seemed to swallow up even the more than forty thousand prisoners who lined up on it by blocks to be counted. The Appel took only a little over an hour, an amazingly short time for such a large count. Afterward we walked around the camp to get the lay of the land. The guards didn't seem to object to prisoners milling about, and we mingled freely with people from all over the camp. I had never seen such a variety of nationalities, from every part of Europe, by the thousands: Poles, Russians, Jews, Gypsies, Belgians, French, Dutch, Danes, Czechs, Bulgarians, Spaniards, Yugoslavs—each speaking his own language, a true Tower of Babel. There was also a large contingent of Norwegian students, who, we were told, had been sent to Sachsenhausen after they had demonstrated against the traitor Quisling. The German prisoners wore triangles of different colors, each representing a code for the type of "crime" they had committed against the Third Reich.

Sachsenhausen contained close to a hundred barracks, many housing up to five hundred men. There was a large kitchen and a bathhouse. A large barracks was marked "Pathology," and here medical experiments were performed, frequently on German homosexuals. There was even a running track offering a variety of different surfaces, so that the many local shoe manufacturers could use the prisoners to test the effectiveness of various materials. Some prisoners had to walk forty kilometers a day on this track, checking wear and tear of different shoes. Sometimes, just for fun, the guards would give the prisoners who had been selected for the tests shoes several sizes too big, so they could enjoy the spectacle of their stumbling and tripping as they tried to run. There was a station Z, where the SS exterminated "undesirable" prisoners. There was even a permanent gallows. Everywhere were big signs exhorting us to diligence, obedience, cleanliness, and order. Our heads were spinning. This place was incredible. It was as if a talented writer had written a weird, crazy, futuristic, nightmarish movie script, and then the producer actually built a huge set for it.

How was our professor ever going to find us here? He would never be able to cut through this superstructure to reach us. We went back to our barracks in a profound depression, too despondent even to talk. I went directly to my bunk and tried to fall asleep, but the images of Sachsenhausen kept crowding my mind. Every hour or two I would wake up, as though in shock at finding myself there.

Next morning it was bitterly cold. I shivered for almost two hours on the Appelplatz in my thin uniform. In Ravensbrück I hadn't much minded the Appel, knowing that soon after it was over I would be back in our nice warm barracks. Not here. Things looked bad for us; we knew no one, had no connections, no money, no way of getting extra food. It was obvious that many prisoners didn't live on camp rations alone. The young Norwegians, for instance, all looked healthy and well fed—strapping specimens of the Nordic type Hitler so admired—and in fact we learned that they and some of the others regularly received food parcels from their families. No wonder they looked so good! We, on the other hand, were the starving pariahs, reduced to skin and bones, on the way to becoming Musulmen.

We were assigned to an outdoor commando and spent the day loading and unloading trucks in subzero temperatures. The SS guards were especially rough, beating us for no reason at all. If something didn't happen soon, we would die. What kept us alive for the moment was the knowledge that the Russian army was on the Oder River, only thirty-five kilometers away. It was only a matter of weeks now, maybe no more than days, before they began their final assault on Germany.

The days dragged slowly. We always worked outdoors, at a different place almost every day, but wherever we were it was bitterly cold. We no longer had the strength to do the jobs we were given, and the guards were always beating us up. Hunger was constant. Only the certainty that both the Western Allies and the Russians would soon be launching their final offensives, that the war would be over and the matter of our survival decided one way or the other, kept us from total despair. We had little hope that our special commando would ever resume its activities; its existence could no longer be justified by any stretch of imagination. There was a strong feeling in the air that time was running out for Hitler.

Some of the other prisoners told us stories about Sachsenhausen. One, a Russian prisoner of war, had worked for over a year as a cleaner in a barracks where a group of more than a hundred Jewish printers were busy producing high-quality counterfeit British pound notes. They had recently succeeded in breaking the code for producing the special paper used by the United States Treasury, but were not quite ready yet to do the actual printing. The Jews in this printers' commando were treated well, he told us. The whole group had been shipped out of Sachsenhausen only two or three days after we arrived. Here was another special commando, except that they were the real thing; what they were doing was genuinely useful to the German war effort—a fact that dampened our spirits still further. If the SS had found it necessary to evacuate the forgers' commando, it was highly unlikely that they would let the Chemiker Kommando resume its "work" so close to the front.

A number of well-known political prisoners were incarcerated in Sachsenhausen, among them the former Austrian chancellor Kurt von Schuschnigg, and Hans Luther, the former head of the German Foreign Office. They were kept in an isolated barracks and we never saw them. A neighbor of mine, a German political prisoner who had been in Sachsenhausen for more than five years, told me that Jews and homosexuals were treated with particular cruelty. He estimated that ten thousand or more German homosexuals had been killed by the SS in Sachsenhausen since he had arrived in the camp. He told us too that sometime in 1942 the SS had locked a group of Jews in a barracks before shipping them to Auschwitz. Learning of this, a few German Jewish prisoners formed a clandestine resistance group, which broke ranks during an evening Appel and actually started to push and shove the SS guards, demanding that they free the Jews in the barracks. The other prisoners looked on in astonishment at this collective act of desperate—and futile—courage. To everyone's amazement, these rebels were not executed immediately, but a few weeks later they were shipped to Auschwitz with the others.

My German neighbor was outspoken in his criticism of the Nazis, and of Hitler in particular. He never referred to him by name, always as *Der Hund* (the dog). "The time is coming soon, the dog will pay," he used to say to me. Sam warned me against becoming too friendly with this man, lest one of the other prisoners denounce him to the SS, which might endanger my life too, by association.

One great help in this difficult time was a contact I had established with a prisoner who was well informed on what was happening on the war fronts. He worked outside the camp in a shoe factory, where he had become friendly with the owner, who had a shortwave radio and listened regularly to the BBC. In the West, I learned, the Allies had begun their offensive and were advancing inside Germany. A massive new Russian offensive was expected any day. The BBC was predicting that the war would end in a matter of weeks, which increased our tension to an almost unbearable pitch. The moment of decision was at hand. Hold on! Hold on!

One day late in February we were at the morning Appel, which seemed to go on forever in the bitter cold. As it ended, I heard an announcement which I couldn't quite make out. My German neighbor, who was standing next to me, said, "You're a mathematician, aren't you? They're looking for you." Sam was standing on my other side, and he too thought he had heard them say "mathematicians." My heart leapt. Could it possibly be true? Had our professor actually managed to find us again? We ran like mad to our Stubenälteste, who grudgingly admitted that the SS were trying to locate a special group of mathematicians, and told us to go to the main office of the camp. We ran there, and the clerk confirmed that a professor from Berlin had been given special permission to set up our Kommando again. He told us to wait. After about an hour we saw the professor coming toward us. Stark was speechless from excitement; I couldn't believe my eyes. Once again, just when we needed him the most, our professor had appeared out of the blue to come to our rescue, like some mythical magician. It was really too good to be true. The mere thought of not having to work outdoors, half frozen, day after day, filled my heart with happiness. The professor greeted us, arranged with the camp officials for a table and benches to be set up in our barracks, gave Stark an envelope with new sheets, said good-bye, and went away.

We spent the rest of the day taking it easy, chatting and speculating about how long this new stage of our Kommando would last. With the Russians almost upon us and Germany so near collapse, how was our professor able to keep his "sting" going? Stark was full of admiration. "You've got to hand it to him. He must have powerful connections." For the first time since our arrival in Sachsenhausen, I enjoyed a good night's sleep.

In the morning even the cold didn't bother me, since I knew that as soon as the Appel was over we would be back in our barracks. Even if the war went on for several more weeks, our chances of surviving had vastly improved.

When we returned to the barracks we found that our Stubenälteste didn't at all relish the thought of eight Jews hanging around his barracks all day, and was loudly giving vent to his doubts about us and our Kommando. He attacked men like our professor, who shirked their duty to fight when Germany's very life was threatened and fifteen-year-old boys and old men were being sent to the front. We were careful not to say anything that might anger him further, and waited patiently until he was finished with his tirade. He then ordered his assistant to set up the table and benches, and left the barracks in disgust.

In no time there I was, back at my machine, banging away at the keys. This was just what the doctor ordered—rest. Our spirits rose. Our only worry was our conspicuousness, even in a camp as large as Sachsenhausen. There were too many SS officers roaming around, and any one of them might take it into his head to question the need for our Kommando at a time when Germany was so near to collapse.

In the days that followed, work in the math Kommando was a respite, a balm to our nerves, which had been frayed by physical abuse and hard labor—too hard for our starving bodies. Yet the tension was becoming harder to bear every day. The clock of our destiny was ticking away relentlessly; we knew that we were at five minutes to noon, when, after all we had endured, all the incredible luck that had brought us through this far, our fate would be decided in one brief moment—either a life of freedom, with all its joys, or brutal death. Every fiber of my body ached to survive, if only to know the excruciating pleasure of witnessing the downfall of Hitler and the SS, cornered like rats, fleeing the sword of justice but ferreted out one by one and made to pay for the bestialities they had inflicted on their fellow human beings. I wanted to be free to go where I pleased, not to be denied life just because I was a Jew. I wanted to meet and embrace those brave men who were fighting to liberate us and restore sanity to a world gone mad. I wanted to find my brothers and sister, hug and kiss them, and together shed tears of sorrow for our parents, who had been forced to lie down naked, to be killed in cold blood. I wanted to shed tears of happiness for them, that their children had survived and would continue the family line. The thought of the decisive days at hand dominated my every waking moment, to the exclusion of everything else.

Meanwhile, we went on with our work. The professor visited us once a week, bringing with him new sheets of meaningless numbers, but his visits were becoming shorter. We could sense his discomfort; he became especially uneasy whenever the Stubenälteste was watching us from a distance.

It was the end of March when we began hearing the first sporadic exchanges of artillery. Although we knew that we were within reach of the Russian long-range cannon, the fact that we could hear them actually in action caused wild excitement in the camp. Our Kommando was confined to our barracks, which meant we had no direct contact with the outside world and were dependent on our neighbors to bring news in to us. But even without them, we would have sensed that something was afoot, for things were changing within the camp. Some of the guards who were known for their cruelty began treating the prisoners a little less harshly; the German civilians in the factories where some of the prisoners were working suddenly became much more friendly, even sympathetic, and openly criticized Hitler and the Nazis. Clearly they were trying to accumulate witnesses who would testify to their "humanity" on the rapidly approaching day of judgment.

On the Western front, the Allied armies crossed the Rhine at points along virtually its entire length, and were thrusting deep into Germany. The end of the war was very near now. Hitler, almost totally paranoid, was buying himself time measured in days, and ruthlessly sacrificing the German people. Old men and children were drafted into the army and forced to fight in a hopeless cause.

In the first days of April the tension continued to rise among prisoners and guards alike. But through it all our professor continued his visits, regularly bringing new work for us. Word came that the Allies were approaching the Elbe River in the middle of Germany, and the final Russian drive to Berlin was expected any hour.

I was now sure that we were in the last days of the war, and tried to envision all the possible variations in the basic scenario of what would happen to us. My main concern was a possible order to separate the Jews from the other prisoners, which would have been a clear signal that they meant to kill us; I didn't think they would try to kill over forty thousand prisoners, of whom only a few thousand were Jewish. Anticipating this possibility, I went carefully through the entire camp looking for some place, any small hole, where Sam and I could hide out for the last few days of the war. I wasn't worried about food; we could last seven to ten days without it. The main problem was water, and I was able to get some containers that would hold enough water for that length of time. One evening after the Appel, I walked for several hours all over the camp looking for a pile of wood, a hole under a barracks where we could squeeze in, anything. But the whole camp was so standardized that I couldn't find a single place where we might hide.

The next day the loudspeakers began to blast a message, the same words over and over: *"Der Hund ist Tod."* (The dog is dead.) This was their way of announcing President Roosevelt's death. In their frenzy and fear of the imminent defeat, Goebbels and his propaganda machine tried to exploit the President's death as somehow signaling a reversal of the inexorable Allied advance. These murderers of millions were so terrified of the day of judgment that they managed to persuade themselves that, with Roosevelt, their archenemy, gone, perhaps they might be able to form an alliance with the West against Russia. What they couldn't accept was the fact that the entire civilized world was united against them. I was sorry that President Roosevelt would not be alive when victory came, but for the moment I was too preoccupied with our own survival to mourn him. What we needed was to find some way to avoid getting killed just as the war was ending.

One day, while we were working away at our numbers, a messenger came in with a note for our Stubenälteste. Told that he was out, the messenger went into the small room where the Stubenälteste worked and slept, and came out again empty-handed. I was so apprehensive of an order, which might come at any time, to kill all the Jewish prisoners that I decided to take a great risk and get a look at that note. I glanced out the door to make sure no one was approaching the barracks, then ran quickly into the Stubenälteste's room. The note was lying on top of his small table. I picked it up, read it, and felt faint. The top line read, in italics: *Re: Jewish Prisoners.* Underneath, in smaller type, was a list of instructions, and the first instruction was to compile a roster of all the Jewish prisoners in the barracks.

I was overwhelmed by a sinking feeling of fear, frustration, and desperation. I ran out and told the terrible news to Sam and the other mathematicians. Gloom fell upon us; no one could do any more work. Arno suggested that perhaps the directive had a different purpose, but we all knew that was unlikely. I was terribly depressed and couldn't sleep all night.

The next day, after the morning Appel, the SS announced that none of the outside commandos were to leave the camp that day; prisoners who were employed inside the camp were to continue on the job. When nothing was said about Jews I breathed again, but was fearful that at any moment I would hear the dreaded words, "All Jewish prisoners—step out."

When we returned to our barracks after the Appel, to our surprise the professor came in. For the first time since he had appeared in Sachsenhausen the barracks was full of people who hadn't gone out that day, and some of them openly jeered at the professor and his "Kommando." One made a crack about him and his Jews being Hitler's secret weapon. The professor ignored these remarks. He collected the completed sheets from Stark and gave him a new batch. Then he took some paper labels from his briefcase, gave them to Stark, and told him that "in view of the situation" (he didn't elaborate), he wanted to make sure the machines would be returned to their "rightful owners." He asked Stark to attach the labels to our machines, said good-bye to us, and left. We looked at the labels. Each was typed "Property of the University of Kraków" (Poland). Despite our anxiety, we burst out laughing. Here was Germany collapsing, and the professor was worried about the rightful ownership of a bunch of obsolete old machines! He must have been making sure that after the war no one could accuse him of having stolen them.

The other prisoners were so noisy that it was impossible to work, but we continued to sit at our table the rest of the day. Now Jews and Gentiles alike were apprehensive and nervous. My German neighbor did nothing to relieve the tension; he kept repeating, "The dog [Hitler] is going to kill us all. He knows he will die, and he's going to take us all with him." That night too I couldn't sleep.

We spent the next day again at our tables, even though we couldn't concentrate enough to do any work. The Stubenälteste came over to us and shook his head. "You're still going on with that crap!" Stark told him that we had to follow orders. He only laughed and walked away. I had to admit we were a ridiculous sight. No one else in the entire camp was working except the people in the kitchen and a few cleaners, the Russian artillery was booming within earshot, but there the eight of us were, still diligent at our tables. The atmosphere was charged with electricity. The other prisoners were milling around aimlessly; arguments and fights were frequent. I began to feel a little better about the order I had seen in the Stubenälteste's office. If they were going to separate the Jews in order to kill them, it would have happened in the last two days.

That night I was so exhausted from lack of sleep that I conked out as soon as I hit the bunk. Very late I was awakened by the noise of another artillery barrage. It went on nonstop for hours, so intense and continuous that there was no mistaking it—this was the long-awaited final Russian assault on Berlin. Fatigue forgotten, I was seized with an enormous excitement. This was it!

Over the following four days nothing changed in the camp. There were no Appels. The barrage of artillery from the east continued on and off, and it was growing louder. The Russians had broken through and were coming closer. Ludicrous as it was under the circumstances, we kept plugging away at our numbers, afraid to take any chances that might give anyone an excuse to accuse us of disobeying orders. From time to time I went outside to see what was happening. The prisoners kept milling about in the yard, and rumors were running like wildfire. The Allies were approaching from the west. Hitler had ordered a "scorched earth" policy before the oncoming enemy. There was to be no retreat; the Germans had been ordered to fight to the last man.

There was no telling what was true and what wasn't. No one had any contact with the outside world, but some of the SS guards inside the camp were passing information to a few of the prisoners. Everyone was talking evacuation, which I found hard to believe. Where would they take us? The Russians were coming in from the east and south—they were probably only fifteen kilometers from Berlin by now—the Allies from the west, so the only possible direction to go would be north, but to what destination? It didn't make sense. If they wanted to kill us all, the best place for that was right inside the camp, where we were surrounded by high walls and machine guns.

On the morning of April 20 an announcement came over the loudspeakers that was repeated incessantly: All prisoners were to line up at the gate by nationality in columns of five. There was going to be an evacuation. Poles, Russians, French, Norwegians, Dutch, Jews, and so forth were to form separate columns. As they began to assemble, chaos ensued, with prisoners running around like crazy trying to find the column for their nationality.

The decisive moment had arrived. When I heard that Jews were to form a separate column, I said to Sam that we were not going to join it, no matter what. He agreed, and we tore off the yellow triangles that branded us as Jews, making sure no telltale threads remained, leaving on the red triangles signifying political prisoners. We had no idea whether they would be verifying nationalities at the gate, but with over forty thousand prisoners running all over the place, I couldn't see how they would possibly have time to check. In any case, we were taking a lesser risk by not following these orders than by joining an all-Jewish column, which we were convinced would be the first to be killed.

Slowly the long columns were beginning to form. Since if there was any kind of check at the gate it would probably be by language, and since Polish was the only language Sam and I spoke perfectly, we went over to the Polish column. Several thousand Polish prisoners had already lined up. When we tried to join the column, a few rabid Polish anti-Semites recognized us as Jews and started to scream, *"Parszywi Żydzi, idźcie do swoich!"* (Rotten Jews, go to your own!) The last thing we needed was to attract any attention from the SS guards, so we quickly moved away and joined the column farther down, where the Poles didn't object to our mixing in with them. We were as quiet and inconspicuous as possible, positioning ourselves in the middle of the column so as not to be too visible.

I was literally counting the seconds in my anxiety to get moving; once we were outside the camp, in a column of non-Jews, our chances to live would be greatly improved. The column on one side of us was Russian; on the other, German. In our column alone there were at least four thousand Polish prisoners. We were happy to finally see the prisoners up front starting to move out the gate. I could see that up ahead the guards were distributing food to the prisoners as they left the camp. All this activity was accompanied by the thunder of the Russian artillery; clearly the SS was in a great hurry.

It took more than an hour before Sam and I reached the gate, and we were careful not to catch anyone's eye, still fearful of being unmasked at the last minute as Jews. We each received a large piece of bread, about three or four times our daily ration, a small jar of marmalade, and a small package of margarine, which the guards warned us had to last us three days. When I actually walked through the gate, a feeling of enormous relief came over me, as if someone had lifted a great weight from my shoulders. As we marched off, for the first time since the start of the Nazi extermination of the Jews in 1941, I felt that we might have a fair chance to survive: As far as the SS guards marching alongside us were concerned, Sam and I were not Jews. I said to myself, "I shall not die. I shall live. I shall tell the story!"

The March

■

We were on a road leading north, in a column of five prisoners to a row, half a mile long. The SS guards were walking on both sides of the column, fingers on the triggers of their machine guns. Two or three were marching ahead of the column and a few behind it. An officer on a motorcycle was riding up and down the road making sure everything was in order. Many military vehicles of all kinds were driving past. Some of the German formations seemed still intact, while others looked like the remains of a fighting force that had taken a bad beating. There were many stalled or abandoned vehicles lying on the shoulder of the road. Civilians were walking along carrying bundles; some had horse carts packed with their belongings. Allied planes and a few Russian ones flew continuously over our heads, but we didn't see a single German plane. From time to time, when one of the Allied planes spotted a group of German military vehicles, the pilot would dive down and strafe them. It did my heart good to see Germans jump and dive for cover. Somehow we weren't much concerned for

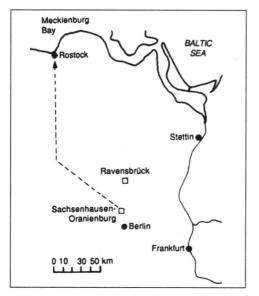

Area of Germany between Berlin and the North Sea which shows the route of the Sachsenhausen death march.

our own safety; our column was very visible from the air, and our striped uniforms made it obvious that we were prisoners. Whenever the planes flew low over us, the guards stepped up to the column, feeling safer from air attack when closer to us.

After a while they led us onto a secondary road parallel to the main one, where things were much quieter. The peasants in the fields, almost all of them old men, women, and children, looked with curiosity but no surprise at the endless column of prisoners in their striped uniforms. I now weighed less than a hundred pounds, Sam, about eighty-five or ninety, and most of the others were in a similar state. But the guards kept us marching at a brisk pace.

It was not yet noon when an elderly Pole marching a couple of rows ahead of us suddenly tripped and fell. He got up again with the help of the others around him, but he must have sprained or twisted an ankle, because he continued walking only with great difficulty, heavily favoring one leg. For a mile or so his neighbors on both sides supported him, but he was in constant pain and after a while couldn't walk at all—he had to be literally carried. An SS guard saw that he was holding up the column, and with his gun motioned him to step out of the ranks. When one of the prisoners who was carrying him wanted to stay with him, the guard pointed his machine gun at him in turn and ordered him to keep moving. The guard then pushed the man over to the side of the road and raised his machine gun. Realizing that he was going to be killed, the man fell on his knees and joined his hands together in a gesture of prayer. The SS guard, his gun about two feet from the man's head, let loose with a burst of fire, and the Pole keeled over and lay still on the ground. Seeing that the other prisoners were slowing down, their heads turning to look at the man lying on the ground, the guard ran back to the column and started hitting the marchers within his reach to hurry them along.

Our mood changed abruptly. Conversation stopped, and all of us walked carefully, making sure not to stumble. Sam and I took turns holding each other's arm. The incident had driven home to us that we were all still in mortal danger. Even though the war was in its last days, the SS obviously had orders not to let a single prisoner out of their control. The rule for this march was: Walk or die.

We continued walking nonstop for several more hours. Some of the weaker prisoners, unable to keep up the pace, began to fall back toward the end of the column. This, we knew, meant a bullet in the head. The stragglers at the end of the column were using their last drop of strength in a desperate effort not to get separated from the rest. Some were wheezing, gasping for air; others stumbled on until finally, all strength gone, they fell one by one to their knees, or simply dropped. Like angels of death the SS men at the rear of the column were looking for stragglers and shot them where they fell as if it were the most routine thing in the world. Their faces were blank. There was no hate in them, no pity, just business as usual. By the time they ordered us to stop for our first break, five or six prisoners from our column were gone, their bodies left behind on the side of the road, riddled with bullets.

Strangely, even though it was now clear that the march was going to be a murderous affair, I still felt far safer than I ever had in the camp. Here they didn't know I was a Jew, and if they were going to kill me it would be because I couldn't walk, not simply because I was a Jew. To my mind, killing a man because he couldn't keep up the pace in a forced march somehow wasn't as bad as killing him because he had been born a Jew. Such reasoning may seem lunatic, but under the circumstances it made perfect sense to me. Having lived for so many years under the gun, when any one of the guards had the clear and unquestioned right to murder me at any moment, at a whim, even for fun, even though I had done nothing to provoke it, for the sole reason that I was born a Jew, I had grown to yearn to have my right to live judged by some other criterion, any other— even whether or not I was able to walk.

Sam and I divided our food rations carefully into twelve portions, and we ate one portion during our brief rest. We knew that our lives depended on making it last as long as possible, on conserving every last bit of energy. However we saw many other prisoners, no hungrier than we, consume their entire three or four days' ration in a few minutes.

We found that Warshawski, our fellow mathematician, was in our column as well, and when the guards ordered us to resume our march, he walked alongside Sam and I. Despite the shooting of the stragglers, I was more optimistic than ever about our chances to make it. The odds seemed good that the SS would not kill so many people, especially since as far as they knew there were no

Jews among us. Besides, even if they had planned to execute us all, it would have been almost impossible for them to manage it. They couldn't mow us all down at once out there in the open; thousands would escape, and their own lives would be greatly endangered. I even overheard some of the Poles discussing the possibility of suddenly jumping the guards, but they had their machine guns at the ready; whoever attacked them first would surely be killed, and no one was willing to die moments before liberation, to save the others. Besides, even if a substantial number of prisoners managed to escape, the SS might still have time to hunt down many of them.

As the sun began to sink slowly in the west, the guards led us off the road to a large farm, which was to be our resting place for the night. They pushed perhaps a thousand of us into a large barn. There wasn't enough room for all of us to lie down, and some had to lay their legs over others' bodies. Sam and I were especially cautious with our food, waiting until it was completely dark before we ate our next portion, and being very quiet about it. We were afraid that some of the prisoners who had no food left might jump us and take ours by force.

The hay in the barn smelled good, and even though we were packed in so tight, I had a good night's sleep. Early in the morning the guards ordered us out, and we were once more on the march. Fortunately it wasn't raining, and the weather was mild. We turned onto another road, on which we could tell another column was marching ahead of us; every few hundred feet we saw the bullet-ridden bodies of prisoners lying at the side of the road.

All day long the SS played their deadly game of march or die, with the killings increasing every hour. Some of the prisoners' shoes were either too big for them or too small, and they were beginning to develop painful blisters; many walked barefoot, carrying their shoes tied together around their necks. Occasionally we heard the rumble of artillery, but now it seemed more remote and sporadic than it had just before we left the camp. I didn't feel as hungry as I had in the camp either, perhaps because I was so absorbed in the life-and-death game with the SS. We were marching now on winding country roads; evidently the SS wanted to stay away from the highways. I felt good, and Sam was holding up fairly well too. We were on the north German plain, which was sparsely populated, and, luckily for us, very flat. The roads would have been much more thickly strewn with our bodies had the terrain been hilly. That night the guards again brought us to a large farm, but this time they let all of us sleep outside, so at least we had plenty of room to stretch our legs.

This went on day after day, except that the number of victims kept increasing hourly. Sam and I had enough food for four days, but many of the others had had nothing to eat since the first rest stop, and more and more were unable to continue the march. The pace was slowing, which helped a little, but still many prisoners, especially the older ones, were unable to keep up and were shot down in cold blood. The lack of any visible emotion in the killers continued to amaze me. Many of the victims fought for their lives until the very last minute, pleading in vain with their executioners for mercy, while others, having witnessed too many earlier killings with no mercy shown, accepted their deaths with resignation. Some prisoners were so hungry they started eating roots and even grass, which caused many of them to develop dysentery, weakening them still further. Most had started the march in fairly good spirits, but now many were losing hope. The battle-front seemed more remote, and we had no idea whatever as to what was going on.

By the sixth or seventh day, Sam was weakening; he had to hold on to my arm most of the time. If we didn't get some food very soon, we wouldn't be able to make it. We were marching in a heavily wooded area, and at night the guards were letting us rest on the edge of these woods.

The killings became very frequent now, as more and more people were collapsing from exhaustion. At least seven hundred in our column were shot to death in two days. We could see hundreds of other corpses alongside the road, left by columns marching ahead of us. The countryside was beautiful; spring was in full bloom. The incongruity between the radiance of the nature around us and the slaughter of innocent people was hard to reconcile.

It was still broad daylight at the end of the seventh day, April 26, and we were lying on the ground, exhausted and hungry, in a corner formed by the country road and a narrow cow path, when suddenly a small white truck appeared and turned onto the path. More trucks just like it, perhaps eight or nine in all, followed and stopped, lined up next to each other. They all had red crosses painted on their sides. It seemed like a mirage. A wild thought struck me: maybe they had brought food for us! But that could only be my hunger talking. It was too incredible even to contemplate. Why would the Germans want to feed us now? It was totally inconsistent with all their other actions, and, anyway, they themselves were short of food. Besides, why white trucks with red crosses? We saw a few civilians from the convoy talking to the SS officer in charge. Then the guards ordered some of the stronger prisoners to open the back doors of the trucks, and to my astonishment they started unloading corrugated white boxes marked with red crosses.

A surge of joy rushed through our ranks. Food! It looked like food! And in seconds we heard that it was, as the prisoners unloading the trucks passed the word along to the others. Most of us had risen to our feet. They were piling the boxes up. Hundreds of them were being unloaded, so it couldn't all be for just the SS; it had to be for us!

The guards ordered us to line up, and soon the prisoners at the head of the line were receiving one box for every four people. The guards warned us that the prisoners themselves were responsible for dividing the food evenly, and that anyone who started a fight would be immediately shot. Sam and I were standing far down the line, but it was moving fast. We heard shouts of joy from the prisoners as they tore the boxes open, and cries of "Chocolate! Cheese! Meat!"

I was dizzy from excitement. It was a miracle, a real miracle was happening before our eyes. Someone wanted to save us! Having known for so long nothing but brutality, hardened by the daily inhumanity of the camps, the thousands of deaths, it was hard to take it in, this evidence of some good in man. What did it mean? Who had sent this food? How had they found us in the middle of nowhere?* Warshawski, Sam, a friendly Pole, and I received our box, and when we opened it we saw that it came from America. It was neatly packed with two different kinds of cheese, a can of sardines, three or four packages of crackers, including Ritz, a bar of Hershey's chocolate, a can of Spam, a can of powdered milk, and a long package of small square slices of pumpernickel. We could not believe our eyes. I suggested that I divide everything in the box into four parts, and we would alternate choosing our shares. Everyone

---

*As I found out after the liberation, it was the Swedish Red Cross that delivered the food packages to us. The Swedish Count Folke Bernadotte, who organized the delivery, and a few others, were able to get approval for this mission of mercy from Himmler, who was trying to ingratiate himself to the Western powers, hoping that his cooperation would somehow save his life. Himmler was captured at the end of the war and, realizing that nothing would save him, committed suicide by crushing a cyanide pill in his mouth.

A note of interest: there are several eyewitness stories about Himmler personally observing, through a small window, the suffocation of hundreds of Jews in a gas chamber during his visit to the Auschwitz extermination camp.

agreed, and so I set to work, conscious of my heavy responsibility to make sure each share was exactly even.

I divided the crackers first, so we could get something inside us immediately. Next came the sardines, because we had no way to store them. We tried not to cram the food into our mouths, but it was hard to hold back. Our bodies were starved, every cell aching for nourishment. The sardines tasted fantastically good. Each morsel was a little piece of heaven, and every part of my body was crying out, "Thank you! Thank you!" to the food as it traveled through.

I used a spoon which I sharpened on a stone to divide the cheese and the Spam. We had never heard of Spam. It was delicious. How clever of the Americans to invent such a wonderful new kind of food! The chocolate was difficult to divide because it was very hard and crumbly, but I finally managed to cut it up into four equal parts. The powdered milk presented a storage problem, but we had some of it mixed with water and saved the rest. I kept the chocolate for last. It was so good I longed to eat my whole share at once, but Sam and I had decided that this food had to last us at least three days, and we each divided our share into little bits.

Since I was stronger than Sam at this point, when the march resumed the following morning I offered to carry his food as well as my own. As we walked along we could talk of nothing but the "miracle." No one told us how the food had gotten to us, so we could only speculate. Something very unusual must be going on; never before had the SS permitted anything like it. Maybe Hitler was dead; were he still alive, he would never permit anything like that. Or perhaps the war was over. But if so, why were the guards still here? Perhaps the International Red Cross had arranged this, and if so it was a sign that a crack had appeared in the wall with which the SS had isolated us from the rest of the world. Whatever its source, the food not only fed our starving bodies, it gave a lift to our spirits as well. We had not yet reached the end of the road, but at least there was someone out there who cared. Knowing this, I felt more at peace than I had in a long time, and I fell sound asleep.

When I woke up, it was almost morning. As usual, I looked around to make sure Sam was nearby. I couldn't see him, and called his name. There was no answer, but the sound woke Warshawski, who said, "Don't worry, he probably went to relieve himself." I waited five, ten, fifteen minutes, but there was no sign of Sam. What could have happened to him? I decided to take a look around. Telling Warshawski to stay where he was so I could orient myself by him, I started walking all around, wherever there were prisoners lying, calling out, "Sam! Sam!" It was dawn, and I could see better now. I covered the whole perimeter without getting any response. I returned to where I had started and there was Warshawski, but no sign of Sam. I knew he wouldn't even think of trying to escape without me; in any case, he was too weak. Perhaps sometime during the night he had gone to relieve himself and had somehow got lost and wandered off, past the guards? Suddenly I remembered that I had all the food for both of us. I got panicky—he was so weak already!—and ran once more around the perimeter in case I had missed him the first time. Nothing. The SS ordered us to line up, and the first prisoners in the column started to march off.

I was frantic. I had no choice but to join the column, but as we set out I moved up the ranks, row by row, until I reached the head of the column, then gradually fell back to the end so that I had been able to scan each row. A guard saw me and demanded an explanation. I was so upset that without thinking I told him that my brother had been in the column and had apparently got lost, and that I had his food. The guard helpfully suggested that perhaps Sam had died during the night. "What are you worrying about?" he said. "You've got the food. Let *him* worry!" and laughed heartily at his own joke.

For the first time in years I had tears in my eyes. Warshawski was very kind and kept reassuring me that since we had heard no shots, Sam must be all right. He even suggested that Sam might well be better off than we were, if he was out of the hands of the SS. But I knew that Sam was too weak to be on his own.

About the middle of the day they gave us a brief rest. When we got moving again, I saw a column of prisoners marching on a parallel country road a couple hundred yards away, in the same direction we were going. Suddenly I noticed a prisoner at the end of the column, about at our level in the line of march, whose gait and height reminded me of Sam, and who kept looking in our direction. "I may be crazy," I said to Warshawski, "but I think that guy over there is Sam." "You're crazy," said Warshawski. "Most of us, in our striped uniforms, look alike from a distance, and anyway, how would Sam have got himself into another column? Besides," Warshawski pointed out, "what can you do about it?"

But I kept looking at the man, and was overcome by the certainty that he was Sam. I said to Warshawski that I was going to tell the SS officer in charge of our column that one of the prisoners on the other road was my brother, who had somehow gotten lost, and that I had his food from the Red Cross box. Warshawski tried to dissuade me; he thought I would be risking my life to say anything. "Even if he were to believe you, what if he goes over to the other column and finds that the guy isn't Sam after all? He might just shoot you."

But I decided to take the chance. I prepared a short speech in German and rehearsed it thoroughly. The next time I saw the SS officer approaching on his motorcycle, I stepped out of the column with my hands raised in front of me. He stopped in surprise. I saluted (to this day I don't know why) and said, "Herr Obersturmbahnführer,

I wish respectfully to report that a prisoner in the other column belongs to this column. He is my brother, who somehow got lost, and I feel very badly because I have his food supply and he has no food. I would be very grateful if Herr Obersturmbahnführer permitted him to rejoin our group, where he belongs. Thank you." Then I saluted him again.

The speech in my broken German, together with the salute, must have been comical, because the officer laughed and said, "We shall see about that," and drove off. I rejoined the column, the other prisoners staring at me curiously. They hadn't been able to hear what I had said, but that was the first time since we marched out of the camp that any prisoner had spoken to the SS commander. As I walked on, holding my breath, I saw the officer ride over the field to the other column, where we could see him talking to the SS man in charge and pointing toward us. Then he rode over to the prisoner I had pointed out to him. I thought my heart would burst from the tension. But then I saw the prisoner leave the other column and cut across the field toward us, a short distance because the two roads were drawing closer. It *was* Sam! I was overcome by a great surge of joy. As he approached I waved my arms to let him see where I was and we fell into each other's embrace, hugging and crying. Warshawski was crying too. "You have a good brother," he said to Sam.

Another miracle! Sam was still bewildered, and when he calmed down he said he didn't know himself how he had gotten separated. He had gone to relieve himself, apparently got lost, and then became mixed up with the other group, which, unbeknownst to us, was resting nearby. The amazing thing was that no guard had spotted him wandering outside the perimeter and shot him.

The march continued, and so did the killings. The distribution of the Red Cross boxes evidently hadn't changed the SS's standing order: Any prisoner who couldn't keep up with the pace was to be shot to death. They were not letting anyone out of their hands alive. However, the shootings weren't quite as frequent now as they had been the day before the food arrived. Those parcels had given us a life-saving infusion of energy and hope. Now once more, as at the beginning, it was legs giving out or injuries to them rather than failing strength that were the main causes of the killings. The column was moving more slowly now, too, and the guards were not hurrying us so much.

Again we stopped for the night at the edge of a forest. The moment of liberation was very close, and we had some food again. If only our legs would hold up, we had a good chance of making it. I slept well that night, and the next morning, April 28, I felt better than I had in a long time. That day went by uneventfully. Sam, Warshawski, and I stayed close together. We ate a little more of the food from the Red Cross, and it was heavenly.

The next morning, after we had marched for an hour or so, we saw a number of dead horses lying on the road, evidently victims of Allied strafing. Frenziedly the prisoners ahead of us were throwing themselves on the carcasses and cutting off hunks of flesh with their stone-sharpened spoons. Some were even trying to tear off pieces with their fingers and teeth. As long as the prisoners stayed on the road, the guards didn't interfere. When the crowd around the carcasses had thinned out a little, Sam and I and some of the other prisoners toward the end of the column cut off some meat for ourselves. It was a grisly business and our spoons weren't sharp enough, but we persisted and got at least a couple of pounds. None of us had anything to put it in, so we stuffed our jackets inside our pants, tightened the pants, and carried the meat inside the jackets above the waist. The meat was bloody, and soon our jackets were soaked with blood. The column looked like a bunch of butchers on the march.

Still there was no relief from the killings; prisoner after prisoner was shot down. It seemed utterly senseless. By now we couldn't be far from the North Sea, and a mad thought struck me: Perhaps the Red Cross had boats waiting to take us to Sweden.

That night we stopped near another forest. A few of the prisoners had brought matches with them from Sachsenhausen, and soon there were hundreds of little fires going. We all sat around them cooking our horsemeat, using the sharpened ends of wooden sticks to hold chunks of it over the flames. This was the first meat I had tasted in almost two years. It was very tough, but I kept at it, doggedly chewing each piece as long as I could, knowing that this extra energy could mean the difference between life and death. We ate only part of the meat, saving the rest, for it was still impossible even to guess how much longer we would have to hold out. Why was it taking the Allies so long to reach us? Most of the prisoners were very subdued, as if the long march had dulled our senses; the last few days we had been shuffling along in a sort of stupor.

On the morning of April 30, we were about to resume our march when the little white Red Cross trucks appeared again on the road. Sam and I still had some food left from the first parcel, but many of the others had long since eaten all their share. We greeted the trucks with cheers, not only because of the food, but also because their arrival meant that someone on the outside knew we were alive, cared about us, and was in touch with the SS on our behalf. This time each box had to be shared among five prisoners, so the portions were a little smaller. But with the horsemeat and what was left over from the first box, our food reserve was building up and Sam and I could afford the luxury of eating a larger part of our portion.

Once again Allied planes appeared, in large numbers and flying very low. We could see them diving in and out over a wide road not far from us that had on it a heavy concentration of German tanks, armored cars, and trucks. They could see us very well, and were clearly taking pains not to hit the column—which was no help to the unfortunate ones who couldn't keep up, and who were still being executed with the same cold, mechanical ruthlessness as before.

When we stopped again for the night, fires soon started up again to cook more of the horsemeat. I didn't eat much of it this time, since I preferred the food from the Red Cross box. Again I slept well in the open air; it was quite warm for that time of year. When the morning of May 1 came, someone suggested that maybe the Russians had been holding off until today, their big national holiday, to liberate us. We marched off once again, still surrounded by the guards. This evacuation, if it could still be called that, was taking much longer than anyone had anticipated. Prisoner after prisoner was killed, the bodies still littering the road. I knew that if it hadn't been for the Red Cross food, it would have been far worse; many more prisoners would have been dead by now.

I looked around. We were all filthy, unshaven, our striped suits soaked with blood from the horsemeat. Many were stumbling along, unable to walk. I occupied my mind with wondering how those food parcels had reached us, but could arrive at no explanation. We came upon more dead horses lying on the road and replenished our supply of meat, throwing away what had been left from before; it had started to go bad.

In the evening we stopped at the edge of another forest, and the SS guards stationed themselves as usual around us to make sure no one escaped. Now that we had a fresh supply of meat, hundreds of fires started again. A Pole who had been walking along with Sam, Warshawski, and me during the last few days, who had been a truck driver before the war, ate prodigious quantities of the horsemeat with relish, but I had to force myself. That truck driver was a good-natured fellow who probably suspected that we were

Jews but never asked outright, and we of course volunteered nothing. For dessert I ate a little more of the chocolate I had left, promising myself that if I survived, I would eat nothing but chocolate for the rest of my life.

Night fell, the fires were extinguished, and we went to sleep. From time to time I woke up at the noise from the military vehicles moving along the road. Early next morning, before we had to set out on the march again, the fires were started up to cook some more of the horsemeat. We were all sitting around our fires, holding chunks of the meat on sticks over the flames, when a voice came from the edge of the forest: "The guards are gone."

Free

◼

At first no one reacted; it was as if we hadn't heard it. But the voice kept repeating, "The guards are gone. There are no more guards!" When it finally sank in, our reaction was very odd. No one shouted with joy. No one screamed with excitement. No one jumped up and down with happiness. There was no hugging or kissing, no tears, no laughter. Most of us just went on cooking our horsemeat.

Perhaps our minds had been numbed by the long death march, and we had been too drained emotionally for any kind of response. I felt a surge of hope and happiness in my heart, but it was mixed with a certain incredulity and caution. Could it be true? Would the guards just run away at night, disappearing like a bad dream? Suddenly I knew I couldn't wait another minute to find out. I had to know for sure.

"Let's not just sit here," I said. "Let's see what's happening." I started walking toward the road, Sam, Warshawski, and the truck driver following me, past groups of prisoners who were sitting or lying around their little fires. We came to the edge of the forest, where we could see the road. It was true—the SS guards were gone, vanished as if by magic! The road was clogged with abandoned German military vehicles standing bumper to bumper as far as the eye could see: tanks, half-tracks, jeeps, cannons, and trucks of all sizes, but there wasn't a single German soldier or SS man in sight. It was an eerie scene: thousands of machines, and not a soul to man them.

My heart started to pound with joy. It was true. We were free! Now we shouted with laughter and hugged one another. We were free, free, free! For years we had longed for, scarcely dared hope for, this wonderful moment; hoped against all reason, against all odds, amid the most nightmarish conditions. And now that the impossible dream had finally come true, and the gift of life was given back to us, we could not savor it fully, taste it all in one big gulp. We just weren't capable of taking it in all at once. My thoughts flew to Fred, Felek, and Hanka. If only they were alive too!

Many other prisoners were emerging now from the forest onto the road. Some of the German army trucks were loaded with food, and we started to break open cases of canned fish, meat, margarine, marmalade, biscuits, and all sorts of other good things. Some people were going crazy, stuffing themselves with all the food they could cram into their bellies. Sam and I and a few others tried to warn them not to overeat; our stomachs were not used to so much food, and they might make themselves ill. Only a few paid any attention to us; they seemed to be trying to make up for all the years of starvation in one giant meal.

Sam and I were so loaded down with cans and packages of food we could hardly walk. Suddenly a jeep appeared with two soldiers driving along the side of the road. We scattered, but as it drew nearer we could see they were not German. Their uniforms were beige instead of the German green, and they were waving at us and smiling. They were British. No one among us understood a word of English, and apparently they spoke no other language, but they made the V for Victory sign. We surrounded the jeep and shook hands with them, and they took out a carton of cigarettes and passed them around. They were Lucky Strikes, the first I had ever seen. The soldiers kept pointing toward the road in the direction from which they had come, apparently urging us to go that way. Then they drove away, laughing and waving to us.

We sat down at the side of the road and ate some more of the food from the trucks. So the Western Allies had beaten the Russians to the punch, and liberated us first. It was a surprise; we had always assumed it would be the Russians, because before the final offensive had begun the Russians had been much closer to us—all the camps were in the East. As we were discussing this, a motorcycle approached and stopped. The rider had a red star on his helmet; he was a Russian. Within a single hour, we had met our liberators from the West and from the East!

It was a historic moment. This time we had no trouble communicating with our liberator, who wanted to know how far it was to Rostock. Of course we had no idea. He was friendly but more hardened by war, and seemed to be in a hurry. He didn't greet us with the same happiness at our being freed that we had sensed from the English, which was disappointing.

The Polish truck driver found a key in the ignition of one of the small German trucks and got the engine started. We decided to drive to the nearest town. The road was jammed with vehicles, but the fields around were very flat, so we drove alongside the road, just off it. After a few hundred feet we saw a sign: "Rostock—7 kilometers." We continued in that direction, and ten minutes later we were in the outskirts of Rostock, a fairly large town, with ruins everywhere. The Allied bombers had done a thorough job. There were a few German civilians on the streets, and they looked alarmed when they saw us.

When we got closer to the center of town, we saw groups of German soldiers standing about. As we approached the central square we had to slow down to a crawl because the streets were increasingly crowded with soldiers. Finally we entered the central town square, and it was a spectacular sight, literally jampacked with tens of thousands of German soldiers milling around aimlessly.

Sam, Warshawski, and I were standing in the open in back of the truck and saw it all. It looked like Times Square in New York on New Year's Eve (as I was to see it before long), except that here in Rostock they weren't celebrating; they looked dispirited and exhausted. Some of them were just standing about with their mouths drooping, their eyes vacant, and a generally hangdog air. They certainly looked like the remnants of a defeated army. Rifles, machine guns, and hand guns were piled up in several spots around the square, although a few of the soldiers were still carrying their weapons. There was not a single Allied soldier in sight. It was a great thrill to see the hated German army in such a bedraggled condition. We were jumping up and down, shaking our fist at the Germans and making throat-slashing gestures with our hands. We were still wearing our striped prison uniforms, and it was just plain dumb luck that one of the soldiers who still had his gun didn't take a shot at us. Perhaps the spectacle of such total dejection somehow made us feel they lacked the spirit to do it. Still, it was incredibly stupid of us to run such an unnecessary risk on the very day of our liberation.

We were slowly making headway through the crowds when suddenly we noticed a lone Russian soldier surrounded by many German soldiers. Coming closer, we saw his jacket lying on the ground, with hundreds of watches piled on it. He was ordering all the Germans around him to hand over their watches to him, and they were sheepishly following his orders.

We left the square and drove around until we saw a group of English officers. These spoke broken French, which I could make out, and they directed us to a temporary shelter, where we found other English army officers who had been assigned to give aid to liberated concentration camp inmates.

We spent the rest of the day taking it easy and talking to other ex-prisoners. We were in a state of nervous excitement and exhaustion. Our hearts were filled with joy, but it was mixed with sadness. I thought of my parents and their cruel death, and of Fred, Felek, and Hanka. I was worried about what might have happened to them, and longed to find them alive and well.

Sam and I had been assigned a small room in the shelter, and I went to bed early that evening. I was dizzy with the thoughts and images that were whirling in my mind, but I finally fell asleep.

I woke up early in the morning not knowing at first where I was. A ray of light was shining through the window, and suddenly I remembered that I was free! The stone in the pit of my stomach that I had felt every time I woke up in the camps and realized where I was was gone. I started to cry. I had cried like that only once before—on October 28, 1942, the day my father and mother were murdered.

After a while I dried my tears and got up. I went to the door and looked outside. It was a beautiful morning in May. The sun was rising and the birds were singing. A new day was about to begin.

Epilogue

■

We spent about two weeks in Rostock recuperating from the effects of our imprisonment in the camps and the death march. The shelter was not very comfortable by normal standards, but compared to what we had known before, it was luxury. There was plenty of food, and we gained weight rapidly and soon started to look like human beings again. The UNRRA (United Nations Relief and Rehabilitation Administration) and the other international relief organizations treated us very well. But it was heartbreaking to see so many ex-inmates die after they were liberated. Some never recovered from the effects of extreme malnutrition; others died from the dysentery they had developed from eating grass during the death march, or from overeating after they had been freed. A few of the liberated prisoners took revenge on the German civilians around Rostock, beating them up and robbing them, but most of us didn't. How could we tell a good German from a bad one? Suddenly it was impossible to find a German who had ever been a member of the Nazi party. I never even considered trying to hurt any Germans at random; what if one of them happened to be a person like Willie, the brave German political prisoner I had known in Ravensbrück?

There were rumors that the Russians were going to take over Rostock and the surrounding area now being occupied by the Allies. Sam and I were impatient to find out what had happened to the rest of our family, and as soon as we felt strong enough we decided to go back to Poland. We said good-bye to Warshawski and the others we had become friendly with, and went to the railroad station. Since no passenger trains were running, we struck out in the general direction of central Poland, traveling in cattle cars, army supply trains, and any other transportation we could find. When we were chased out of one, we changed over to another, as long as it was heading east.

We had heard that Warsaw had been completely destroyed, but that there were still Jews in Łódź, the second largest city in Poland. By chance in Łódź we found Motie Orenstein, a second cousin, who kindly invited us to stay in his apartment. While there we heard rumors that the entire contingent of Hrubieszów women who had been sent with us to Budzyń from Jatkowa had been murdered in Stuthoff, a concentration camp near Danzig. Hanka had been among them. Someone had heard that Fred was in Amberg, in Germany, and that Felek had been killed in the last days of the war. We had no confirmation of any of this, no witnesses. We learned too that a few Jews had gone back to Hrubieszów. Anxious for more information, we decided to return to our hometown. We found it virtually undamaged by the war, but out of the prewar Jewish population of Hrubieszów, some eight or nine thousand, we found only five Jews left in the town.

We stayed a few days in Hrubieszów, where we heard that the local Poles who had taken over the houses and property of Jews were worried now that those who had survived the war would return and reclaim them. We were told that three Jews who came out of hiding were killed by Poles. A man whom we had known well before the war came to see us and advised us to leave town. He heard talk that Poles who were living in our father's building were planning to kill us. Sam managed to sell one small store in the building to a tenant at a ridiculously low price, and we left in a hurry, heading back to Łódź. (The other Jews also left Hrubieszów, and today there is not one Jew living in our hometown.)

We stayed several more weeks in Łódź, hoping for further news about our family, and in the meantime began to think about what to do with our lives. I wanted to leave for the American Occupation Zone in Germany, try to find Fred, and emigrate to the United States. Sam decided to stay in Poland, feeling that as a lawyer he could practice his profession only there, that in any other country he would have language difficulties. "In my profession," he said, "language is our most important asset. What could I do outside Poland as a lawyer?" I told him that I didn't want to live under the Communists, and furthermore that I was convinced that the great majority of Poles hadn't changed and would always remain anti-Semitic. Although only about fifty thousand Jews remained in Poland out of the three million, three hundred thousand who had lived there before the war, that was still far too many for most Poles.

One day when I was sitting on a bench in a park in Łódź reading a newspaper, I overheard a conversation between two Polish women who were having their lunch on the other side of the bench. "At least Hitler did one good thing: he got rid of the Jews," one of them remarked. The other commented, "Yes, but he should have finished the job."

That was the last straw for me. I went back to the apartment and told Sam that I was leaving for Germany immediately, to look for

Fred. Sam was still determined to stay, so I got ready to leave and we hugged and kissed each other good-bye. It was a sad moment; we had never been separated since Felek and he had come to Ołyka for their summer vacation early in June 1941, just before the Germans attacked Russia.

I traveled through southern Poland, Prague, and western Czechoslovakia, finally arriving in Amberg, where I found Fred in a rehabilitation center for former concentration-camp inmates, wearing an UNRRA uniform and working as a doctor. He looked wonderful. Emotion overcame us completely. We both burst into tears, and hugged and kissed each other over and over. He confirmed the rumors we had heard that Felek had been killed by the SS. With a breaking heart I listened to his story.

About a week or two after Sam and I had left the Płaszów camp with the other "mathematicians," the SS had evacuated the rest of the Chemiker Kommando to the Flossenbürg concentration camp in Germany. As with us in Sachsenhausen, it had taken a while but eventually their professor too had appeared, set up their Kommando in an empty barracks, and set them to work again on the same phony projects as before. After a few weeks the part of the Kommando that was working on the "immobilizing gas" was moved to Kraków, in Poland, where they continued their work until they were evacuated to Auschwitz. The others, including Fred and Felek, continued on in Flossenbürg until the end of April. Their professor ran out of projects for them, so during the last two months he arranged for crates of old World War I books on military strategy to be shipped to them, their new assignment being to search for weapons left over from 1918 that might have been stashed away somewhere and overlooked by the German army, and if found could still be brought out and used. The "sting" was still going on. At the end of April, Fred, Felek, and about two thousand other

Jews from Flossenbürg had been put on a train that was destined for the Dachau concentration camp.

A few of the prisoners, knowing that the Allied planes were continuously bombing German trains, attached their striped jackets to the roofs of the cars as a signal to the pilots that theirs was a prisoner-of-war transport. This worked for a few days; the Allied fighter planes were concentrating on attacking the locomotive, hitting none of the cars behind with the prisoners. The train made very slow progress because the locomotives kept getting hit and had to be replaced several times. The last attack occurred in the station at a small town, and this time the Allied pilot strafed the cars as well. About thirty prisoners were killed, and another hundred and thirty wounded, among them Felek. A bullet shattered his knee. The SS officer in charge of the transport decided that this time he would not try to get a replacement for the locomotive, and ordered the evacuation to continue on foot. The wounded prisoners were taken out of the cars and moved to one side of the track.

When Fred saw that the wounded were going to be left behind at the station, he went to the officer and told him that he was a doctor, and that many of the wounded needed immediate help. He requested permission to stay with them, but the officer refused, saying that it was unnecessary because the Americans would be arriving very soon and would take good care of the wounded. Fred persisted, telling the officer that some of the wounded couldn't wait for the Americans but needed immediate help, and that as a doctor he had an obligation to stay with them. But the officer was adamant and ordered Fred to join the other prisoners, who were about to leave, surrounded by SS guards. So Fred was forced to leave Felek.

They marched for several days with nothing to eat. The prisoners who were unable to continue were killed on the spot, as had been the case with us. At night they were locked up in barns. Fred developed an infection in his elbow and became feverish with hallucinations. On the fourth morning of the march the SS guards ordered the prisoners to form a column. Fred was in the first row of five, with his friend Dr. Schindel. Suddenly a tank appeared on the road in front of the barn, only a few yards away. Fred noticed that, instead of the German cross, it bore a star. "Americans!" he screamed. He and the other four prisoners in the first row lunged toward the tank. The guards had seen the tank too. They threw down their weapons and started running into the fields. Some of the stronger prisoners ran after them and caught a few of them, whom they killed with their bare hands in a matter of minutes.

Fred simply sat down and leaned against the tank, feeling no emotion, only total exhaustion. An American soldier leaned out of the tank, patted him on the shoulder, and gave him a pack of Lucky Strikes. Fred started to weep. The soldier told the prisoners to return to the town where they had left the train; the American troops there had facilities to take care of them.

They walked back to the town, where they found that the SS had killed all hundred thirty of the wounded prisoners immediately after Fred and the others had been marched off. They machine-gunned them right where they were lying by the side of the tracks, and buried them in a mass grave. Immediately after the town was liberated the American officer in charge ordered the townspeople to open the grave and take the bodies out. He ordered caskets to be made for the murdered prisoners, but there weren't enough workmen available to make a casket for each one, so two bodies were placed in each casket and they were buried again. So died my brother Felek, a few days before the liberation.

I stayed with Fred for a couple of weeks, and then we heard rumors of new pogroms in Poland. Once again the Poles were killing Jews; many of them were slaughtered in Radom. I hoped that now Sam would be willing to leave Poland, but I wasn't sure that he could get out by himself; it was becoming more difficult to cross the borders.

I decided to go back to Łódź. I traveled about ten days by train and on foot, and arrived at Motie's apartment only to be told that Sam had left for Amberg two days before. I stayed and rested in Łódź for a few days, and heard fresh rumors that Hanka had been killed in the Stuthoff massacre, but I refused to give up hope.

I couldn't wait to get out of Poland, and promised myself that once I did I would never return. How could I bear to live in a country where Jews were so hated that even the slaughter of millions of us, children and old people too, didn't soften the hearts of those with whom Jews had lived side by side for centuries?

Once again I started out on the long trip to Amberg. I stopped off for a while in Prague, where I met and became friendly with a Czech girl. We grew to like each other, and she wanted me to stay in Czechoslovakia. One day while walking with her in Prague, I ran into Hy Silberstein. He was on his way to Poland, but I convinced him that there was no future for him there, and he decided to go back to the displaced persons camp in Germany, where a few days later his brother Abram found him. Abram had lived in Palestine before the war. Along with the future leaders of the Israeli army, he had been trained in survival warfare by General Orde Charles Wingate, joined the British army, then the Jewish Brigade, and was promoted to the rank of major in the British army. He had been decorated many times during the war. Field Marshal Bernard Montgomery, commander in chief of the British forces, wrote him a personal letter commending him for his bravery. Somehow Abram was sure that Hy had survived the war, so he traveled all over Germany looking for him, and finally found him in a DP camp.

I was very fond of the Czech girl, but wasn't yet ready to get tied down, and decided to rejoin my brothers in Amberg. Soon after I returned there we received confirmation of Hanka's death from Pola Ries, one of the thirteen survivors of the Stuthoff death march.

After the Russian armies had cut off East Prussia from the rest of Germany in January 1945, the SS started to evacuate Stuthoff and all its satellite camps. They marched thousands of Jews, most of them women, in the bitter winter cold and howling winds toward the Baltic Sea. At night the prisoners slept on the snow, without cover. Thousands froze to death. Those who were unable to walk on were shot. Of all the death marches, this one was by far the worst. Those who survived the twelve days of this hell were literally driven into the Baltic Sea, where a thin layer of ice had formed at the shore. The ice couldn't support the weight of so many people, and they drowned in the ice-cold water, while the SS shot them from the shore. So died my sister Hanka, not quite nineteen, just a few days before the Russians arrived.

The United States government opened its gates to more than a hundred thousand survivors of the Holocaust, and through our Uncle Morris (Moshe) Orenstein in New York, Fred, Sam, and I obtained visas. We spent about two years in various DP camps and in an apartment in Stuttgart along with Fred, who was practicing medicine there, waiting for our immigration papers to be approved. I spent the time reading, playing chess, going out with girls, and learning English words; I memorized over two thousand words from an English dictionary. Finally, on September 24, 1947, we boarded the SS *Fletcher*, a Liberty ship, in Bremen. After a stormy passage we arrived in New York harbor on October 2, 1947, and as the ship moved into the harbor we were on deck marveling at the Statue of Liberty and the New York skyline. Uncle Morris and Adele Bigajer, a girl I had met in one of the DP camps in Germany, were waiting for us, and Morris took us to a room in Manhattan that he had rented.

This was all very exciting and promising, but I still had one big question: Was there any anti-Semitism in the United States? I had heard conflicting stories about it. To settle the matter, I immediately bought two newspapers, the *New York Daily News* and the *New York Mirror* (now defunct). I had been told that these two papers were somewhat anti-Semitic. I read both of them straight through, which took me far into the night, and found not a single anti-Semitic reference in either one of them. I sighed with relief. The stories of American anti-Semitism were exaggerated.

I soon found that even though I had memorized the meaning of more than two thousand words, I still had trouble understanding people. There was more to it, I discovered, than vocabulary; there were also the many idioms. But I learned fast. I was working hard; my first job was with Jonathan Logan, the dress manufacturer, lugging bales of cotton. I married Adele, worked at a few other jobs, and bought and sold a grocery store. Then Uncle Morris suggested that we go into business together. He put up $40,000, and I ran the business. In 1956 my daughter Annette was born, and in 1958 my son Mark.

Our business grew from a small novelty company to become one of the largest toy manufacturing companies in the country. I became a millionaire. Then I made some bad marketing mistakes and lost all my money. My marriage wasn't working out, so Adele and I were divorced. I was lucky to meet and then marry Susie Vankovich, a girl from West Virginia. It was Susie who urged me to write this book. I gave up manufacturing and became an inventor of toys.

My new business was quite profitable, and I became active in charity work, particularly with the Metropolitan New York Coordinating Council on Jewish Poverty. Susie and I are interested in helping the elderly poor of New York, both Jews and non-Jews. We arrange for iron bars to be installed in the apartments of the poor, who are burglarized frequently; we buy beds for those in need of them; we provide money to move the elderly out of dangerous neighborhoods; and in general we do what we can to make their lives a little easier.

Recently a federally funded building with a hundred and forty small apartments for the elderly poor was under construction on Manhattan's Lower East Side. There was no provision in the funding for a security system, guards, air-conditioning, or luncheon facilities, all of which are essential to the elderly, so Susie and I provided the money for these things. In appreciation, the management of the building named it the Lejb and Golda Orenstein Building, in memory of my parents. The eleven-story structure is on Bialystoker Street in Manhattan, between Grand and Delancey Streets. Above the main entrance is a sign, "Lejb and Golda Orenstein Building," and there is a commemorative bronze plaque in the entrance hall. It gives the names of my parents and of Felek and Hanka, and the date on which each of them was murdered by the Nazis.

It seems a fitting memorial to them, even though it is in a country they never saw, for this is the country that gave us, the surviving children, freedom and a new life.

Postscript

■

Information on Key People Mentioned in this Book

Murdered by the Nazis:

The Orenstein Family: all except my brothers Fred and Sam, cousins
   Motie, Elezer (Bucio's son), and Rose Toren.

The Strum Family: all except cousin Józiek (died of cancer in 1981).

The Peretz Family: all except son Lolek (now in Israel).

The Lichtenstein Family: all.

The Burstyn Family: all.

The Silberstein Family: all except Hy.

Survived:

Bencio Fink and David Rotenberg now live in Israel.

Chaim Ajzen and Tobka Becker joined the partisans, were married,
   and now live in Australia with their two children.

Jurek Topaz now lives in the United States.

The "mathematicians" all survived, with the possible exception of the lady who worked with us in Płaszów but did not rejoin us in Ravensbrück.

The Nazis:

Hans Wagner was captured after the war, sentenced to death, and hanged.

Demant was sentenced to life in prison by a German court.

Waldner, the Gestapo chief of Hrubieszów, was freed by a German court.

Alex disappeared after the war.

Dr. Gross was tried and hanged in Poland after the war for collaborating with the Nazis.

I have received word from Mordechai Paldiel, Director, Department of the Righteous, that Mrs. Lipińska was nominated for induction into the "Avenue of the Righteous Gentiles." The "Avenue of the Righteous Gentiles" is a path near Yad Vashem (Israel's memorial to the six million Jewish victims of the Holocaust), which commemorates Gentiles who saved many Jewish lives at tremendous risk to their own and their families' lives. There are trees planted and marble plaques for each of the Righteous Gentiles. This is an exceptional honor for Mrs. Lipińska.

ABOUT THE AUTHOR

Henry Orenstein is a philanthropist, inventor, entrepreneur, and Holocaust survivor. After surviving World War II, much of it in various concentration camps, Orenstein became a toymaker who convinced Hasbro to start producing Transformers in the U.S. He holds over 100 other patents, the best-known of which gave Orenstein the exclusive rights in the United States to detect and display a player's hidden cards to the audience in poker games, one of the principal reasons that televised poker is so popular today. Orenstein is the creator and executive producer of the Poker Superstars Invitational Tournament as well as the popular TV show *High Stakes Poker*. In 2008 he was inducted into the Poker Hall of Fame.